On Good Ground

THE STORY OF THE SISTERS OF ST. JOSEPH
IN ST. PAUL

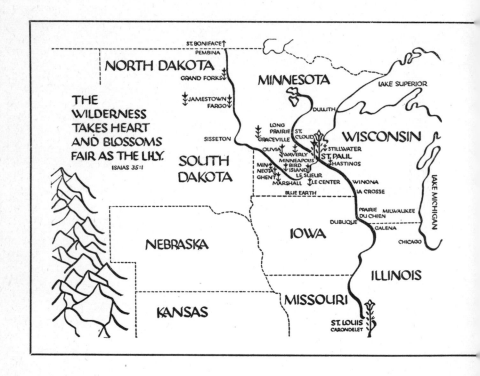

RIVER ROUTE OF THE SISTERS OF ST. JOSEPH FROM CARONDELET TO ST. PAUL IN

1851 AND THEIR PERMANENT FOUNDATIONS IN THE ST. PAUL PROVINCE, MARKED

BY A LILY, SYMBOL OF JOSEPH OF NAZARETH, PATRON OF THEIR CONGREGATION

ON GOOD GROUND

The Story of the
Sisters of St. Joseph in St. Paul

SISTER HELEN ANGELA HURLEY

PUBLISHED BY THE UNIVERSITY OF MINNESOTA PRESS, MINNEAPOLIS

Copyright 1951 by the

UNIVERSITY OF MINNESOTA

PRINTED AT THE NORTH CENTRAL PUBLISHING COMPANY, ST. PAUL

London • *Geoffrey Cumberlege* • *Oxford University Press*

TO MY PEOPLE
THE MEN AND WOMEN OF MINNESOTA
AND NORTH DAKOTA

who shared with me the experience of birth
on a Red River Valley homestead,
of life in villages, towns, and cities,
of education in public grade school, Catholic high
school and college, state university, and
Catholic graduate schools,
of teaching in public and Catholic high schools,
of thirty years of convent life,
and of half a century of friendships beyond
race and color and creed

THIS BOOK IS AFFECTIONATELY DEDICATED

Foreword

In this history of the Sisters of St. Joseph in the province of St. Paul, the author has succeeded in producing what is at one and the same time a work of good historical scholarship and a story that will hold the interest of the general reader.

From the point of view of local history writing, this book represents the accomplishment of no easy task, built up as it is from scattered and fragmentary sources. It has been necessary to gather records from here and there, with disappointments now and again caused by lacunae in the evidence. The working out of an intelligible and interesting pattern has required no small amount of research and of patience and ingenuity.

The paucity of records in the case is not due simply to carelessness and indifference to the convenience of historians in days to come. The years covered by this narrative were arduous ones, when there was much to be done and hardly persons enough for the doing of it; when time and energy were so absorbed in the doing that little of either was left for the recording.

Since the Sisters of St. Joseph came to St. Paul at the very beginning of the diocesan history, in the same year as its first bishop, they have been from the start and through the subsequent years zealous and successful coworkers with the bishops who appear in this narrative, Cretin, Grace, and Ireland. With Archbishop Ireland especially their purposes and efforts were so linked that he appears in the narrative as an absolutely indispensable figure, a counterpart with his own valiant sister, Mother Seraphine Ireland, provincial superior of the Sisters of St. Joseph in St. Paul.

The reader will find pleasure and profit in this rehearsal of a goodly part of the effort that went into the upbuilding of our state of Minnesota, especially in the fields of religion and charity and education; he will be reminded, as we all well need to be, of the ideals of courage and perseverance of our forebears in the achievement of what Minnesota is today.

This volume deals only with the history of one religious community, the Sisters of St. Joseph. It is, however, suggestive of the here untold work of other communities in the same area whose names, along with those of the many here individually unnamed Sisters of St. Joseph are written in the Book of Life.

To them and to all of every religious denomination and of every nationality and race who out of the past are our benefactors, we of the present have reason to be grateful.

WILLIAM BUSCH

St. Paul Seminary

Acknowledgments

THIS book was begun in 1942 when a student at St. Margaret's Academy in Minneapolis asked me how there could ever be peace in the world. That young lady — and thirty years of other students who have demanded answers — will know without my saying it how much my book depends upon the affectionate response of all of them.

The true background, however, derives from the very small town in North Dakota where my family went to live when I was four years old. There the educational feature par excellence was the fact that ours was one of three Catholic families in the village. While we sang "Jesus Wants Me for a Sunbeam" and listened to the King James Version and the Lord's Prayer the "other way" every day in school, we had our private fun too.

My mother taught us how to be amused privately at the little old lady who would say, "Come in! Come in! You may look at the flowers. I like little Catholic girls as well as little Baptist girls" and at the caller who complained of the Methodist sermons, "Dancing and cards! Cards and dancing! Is them the only two sins they is?" My mother also approved highly of the W.C.T.U. and she had us memorizing pieces about two glasses filled to the brim (I forget with what) and she was careful that no one be scandalized by too much dancing and card playing on our part.

The real distinction in faiths was that of a Sunday afternoon all the children on our street sat on the front porch

ix

reading the Bible while we played croquet among ourselves
in our own back yard. The only acute suffering I remember
was not being permitted to go to Epworth League. Even the
subscribers to the *Menace* were our dear friends and if there
was a difference between us, it was simply that they did not
realize we were a minority.

My friend Rose Wilder Lane, who has such an accurate
memory of her childhood in Dakota Territory and who has
written the world's best books about the weather, *Let the
Hurricane Roar* and *Free Land* (or is one of them about
oyster crackers?) cannot remember whether there were any
Catholics in her village. And when I ask her to tell me what
she thinks of sisters, she sets down something that sounds
to me like a lovely picture of a beehive. Here is just another
angle from that of the dear old rheumatic in our town who
said to me on my first visit home after I entered the convent,
"We used to lock the door when we saw the ladies with them
things on, but I'm not afraid of you when you come with
your mother."

Another humiliating peculiarity of our family was that my
father was one of the few Democrats we ever encountered.
Therefore, since politics was rather taboo as a topic outside,
we were drenched in it within, from pictures of the gerry-
mander in our county drawn on the tablecloth to the daily
recitation of the contents of four newspapers. Beginning
with the Russo-Japanese War, when most of us could talk a
little, the table was split right and left on every question.
If we derived an impression that meals were for argument,
we also learned that there are two sides to everything.

Those remote influences — among which I must record my
ever generous brother, Stephen E. Hurley, and sisters, Catherine and Marcella, all of Chicago — have determined the
trend of my book, but it has been blessed with more recent
and immediate help as well.

As an expert both in the liturgy and in local church history, the Reverend William Busch has contributed much

more than mere painstaking attention to the manuscript and he could have expended no more enthusiasm on a book of his own than he has devoted to mine.

Ralph Backlund, producer for the Columbia Broadcasting System in New York and prize-winning author, was so lavish with time-consuming editorial labors and expert advice that I have no words to thank him adequately.

A cheering section which had much to do with the final expansions and contractions was made up of Monsignor Edward Geraghty, Father Robert Hovda, Gerald Compton, Gordon Zahn, Richard Leonard, the William E. Carlsons, Doctors Harold and Euphemia Haynes, Margaret Shelley, Mr. and Mrs. Clarence Mitchell, Edgar Crane, and others whom the limitations of space restrain me from naming.

I am indebted to many of the Sisters of St. Joseph in the province of St. Paul for critical readings. One half of the sisters going through the manuscript removed all the commas; the other half restored them, and added a few. All of them said that much of what I have written was news to them. They cannot, therefore, be held accountable for my careless inventions and discrepancies, and we may perhaps leave the commas to God. Or to the University of Minnesota, aged but still hard-working mother of the state's comma placers.

More though for the university. There I found out from Professor Robert E. Cushman disturbing things about civil liberties and what, if anything, I know about writing. From Professor Quincy Wright I first learned of international peace. The late Mason W. Tyler once took a full class hour for a defense of Pius IX as an international leader of a spiritual dominion, who could not be expected to take sides in a war.

It was in Professor Tyler's class, too, that a boy called out one day, "You may say what you like about Bismarck's blood and iron policy, but if a person wants to get any place, it's the only way to success."

After a dramatic moment of silence, Mr. Tyler said quietly, "Success? What do you mean by success? When you say the word, my mind goes back two thousand years to a little city where one day a Man was crucified on a hill outside the walls. He was the biggest failure the world has ever known — or the biggest success. What do you mean by success?"

That was in 1922. Years later, Dr. R. W. Murchie told us in rural sociology that the government might have been well advised to have read the Bible instead of destroying little pigs and excess wheat. In the story of Joseph the principles of storage for the needs of others might have been learned. On the same side of the ledger I am under obligations to such leaders in Minnesota history as Dr. Solon Buck, Dean Theodore Blegen, and Dr. William Anderson.

The award of a University of Minnesota Fellowship in Regional Writing enabled me to purchase a microfilm reader for my personal use and to secure much valuable material which would have been unattainable otherwise.

My great debt to Dr. Paul Hanly Furfey of the Catholic University I trust is expressed in these pages by a remembrance that New Testament charity includes social groups as well as individuals.

The Reverend Thomas T. McAvoy, archivist and historian of Notre Dame University, has generously put at my disposal the fruit of his prolonged and scholarly labors in the study of the Catholic minority. In addition, he was kind enough to read my manuscript and to make valuable suggestions. Sister Grace McDonald, O.S.B., of the College of St. Benedict, St. Joseph, Minnesota, has also shared with me the fruit of her researches into Minnesota church history. Valuable documents and invaluable interpretations have been provided by the Right Reverend James M. Reardon, P.A. The Reverend Hugh Nolan, editor of the Catholic Historical *Records* of Philadelphia, secured essential letters and other documents and took a helpful interest in my research.

Lilamae Wick, one of my former students at St. Margaret's Academy, was so kind as to draw the frontispiece and the jacket and cover designs.

To the patient correspondents who furnished me with information from convent archives all over the United States and Canada, I give my hearty thanks. Lucile Kane, curator of the Manuscript Division, Minnesota Historical Society, and all the librarians in the many deposits I have used deserve praise for their good services.

Finally, my worries at the end were lightened by the sympathetic manner in which Mrs. Robert Buelow (Marcella Moore) helped me to prepare the manuscript for publication. And I appreciate the painstaking care with which the staff of the University of Minnesota Press saw the manuscript through the publishing processes.

To these and all the friends included in my dedication I express my gratitude. They have done so much for the book that nothing is mine, save what is defective.

SISTER HELEN ANGELA

Fast of the Assumption, 1951
St. Joseph's Provincial House
St. Paul, Minnesota

Table of Contents

ILLUSTRATIONS

Frontispiece. River route of the Sisters of St. Joseph from Carondelet to St. Paul in 1851 and their permanent foundations in the St. Paul province, marked by a lily, symbol of Joseph of Nazareth, patron of their congregation.

Between pages 176 and 177. Water color sketch of the Chapel of St. Paul made by Robert O. Sweeny in 1852. Mother St. John Fournier of St. Paul. Mother St. John Fontbonne of Lyons. Mother Celestine Pommerel of Carondelet. Grey Nuns traveling through Minnesota. Bishop Joseph Cretin. Countess de la Rochejacquelin. The Ellens — Sister Seraphine Ireland and Sister Celestine Howard.

Between pages 208 and 209. Mother St. John Ireland, Mother Celestine Howard, and Mother Seraphine Ireland in 1885. Sister Wilfrida Hogan. Sister Antonia McHugh. Mother Seraphine Ireland in 1925. Archbishop John Ireland. Reception and Profession Day, 1951, at St. Joseph's novitiate in St. Paul. St. Joseph's Provincial House, St. Paul.

Tout Est à Créer

IN THE YEARS OF BISHOP CRETIN

※ I ※

The Swelling of the Stream

GOD WAS not unknown in the forests and sawmill towns of Minnesota in the 1850s.

His Kingdom may perhaps have been regarded less as a spiritual dominion than as a sound institution which was good for the country, but there was nevertheless a sizable amount of faith in the Power which could stay lethal storms and a similar quantity of hope in the Providence which rewarded the righteous with prosperity. The theological virtue of charity was less discernible in a region where exigency put the emphasis on acquisition of a satisfactory share of the natural bounty and not upon a heedless giving away of this world's goods.

A "vision" recorded in 1853 by a historian aptly named Bond illustrates the fact that mystical experience was limited to what was commensurate with good American common sense. This citizen wrote elaborately of things he prophesied would happen on the Fourth of July in 1876. At the celebration of the joining of the Atlantic and Pacific with iron rails "*via* St. Paul," a figure representing Neptune with his trident would stand behind the altar to "typify that our advancement in the arts and sciences had induced even the 'god of the ocean' to forsake his native element . . . to take the overland route from one part of his dominions to another . . . while the shells and precious stones falling from his

3

chariot seemed to remind us that this great undertaking was destined to be literally paved with the riches of the deep."

The frontier mystic foresaw that when the Christian minister and the president of the United States — a Minnesota citizen — arrived at the triumphal arch, the minister would briefly invoke "the blessings of Jehovah upon the great enterprise before them." In the succeeding ceremonies the bright drops of the Sacramento would flow with those of the "Father of Running Waters" and as serf and Cossack struck a blow for freedom, "the goddess of Liberty flitting and hovering over the scene," a triumphant shout would come "ringing up the noble river to the spot where the multitudinous host were still pouring forth their anthems of praise to the God of hosts."

The quality of Mr. J. Wesley Bond's prophecy was not unduly extravagant, but his reverence for sacred things appeared to better advantage elsewhere in his volume, *Minnesota and Its Resources,* where he wrote:

"From the outset, the means of grace have been abundant in St. Paul. If she should ever go down to a degraded end, through sin and infamy, it will not be the fault of the various religious institutions and denominations of our common country. . . . The catholic church was the first to organize here. . . . In 1841 . . . the log house of worship . . . on Bench [now Kellogg], between Minnesota and Cedar Streets, was erected. The older society at Mendota being called the Church of St. Peter, the one here took the name in contradistinction of the great Apostle of the Gentiles — St. Paul. This gave name to the town; and it is but an act of simple justice to state that to the good taste of the catholic clergy are we indebted for the excommunication of the outrageous cognomen of 'Pig's Eye,' which in its flight from our high and salubrious bluffs, found no resting-place until it reached an entanglement of sloughs, marshes, and mosquito dens, some miles below. In May, 1849, a large and devout congregation worshipped in the log church, under the care of the Rev. Mr. Ravoux, a faithful and zealous man. The following year, Minnesota was set off as a bishopric, with the seat at St. Paul; Father Cretin, of Dubuque, was ordained bishop, and arrived here in the spring of 1851."

To this Mr. Bond added the information that the St. Paul congregation was "mostly of Canadian, French, and Irish extraction."

It was, however, the territory's panorama of adventuring enterprise for which Mr. Bond, like so many of the frontier writers, reserved his note of religious exaltation. The imperial domain turned visions into palpable reality and created a perpetual pageant of gay voyageurs, daring soldiers, painted Indians, hearty lumbermen, scholarly explorers, immigrant farmers, carefree navigators. Paeans to saintly missionaries were reserved for later reminiscent literature. To their contemporaries, religious men and women were somewhat deficient in pictorial qualities.

If, for example, the lack of possessions or reputation alone could identify a Christian, the four Sisters of St. Joseph who arrived in St. Paul on the morning of November 3, 1851, fitted neatly into the category. Obviously, however dedicated they were to the purposes of their "little design," as their founder had called their humble institute, they would cause no stir in a place already bursting with destiny.

A century later the four would be more than a thousand; they would have in their charge forty-seven elementary and ten secondary schools, a great college, five modern hospitals, two orphanages. The Sisters of St. Joseph would be secure in their little corner in St. Paul. But in 1851, *tout est à créer* — all was yet to be done.

The four sisters belonged to a little institute founded by the Reverend John Peter Medaille, S.J., and under the patronage of the Right Reverend Bishop Henry de Maupas in Le Puy, France, on October 15, 1650, for the service of hospitals, the education and direction of orphans, and the visiting of the sick and poor. Since none of the six original members could

read or write, it was some years before education was listed
as a leading work of the society. The leaders wished to per-
petuate the idea which St. Francis de Sales had not been
permitted to carry into effect in founding the Visitation
Sisters, that is, the union of the active and contemplative
life in such a manner that the members of the group might
engage in the works of charity outside the convent while
at the same time leading a life of prayer. There was no inno-
vation in this plan, but rather a return to the "ora et labora"
which St. Benedict had made the guiding principle of
Western monasticism in the sixth century.

For the Sisters of St. Joseph a precious heritage of content-
ment in humble labor and disdain for worldly opinion was
furnished by their model, for the lily of Joseph of Nazareth
was a symbol of fair love and it also recalled the lesson of
the lilies of the field.

The spirit of the institute was indicated by Father Medaille
in a letter written to the first Sisters of St. Joseph in 1650.
"Almighty God has vouchsafed," he wrote, "to manifest to
me in the Holy Eucharist a perfect model for our *little design*. Jesus is there wholly annihilated. We, likewise, my
dear daughters, must labor to establish an obscure institute.
In the eyes of the world, it must be nothing. . . . The
Holy Eucharist is a mystery of perfect union. It unites creatures with God; and by the title of communion which it bears,
unites the faithful among themselves by a common bond.
. . . Our little design and the persons who compose it
ought not to live for themselves, but be entirely immolated
for God and for the neighbor. They must be everything for
the dear neighbor, nothing for self."

In this spirit the Sisters of St. Joseph spread rapidly into
ten or twelve dioceses, especially in the south of France. The
"little design" was being worked into a great tapestry of
annihilation of self and service for neighbor when the French
Revolution all but destroyed it. The houses of the little
society were pillaged, almost all the records were damaged

or carried off. Some of the religious were thrown into prison — a few were made to pay with their lives.

Mother St. John Fontbonne, the superior at Monistrol in the diocese of Le Puy, was the heroine of this period. And a trying period it was. Bishop de Gallard of Le Puy was exiled because ho refused to take the constitutional oath imposed on the clergy by the revolutionary government. The curé of Monistrol, M. Ollier, on December 28, 1790, signified his willingness to comply with the government order. Despite Bishop de Gallard's letter to the effect that the oath was unlawful, since it separated the church in France from the authority of the pope, M. Ollier took it publicly in the parish church on January 30, 1791. That made the position of the sisters difficult, but Mother St. John in the name of her community refused to take the oath. From then on the sisters endured hunted wanderings from cave to prison until they were forced at last to return to their own homes and to wear secular dress.

As soon as the laws permitted, Mother St. John gathered together, at the invitation of Joseph Cardinal Fesch, the archbishop of Lyons, the few sisters who could be found living in hiding, to build up again the "little design" of St. Joseph. This was accomplished in 1807, when twelve postulants were put under Mother St. John's direction at St. Etienne. Her courage was displayed still further in 1830 when she withstood the soldiers who would have desecrated the shrine of Our Lady of Fourvières before any of the sacred articles could be removed. Then in 1836, when she was seventy-seven years old, in answer to a call from Bishop Joseph Rosati in faraway St. Louis, Mother St. John undertook the planning of a mission to America.

The peculiar fitness of the Sisters of St. Joseph for work in the Mississippi Valley had been urged in some detail by their patroness and benefactor, the Countess de la Roche-jacquelin, Félicité de Duras, in a letter to Bishop Rosati in 1835. Up to 1634, all religious women had lived in a strict cloister and they were properly called nuns. Then St. Vincent de Paul founded an order whose chapel, he said, was the parish church, their cloister the streets of the city or the wards of the hospital. These sisters were called "Sisters of Charity" and similar institutes, founded later, such as the Sisters of St. Joseph, often were known by this title — to Catholics as well as to non-Catholics — although each, according to its spirit, had its own appropriate name. The countess called her "little sisters" the children of St. Teresa and St. Vincent de Paul, "because they combined the spirit of recollection and contemplation of the cloistered orders with the charity and zeal of the uncloistered." Or, in the usual description, they strove to unite in themselves the virtues of Martha and Mary.

"But perhaps, My Lord," the countess continued in her letter to Bishop Rosati, "you do not know who the Sisters of St. Joseph are? They follow the Rule of St. Augustine, and they make perpetual vows; they promise, without exception, to perform *all* works of charity. Their rule binds them to all the virtues of the cloister, joined to the virtues demanded by an ardent charity for the neighbor. This was the first idea of St. Francis de Sales which he gave up with regret for the Visitation. Hence, piety, recollection, abnegation, humility, flourish on the one hand; and, on the other, free schools or pay boarding institutions, large hospitals, hospices for the aged or foundling asylums — prisons, relief of the poor, of the sick in their homes, care of the scurfy, of the mangy, it matters not — the care of dispensaries. In certain of their houses they do manual work — sewing or handicraft. At Lyons they make ribands. Ah, My Lord, if you had only seen, as I have, the spirit of poverty — that evangelical *littleness*! I speak truly: I have known them for thirty years — France is full of them.

"I know that you, too, have estimable works; but in your vast new country, where there is so much to do, do you not wish to sow the seed of every kind of grain? This will be the more fruitful if you take the Sisters of St. Joseph, for in this Order a foundation is never a foolish enterprise, such as the unwise projects sometimes undertaken in the Order of St. Vincent de Paul. My little sisters work rather according to reason and the suitableness of the place. I know a foundation which was begun with thirty centimes, in a little stable. But God was there; like the example of the Crèche, the establishment prospered so much others were founded from it."

Bishop Rosati must have found the countess' enthusiasm convincing, for he wrote to Mother St. John asking if a group of the sisters was available for work in St. Louis. She responded by sending six sisters in 1836, among whom were two of her own nieces, and by adding in 1837 two other sisters, who had been detained to study methods of teaching the deaf. This good work Bishop Rosati considered of paramount importance.

Although Mother St. John Fontbonne died in 1843, the same "little design" was repeated again and again as soon as more young women took the veil in France or in St. Louis and there were enough hands to extend the work. One of the original band who went from Lyons to St. Louis in 1836 and one of the two who reached St. Louis in 1837 were among the four sisters who opened the mission in St. Paul in 1851. The other two in the St. Paul group were American-born sisters who had been received into the community at St. Louis.

As Countess de la Rochejacquelin had pointed out to Bishop Rosati, the Sisters of St. Joseph were, by reason of their design, especially suited for service in frontier areas. The plan embodied in their constitutions provided for works of mercy outside as well as within their houses and a strict enclosure was therefore impossible. Their distinctive dress was a symbol that they were endeavoring to live in a Christlike manner. The habit was of black serge; the sleeves and skirt were long and wide, and the fitted waist was overlaid by plaits in front. The headdress was a black veil, worn with band, cornet, and guimpe of white linen. In addition, a cross of black wood bound with brass and bearing a brass figure of Christ on the Cross was suspended from a cord about the neck, and a black rosary was attached to the cincture.

Thus costumed the sisters stirred the suspicions of nineteenth-century Americans for fifteen years in and around St. Louis and for four years in Philadelphia before the expedition to St. Paul. Yet even as poor and unwelcome foreigners they had managed to secure a little sphere of influence in a few schools and orphanages. Beyond that, in St. Louis they had charge of an asylum for the deaf and in Philadelphia of a hospital.

The bishops of the two sees came to rely on them appreciably, although it was perhaps a reliance on those "good for everything" which was accorded them rather than the esteem reserved for experts. For, when Bishop J. N. Provencher of St. Boniface, Manitoba, was anxiously searching for sisters in 1842, he was advised by Bishop Mathias Loras of Dubuque that the Ursulines and others with a strict enclosure were not suited to a new country. The Sisters of Charity of St. Vincent de Paul were excellent, he declared, but their principal work was to direct hospitals and they were hard to secure. The Lovers of the Cross were not very numerous and they probably would not care to go to the Red River country. The only order which, in the opinion of the bishop of Dubuque, would suit Manitoba was that of the Sisters of St. Joseph of Lyons. He said that they had a beautiful establishment at Carondelet, near St. Louis, and that he had already taken steps to get some of the sisters for the northern part of his own diocese, which then included the vast stretches to the north of Iowa and west of the Mississippi. He was so sure that Bishop Provencher would be satisfied with the Sisters of St. Joseph that he had written to Lyons the same day.

This enthusiastic description of the Sisters of St. Joseph

pleased Bishop Provencher so much that he joined the caravan of Red River carts which he was sending to meet them
at St. Peter's (Mendota), but there were no sisters to be
had. The motherhouse at Lyons had been unable to supply
any more sisters for America at that time. He journeyed on
down to St. Louis and was further disappointed that no
Sisters of St. Joseph were available for him after observing
their peaceful, busy life at the motherhouse in Carondelet.
His canvass through the country of all likely communities
finally met with success at Montreal, where the Grey Nuns
agreed to supply his missions.

This was a fortunate circumstance for the historian because the Grey Nuns have left piquant accounts of their
trips through Minnesota from 1846 to 1859. They have recorded faithfully the details of their experiences in Stillwater, St. Paul — where they spent five weeks in 1850 — St.
Anthony, Crow Wing, and St. Cloud, and on the prairies and
rivers to Pembina.

Sisters Gosselin and Ouimet had an extended tour of
fifty-seven days' travel from Montreal to St. Boniface in
1846. It took seven hours to drive by wagon from Stillwater
to St. Paul, where they waited six days for the caravan of
thirty Red River carts and the trek across the prairies.

The whole trip consumed ninety-two days in 1850 for
Mother Valade, Sisters Fisette, Laurent, and l'Esperance,
three lay women, and two men. When they reached St. Paul
from Galena by means of "un bateau à vapeur" they learned
that the caravan had been delayed by bad roads. Father
Ravoux generously offered them his house. It was twenty
feet square and contained two rooms and a garret which was
reached by a ladder. The furniture included two chairs, a
table, a poor bed, a cupboard, and a few boxes.

Mother Valade had the two men repair the house and
make a lean-to for the stove. For the rest of the month the
men were hired by the farmers around St. Paul. Mother
Valade bought some provisions, but the good people of the

settlement brought the sisters milk, butter, eggs, bread, and cakes. The Grey Nuns scrubbed and cleaned the church and mended the vestments and the priest's wardrobe. Father Ravoux provided a class of forty children for them. Sister l'Esperance taught the French-speaking children and Miss Ford (one of the lay women) the English-speaking class.

When at last they set out with Norman W. Kittson's caravan on August 3, they were hospitably entertained on the first night at St. Anthony's Falls by Mr. and Mrs. Pierre Bottineau, whose little ten-year-old daughter, Mary, went off with the sisters in the caravan to begin her education. The fascinating story of the trip through swamps, muskegs, and rivers, with many detours to avoid attacks by the hostile Sioux, with rations of nothing but boiled rice supplemented by wild berries, is admirably told in the long letters written by the sisters to the motherhouse in Montreal.

These were the very experiences for which the Sisters of St. Joseph had been longing for fifteen years. Just as Bishop Provencher had observed when he visited Carondelet in 1843, they had continued to fit themselves into any work which came to hand. The elegant boarding schools for the daughters of the wealthy had already been allotted to the more cloistered — or, it may be, the more secure and cultivated — orders. When Mother Seton's Daughters of Charity amalgamated with the French Sisters of Charity of St. Vincent de Paul, it was decided that they were no longer to take charge of institutions for boys and the Sisters of St. Joseph, as a consequence, were asked to take over the male orphanages.

However, although the sisters had expanded their work as their increasing numbers permitted, St. Louis had offered scant opportunity for brushing with the "savages, heretics and infidels" for whose salvation the Countess de la Rochejacquelin had paid the passage of the six sisters to America, notwithstanding the circumstance that her property was sequestered at the time and she was obliged to sell her jewels to secure funds. The countess, in her letter to Bishop Rosati, ranked the desirable objects of missionary zeal as "savages, poor persons, Protestants, Methodists, and all the unhappy sects."

She informed the bishop that she based her judgment of the American scene on the letters printed in the *Annals* of the Society for the Propagation of the Faith, a publication of the naive little association which Pauline Jaricot had organized by teaching French working girls to give one cent every Saturday to aid the foreign missions. In spite of unbelievable treachery on the part of trusted friends and the insidious deception of enemies, the foundation prospered and was able to send large sums to Asia and Africa. And narratives published in the *Annals* aroused the French-reading Europeans to so much interest in American "savages" that, as time went on, a million francs were sent to Iowa and Minnesota.

While Bishop Joseph Cretin was in St. Paul from 1851 to 1857, he received more than two hundred thousand francs from this French society. All the early houses of the Sisters of St. Joseph were financed in large part by these francs. Without their help, the sisters would have been forced at the very outset to neglect the last plea of the countess: *"Never refuse poor children in your schools!"*

It was Bishop Cretin's call that gave the sisters their chance to work among the "dear Indians" and brought them to St. Paul, but the moving spirit in that and in much of the work that preceded it was Cretin's predecessor, Bishop Loras.

Mathias Loras had come to America as a missionary for Alabama in 1830. When he was made bishop of all the region between the Mississippi and Missouri rivers from Iowa to Canada in 1837, he proceeded to France for help. During the winter of 1838, he returned with a group of young priests, four of whom were to be important to the yet unorganized Minnesota. They were Joseph Cretin, Anthony Pelamourgues, Lucian Galtier, and Augustin Ravoux.

Two months after their arrival in Dubuque, the bishop took Father Pelamourgues with him to visit Mendota, then known as St. Peter's. They found 185 Catholics in the neighborhood and it was decided that a priest must be sent to care for them. The lot fell upon Father Lucian Galtier and he proceeded to his new mission by the first boat in 1840.

The following year — memorable for the building by Father Galtier of the log chapel of St. Paul — Father Augustin Ravoux and Father Joseph Cretin were sent to work among the Indians in Minnesota. However, prospects of success were so limited that it was decided Father Cretin should be sent to the parish in Prairie du Chien and Father Ravoux should work in Minnesota as a missionary to the Sioux without fixed residence. There he remained except for an excursion to Prairie du Chien in 1843 to print on Father Cretin's press his Sioux manual, *Wakantanka Ti ki Chanku*, "The Path to the House of God." When Father Galtier was sent to Prairie du Chien in 1849, Father Ravoux took his place as pastor of Mendota and St. Paul.

The St. Paul mission (officially "St. Paul's") was actually within the Milwaukee diocese, but the bishop of that see was unable to give any assistance except that of an occasional exploring missionary and of Father Anthony Godfert's residence at St. Paul's for a short time in 1844. The Catholics had become so numerous in the settlement that by 1847 Father Ravoux found it necessary to build an addition to Father Galtier's chapel.

Pig's Eye was no longer in use as the name for the village, but it aroused a reminiscent interest for many years. The *Minnesota Pioneer*, a St. Paul weekly paper, on September 19, 1849, told with appropriate flourishes the story of the Frenchman named Parrant. He was "notable for having one eye, unequally matched with its distant yoke mate, and precisely the shape of a pig's eye. . . . His identity became in the process of time stamped with that name." Parrant opened a grocery at the lower landing in St. Paul. There "a gentleman inditing an epistle at Mr. Parrant's desk, dated the letter, for want of a more definite designation, 'Pig's Eye, such a month, 1842'."

The account in the *Pioneer* goes on to relate that the letter received in return was directed to Pig's Eye and thus the name was fixed until the Catholic church was named for St. Paul and Pig's Eye thereafter was used only for the lower settlement two miles above Red Rock. In 1849, there were some forty families of Canadian French voyageurs living along its one street.

Just then, when St. Paul had little to mark it for the Kingdom of God except the name of the Apostle to the Gentiles, another paper, the *Minnesota Chronicle and Register,* announced a new bishopric. On August 29, 1849, an item read, "The Catholic church are about to found a diocese in Minnsota, with the seat of the Bishop at St. Paul. This will insure the building of a splendid Cathedral here, to supply the religious wants of the numerous members of that denomination, and incidentally add to the architectural beauty of the growing town."

This was prompt reporting, since the Seventh Provincial Council of Baltimore had proposed the erection of a diocese at St. Paul, Minnesota Territory, in the spring of 1849, upon the recommendation of the Right Reverend J. M. Henni, the bishop of Milwaukee, who could no longer resist the harassed pleas of Father Ravoux. The Revolution of 1848 had caused disorders in the Holy City and the exile of the Supreme Pontiff, Pius IX, which prevented the petition from being granted before the following year. The bull of erection was dated at St. Peter's, Rome, July 19, 1850. Father Cretin of Prairie du Chien was named bishop-elect of the new diocese, which comprised all of Minnesota Territory — the area now organized into the states of Minnesota and North and South Dakota as far west as the Missouri River. Late in 1850 the bishop-elect left for Europe to procure missionaries and pecuniary means for the field of his future labors.

Something like squatter's rights over souls seems to have informed the long article on "Churches, church-buildings, and clergy of the Territory of Minnesota" which the *Minnesota Democrat* for December 10, 1850, offered its readers. The Catholic mention was brief:

"The first house of worship, erected in the present white settlement was that now occupied by the Roman Catholic Denomination in this town. It was built several years since, when the spot was only a resort of the French Voyageur and wandering Dakota. Though a rude log chapel, it occupied a most commanding situation, and reminds one of the chapels long since decayed that were erected by the zealous Jesuit on the shores of Lake Superior and Green Bay. This pile of logs is soon to be removed we understand, to give place to an architectural pile, worthy of that branch of the Church which has produced an architect, painter and sculptor, like Michael Angelo. . . . This town derives its name from the Catholic log church, near the river, which stood there solitary and alone when the present site of St. Paul was inhabited by Indians."

The "clergy" received no notice except in the column of announcements: "Saint Paul. Roman Catholic Church. In charge of Rev. A. Ravoux. Morning services at 7½ and 10½ o'clock. Afternoon at 2½ o'clock." Father Ravoux was not the sort of person that the Protestant ministers who helped the editors with these recurring historical accounts were anxious to advertise. He had an annoying way of pursuing his discoveries to an embarrassing conclusion. Of his encounters in 1847 with the Reverend Dr. Williamson, a missionary at Kaposia (South St. Paul), he still spoke with asperity forty years later in his *Reminiscences and Memoirs*.

His first objection was to Dr. Williamson's statement that many of the children of St. Paul were "growing up entirely ignorant of God." This was an affront to Father Ravoux who was attending to the spiritual wants of the Catholics of Mendota and St. Paul. The majority of the sparse population were Catholics, the priest protested, knew their religion, and helped to teach their children.

In the course of his prospectus for a proposed school, Dr. Williamson had remarked that "possibly the priest might deter some from attending, who might otherwise be able and willing." Father Ravoux countered that the priest would object, "not because the priest was opposed to education, but because he had reason to know that the Rev. Mr. Williamson would try to spread his religious tenets among Catholic children." The evidence was in a pamphlet in French which Dr. Williamson had given to a Catholic family in Mendota, containing the untruth that "the Catholic church makes a God of the priest, and she accepts fasts, penances, and money instead of virtues."

Father Ravoux laid bare the false statements of the pamphlet on two Sundays in St. Paul and Mendota. He pointed out that although Dr. Williamson was noble-hearted and charitable, he "was not the man under whose influence Catholic children should be allowed." A copy of Father Ravoux's lectures was presented to Dr. Williamson and "no more was heard from that source, of tract distributing or of false statements of Catholic teaching."

Early in January 1851 Bishop-elect Cretin sent to the Central Council of Lyons a report to the Society for the Propagation of the Faith on the conditions in his diocese and the needs thereof. He listed the population as 3000 Catholics, 1000 heretics, and 27,000 infidels. There were three priests, none of them native to the country. A note in the space for listing churches and chapels said, "Two kinds of stables actually serve for the celebration of the sacred mysteries, meriting neither the name of churches nor chapels."

One priest had the care of the whole white population, scattered over twenty leagues. Two Canadian missionaries were among the Sauteux (so named because they were first encountered at "the Soo," Sault Ste Marie) at Pembina, more than a hundred fifty leagues from St. Paul. The bishop-elect spoke of the cession of the rich Sioux lands on the right bank of the Mississippi and their opening to settlers. He thought that the moment for the conversion of the numerous savages within his diocese had arrived, since many Protestant missionaries had withdrawn.

The bishop-elect had also sent an appeal to the Paris office of the Society for the Propagation of the Faith. There he described his future see as he had observed it a year and a half before. Then the little city of St. Paul "had only some cabins." In 1850, however, he reported that it numbered "three thousand souls, two printing shops, three Protestant churches, although Catholics are in the majority."

Bishop Cretin was consecrated on January 26, 1851, by the bishop who had ordained him twenty-five years before, the Right Reverend Alexander Raymond Devie, bishop of Belley, in his episcopal city and chapel. He arrived in St. Paul on July 2, accompanied by five seminarians. They were Francis de Vivaldi, Louis Ledon, John Fayolle, Marcellin Peyragrosse, Edward Legendre. Father James Moran had arrived from Ireland a short time before.

The *Minnesota Democrat* made much of the bishop's installation and gave a sketch of the fifty-one-year-old prelate which was copied by the *Boston Pilot* as an item of interest to the immigrants. The account noted that the bishop had been a parish priest in Ferney, the residence of Voltaire, for fifteen years before he came to the United States in 1838. "Those who know him well," concluded the writer, "and of different sects, represent him as a highly educated and excellent man, an American in all his sympathies, and warmly attached to the free institutions of our country."

His early impressions of the diocese Bishop Cretin sent to the Paris office of the Society for the Propagation of the Faith. It was but human for the bishop to stress the prospects of the country glowingly and at the same time to give a striking picture of its poverty. He reported that public opinion was not unfavorable to the Catholic religion, but he was disturbed by the fact that four Protestant churches "surmounted by elegant steeples with bells" brought the condition of the Catholic buildings into relief.

"Close by the poor dwelling of the bishop," he wrote, "there is an Episcopalian Church of Gothic style, with a spire surmounted by a beautiful cross, which makes strangers think it is a Catholic church. The three ministers who serve that church have placed there an altar, candlesticks, tabernacle, a crucifix and a communion table. It is to be hoped that they will some day be reunited to the true Church. But the Catholic Church is worse than a stable. To stop that sort of scandal, and not being able to erect a suitable building, the prelate has built a three-story house, 84 feet by 44. The lower floor will be used for school; the middle, for the church; the topmost, for the residence of the clergy. Later the building can be used for a college or seminary. It will be finished in October. The total cost is 24,000 francs. . . . Four Sisters of St. Joseph are expected from St. Louis."

The Sisters of St. Joseph were not the first order Bishop Cretin thought of inviting to the wild regions of his newly organized diocese. It was only after the Visitation Sisters, the Sisters of Charity of the Blessed Virgin Mary (the good sisters of Dubuque whom Bishop Provencher could not take because they did not speak a word of French), and other communities had refused his appeals that Bishop Cretin followed the suggestion of his former bishop, the Right Reverend Mathias Loras, and begged the Sisters of St. Joseph to come to St. Paul. This was the opportunity the sisters had been waiting for, and they responded with alacrity.

The completion of the church-seminary-residence fixed the date of their arrival from St. Louis, since the quarters they were to occupy could not be vacated until the new building was ready. On September 9, the *Democrat* announced hopefully that the walls were rising rapidly and that the building would be "one of the handsomest and most elegant pieces of architecture in the North West." The *Pioneer*, however, contributed a sour note on September 11, telling that one of the center beams of the second story broke for want of proper support in the center and fell down with all the other beams into the basement, knocking some holes in the unfinished walls. Nevertheless, the *Democrat* was able to say on September 30 that the brick work of the Catholic school had been finished and the workmen were putting on the roof.

A month later the four Sisters of St. Joseph were on their way to St. Paul.

In a letter of October 29, 1894, Sister Francis Joseph recalled their departure from St. Louis. They constituted "the first colony for the St. Paul Mission," she wrote. In the group were "Mother St. John Fournier, of France, Sr Mary Philomene, of France, Sr Scholastica Vasques, a French & Spanish Creole born in St. Louis, Sr Francis Joseph Ivory, of Loretto, Pa."

Mother St. John Fournier, the leader of the little band, had been mistress of novices in Philadelphia. "In the autumn of 1851," she wrote in 1873 (in one of her animated accounts of her early American experiences for the motherhouse in Lyons), "the doctors [in Philadelphia] insisted that I take a little rest. I decided to go and spend some time with our good Mother Celestine [Pommerel] — Mother Delphine had come from St. Louis to take my place in the novitiate. But shortly after my arrival in Carondelet, Monseigneur Cretin came to ask for some sisters for his diocese of St. Paul. Seeing our poor Mother in great embarrassment, for the classes and different missions were all arranged, I offered to accompany the sisters to help the young superior a little, which greatly consoled dear, worthy Mother, but caused me many hidden tears."

Sister Francis Joseph was undoubtedly the young sister who would have been burdened with the responsibility of the superiorship if Mother St. John Fournier had not offered to go with the group. Born of Irish parentage in the little colony of Loretto, Cambrie County, Pennsylvania, and baptized by the Reverend Demetrius Gallitzin, the renowned Russian prince-convert, Sister Francis Joseph seems early to have acquired a taste for pioneering which made her a sort of advance agent for the sisters of foreign birth and parentage. At any rate, having entered the novitiate at Carondelet on June 12, 1847, she was destined to see the beginnings of foundations in such widely separated places as St. Paul; Canandaigua and Buffalo, New York; and Kansas City, Missouri. In addition to her status as the most American of the group, honors could be accorded her for her courage and enthusiasm. Her reminiscent letters concerning the foundations were all written from forty to forty-five years after the events, yet they are both factual and interesting, if not models of orthography.

Sister Philomena was described by Sister Francis Joseph as one of the "old French members from Lyons (France)." As a twenty-four-year-old postulant in Lyons, Sister Philomena Vilaine had volunteered for the foreign missions. She received the habit on January 3, 1836, and set out for America the next day with five other sisters.

The term *creole* by which Sister Francis Joseph characterized Sister Scholastica was used to indicate French-Spanish-Negro strains. It is thought that this interesting sister was seventeen years old when she came to St. Paul and it is known that she died in 1859 in Mississippi.

Greater diversity of nationality and social condition it would be difficult to find in so small an association and for that reason these four sisters illustrate admirably the new manner of being which their Christian community life gave them. For the band was not starting out merely with a vow to obey Mother St. John Fournier in all things, but to do as Christ bade them do. Nor were the American members resentful of being placed under a woman who knew little of the language of the country. The human accidentals were trifles to them which could not obscure the meaning of Christ.

Of the trip to the new foundation, Mother St. John in 1873 wrote simply, "We embarked (four sisters) and went up the Mississippi. When we reached Lake Pepin, about a hundred miles from St. Paul, the ice was so thick that it was difficult to go on." Sister Francis Joseph's account in her letter of 1894 was more detailed:

"We went on board of the Steamer St. Paul about 8 p.m. Tuesday [October 28, 1851]. We traveled on [with] but a few Short Stops, as the Weather was cold and ice forming on the River. We arrived at Galena Friday the 31st of Oct. We stopped all night, put up at M^r [Nicholas] Dowlings, who was Mayor of the City, that year, his Lady was a Catholic, and was very kind to us. The following morning, being the Feast of All Saints, we heard Mass and received the Holy Communion in the Chapel of the Sisters of Mercy. After breakfast, we went aboard the Steamer and resumed our journey."

The polished wood and brass trimmings of the old river boats made them glittering palaces, and the Mississippi of the 1850s was spectacular with showy craft. The boats were wonderfully and intricately made; gay music and good company generally enlivened the river excursion. Forests still clothed the rugged bluffs, adding a picturesque backdrop for the island-dotted river. Galena was a veritable Damascus, where caravans of wagons met caravans of boats.

The mayor whom the sisters visited had formerly lived in St. Louis. The *Boston Pilot* cited him as one of the few Catholics in public office in the West, though Sister Francis Joseph merely recalls that his wife was a Catholic. He was a prosperous merchant who lived in a substantial house with pillars across the front. It was later owned by members of the Ulysses S. Grant family and, on that account, it has been preserved as a museum.

Luxurious surroundings seem to have made little impression on Sister Francis Joseph's memory, since she continued, "We made about an hour or 2 delay at Dubuque. We got off, and went up to see the Sisters who had been there but a short time." These were the Sisters of Charity of the Blessed Virgin Mary who had left Philadelphia in 1843, just in time to escape the burning of their convent by Nativist rioters in 1844. But now the sisters bound for St. Paul were apparently looking not to the past but to the future, for nothing of these untoward experiences is related in the reminiscences, which proceed with eagerness.

"We then resumed our journey, the [weather] being chilly and damp. We did enjoy the Scenery very much. We made a short delay at Prarie de chine [Prairie du Chien], when a priest (the founder of the St. Paul Mission) came on board, travelled quite a distance with us. I have often heard his name, but have forgotten it. He built the first Church in St. Paul."

The priest, of course, was Father Lucian Galtier, builder of the log chapel from which the city of St. Paul took its name. Since 1849, he had been in charge of the parish at Prairie du Chien. Throughout his life the significance of his St. Paul pastorate was kept before Father Galtier's mind. On one occasion he wrote, "I blessed the new Basilica of St. Paul on November first, 1841. [It was] smaller, indeed, than the Basilica of St. Paul in Rome, but as well adapted as the latter for prayer and love to arise there from pious hearts."

Frequently he was asked to tell how the chapel was built of red and white oak logs cut on the spot, held together by wooden pins. The roof was made of steeply slanting, bark-covered slabs, surmounted by a wooden cross. If the labor had not been volunteered by the French parishioners — La-Bissoniere, Gervais, Bottineau, Morin, Guerin — the whole bill would have been sixty-five dollars. The building was twenty-five feet long, eighteen feet wide, and ten feet high. Tamarack had been used for the rafters and pews and floor. Father Ravoux had built on the twenty-foot addition in 1847, but the congregation had long outgrown the rude church.

Besides Father Galtier, Sister Francis Joseph mentions

some of the other passengers on the boat bound upstream. For example, Major Abram M. Fridley, the newly appointed Indian agent for the Winnebago at Long Prairie, was on board with his family. Both Sister Scholastica and Sister Philomena eventually were to go to Long Prairie, about a hundred miles north of St. Paul, to teach among the Indian children at Fridley's agency. Although unaware of that fact, the sisters undoubtedly asked Major Fridley many questions about the "savages." Probably as a result of this meeting, within a few weeks the major sent his daughter Mary to St. Paul to become a boarding student in the new St. Joseph's Academy on Bench Street.

The *Democrat* briefly announced the sisters' arrival in St. Paul in its issue of November 18: "Four Sisters of charity have arrived at St. Paul, from St. Louis, and will shortly commence teaching a ladies' seminary in the old Catholic chapel. A school for lads and young men is about being opened in the new Catholic building. A corps of learned professors will take charge of it."

Further mention of the sisters was not made in any territorial paper for another eight months. During the week they arrived, Catholic news in the *Minnesotian* was confined to one item: "The new Catholic bell was consecrated on Friday; it is, we believe, the heaviest bell in town, and has a very fine tone. St. Paul has now four church bells, with more coming."

The *Pioneer*, too, offered only Mr. Goodhue's much quoted soliloquy on the bells on November 6: "Church Bells. There is a large new bell, a very fine one, just received and hung up in the rear of the Catholic Seminary — a present from Louis Roberts. There are now four good bells in St. Paul, and another coming for the Baptist Church. We have some good church beggars in St. Paul; and our town has rung in pretty well upon the liberality of donors the past year. Our atmosphere is just right to make the ringing of church bells musical. The Catholic bell is hung upon four posts (the erection of the belfry being for the present thus *post-poned.*) It

rings much louder for being near the ground. The four bells
make a regular gamut of tones — the lowest note being the
Catholic, next above the Methodist, next the Presbyterian,
next the Episcopalian. If the Baptist bell should weigh 800
pounds it will go to the bottom of the scale, which being
eked out with the Mission bell and the little Catholic bell at
the old church will give us quite a gamut."

Sister Francis Joseph's report of the coming of the sisters
gathers significance from the fact that, in the absence of
contemporary newspaper accounts, it is the only record. "We
arrived at St. Paul during the night of Nov. 2nd," she recalled in her letter of October 20, 1894, "when we woke up
to look at our new home. It looked very dreary, the hills were
covered with Snow, the Cap[tain] sent [a] messenger to the
Bishop — about 10 AM. a French Cleric came down for us,
took us to a Lady named Madam Tourpan [Turpin], who
received us very kindly, and treated us to a very good
Dinner. After a rest, the Rt. Rev. Bishop Creten came accompanied by a young Cleric. We then were shown Our
New home, a small fram[e] Shanty on the Riverbank. We
took our first meal, Supper, (Nov. 3) in the vestry of the
Old log Church. We had difficulty to get Water enough to
make our tea as there was but one Well in the town and that
was locked up. We rested in the Vestry until the Students
removed all their Effects from their Pro-Theological Seminary. We then took possession of our new home. Opened
School [on the] following Monday, in the Vestry. I had
charge of the English department, as all the other Sister[s]
were French. That week we received our first boarder [for]
the Embryo Academy, Miss Martha Ellen Rice. We fixed up
an old shed back of the Shanty. M. [Henry M.] Rice
furnished her room, a good bed, &c, very comfortable. The
next month We received a Second Boarder for Our New
Academy. Miss Mary Fridley — daughter of [Major] Fridley,
of the [Winnebago] Agency. The young Ladies did well, and
seemed happy. I left them there. In March, we received a

third pupil Mary Bourtinneau [Bottineau] (a half breed)
from St. Anthony — We had a well attended School, as it was
the Only one, Except the boy's Class in the basement of the
Church, taught by a Mʳ Kelly, who became a priest of the
Diocese afterwards. We had very happy times, yet some days
we did not tast[e] food, until night. In the Spring we moved ˙
the School into the Old Church. We had the building filled."

Something of the sisters' orientation problems may be
gleaned from Sister Francis Joseph's further graphic observations. "To understand the position of the young Community
our first year, you must know (at that time) Minnesota was
an Indian camping ground, the chief settlers were Indian
traders, no farms had yet been planted, no public con-
veyance. (Winter) The Only road or — Way to Settlement
below was the Miss. River which was then frozen, and the
Wolves often attacked travellers as they travelled over the
ice. The nearest place to secure provisions was Debuque
Iowa. (500 miles away) So very often others were as bad off
as ourselves, nothing could be procured for love nor money.
This was the state of things, from Nov. to about the last of
May, When an event occurred, that changed all for the
better. This was the arrival of the first Steamer after the ice
had broken. As the Steamer, the *City of St. Paul*, came
steaming up the excitement was intense. Every individual
in town was on the River bank, with a loud Welcome for
the friend who brought them all comfort — all temporal
difficulty vanished with this event."

The Grey Nuns wrote of the unimaginable beauty of the
prairies covered with wild roses as they traveled through
Minnesota in Red River oxcarts. Sister Francis Joseph was
somewhat more practical, for she went on, "The Spring was
charming, the Prairies all in full bloom. Wild ducks plenty on
the River and Lakes. The Settlers were coming in from all
quarters, times have been good ever since. . . . Once in a
while we received a present of Venison, bear, deer, or
smaller animals, also fish — all very acceptable."

Equally vivid observations on the first winter were given by Mother St. John Fournier in the memoir she wrote to Lyons in 1873. Noting the arrival of the sisters in St. Paul, she told that "Monseigneur Cretin, the good and worthy bishop, gave up for us and installed us in his palace, which was only a cabin of rafters [in the original meaning of rough, heavy pieces of timber] composed of one room and a loft open on all sides." (Bishop Cretin seems to have had a similar problem in describing a log house for French ears. In 1845 he wrote home to his sister from Turkey River, Iowa, where he had charge of the Winnebago mission, that he was "lodged in a house formed of trunks of trees, laid horizontally one over the other, and covered with bark.")

Mother St. John's account is explicit. "Therefore," she stated, "our room served for oratory, refectory, community room, parlor and dormitory. At night, we put our mattresses, two on the table (after it was made) and two on the floor. We opened school in the old church near us. The following spring, Monseigneur built a beautiful brick school which served also as a dormitory for our boarders. The church was some distance from us; there were still neither roads nor streets in St. Paul. They had only cut the trees in a path and left all the stumps. Every morning that winter until the snow came, we made a number of genuflections on the way to church and to conclude, we kissed the ground. When the snow came, we sank into it two or three feet, or we walked on it, as if on ice. It was on one of those mornings that a starved wolf had a mind to take a bite — or the whole — of my person! The next day and all the rest of the winter Monseigneur came to say Mass in his old palace and on the table. I forgot to say that we had nearly seventy day-scholars and seventeen boarders, half Canadian and Half Indian, whom we prepared for baptism."

Life in the city of destiny was clearly recalled by another missionary, Sister Appolonia Mirey (or Meyer), who came from Philadelphia in June 1852. "On my arrival at St. Paul,

I was expecting a grand house," she remembered in 1895;
"to my surprise it was a log Cabin with one room and a shed
Kitchen with a few small outhouses which accommodated
eight boarders, we had to saw the wood for fires having no
coal, we had to place the victuals all on one dish when
cooked and enjoy it the best we could so you see we Kept
the Vow of Poverty very well and indeed we were happy
with all the hard work. . . . I often give the sisters a laugh
telling about those days."

A letter of Bishop Cretin to Bishop Chalandon, the coadjutor of Belley, described the difficulty with which he had
accomplished his work in the first three months after his
installation. He kept no servant and he had no horse. It was
necessary to go a good distance on foot to visit the sick. Although he was asked for missionaries for the savages in three
places he could not get priests or religious to come from
Europe. He was just as much in need of priests to care for
whites, for 20,000 emigrants, mostly from Catholic countries
in Europe, were expected in Minnesota the next season. He
complained that he had not even had money enough to fence
in the free land he might have had if he had been able thus
to establish his title to it.

The testiness of the bishop's report, intended primarily for
the office of the Society for the Propagation of the Faith,
must be condoned in view of the beginning just then of the
long school controversy in Minnesota. The opening salvo was
fired on December 2, 1851. That day the *Democrat* announced that the governor had appointed the Reverend E.
D. Neill, a Presbyterian minister of St. Paul, to be superintendent of the common schools for the territory. Mr. Neill
had also sent a letter to the paper announcing that he had
selected the Parker Readers as the texts which should henceforth be used in the schools of the territory. He had
examined the books and determined that there were no pas-
sages which would arouse religious prejudices. "A fruitful
source of difficulty in our public schools," wrote Mr. Neill,

"has been the reading of lessons from the Protestant version of the Bible."

Mr. Neill justified this burst of tolerance with an appeal to sound economy. "If the State ever expects to have her schools receive the support of the entire community, those who have charge of Public Institutions, cannot be too careful in excluding works that have sectarian bias, and the 'good' of every shade of religious belief should watch that an instruction of that description, is instilled by the teacher. But," wrote Mr. Neill grandly, "at the same time, we would not have any torment themselves with a jealousy of purposes, which have no existence but in their own imagination."

This passage was manifestly designed to encourage Catholics — part of the "entire community" — to send their children to the public schools without suspicion of the intentions of officials. At the same time, the speaker wished to assure the "good" Protestants that the removal of the King James Version of the Bible from the schools did not mean that Catholics were to introduce any of their religion into the curriculum.

What impact the fine phrase "jealousy of purposes" can have had on the four sisters in their chilly one-room convent or upon a worried bishop endeavoring to sort idioms and motives and promissory notes is now a mystery known only to the Father of Waters. Heart-warming, without a doubt, was the news received toward the end of 1851 that the Society for the Propagation of the Faith had allotted to St. Paul the sum of 37,500 francs. At most, the contribution was not more than 7500 dollars, yet it made an actuality of not only the sisters' school but also a hospital, a school for the Indians, and an orphanage.

The bishop was unable to realize the native expectation that Michelangelo in person was to lead the van of Catholic immigration to the territory, but he congratulated himself, nevertheless, that the Sisters of St. Joseph had come to Minnesota to stay.

℀ II ℀

Of Every Tribe and Tongue

ITINERANT missionaries were a curiosity in frontier St. Paul, but their visits supplied inspiration to the small group of sisters. One of the early visitors was the founder of the Dominican Sisters of Sinsinawa, Wisconsin, Father Samuel Mazzuchelli, whose adaptability is suggested by the fact that he was known to his flock in Galena as Father Matthew Kelly. The *Minnesota Pioneer* treated his brief stay in St. Paul early in 1852 in characteristic fashion: "We want this priest, or another equal to him to preach in St. Paul amongst the Catholics — so we hear *them* say. Father Morin [Moran] did not quite do. . . . He hit the devil a good many fair licks, but Mazzuchelli knocks the old un's horns clean off."

Sister Francis Joseph described the same visit otherwise. "Shortly after our arrival in St. Paul," she wrote, "we were honored by a visit from Rev. Father Mazurkehly, a Domini-can, an old Missionary of the Northwest." She recalled that he welcomed the sisters to their new scene of labor and then, stepping to the door of the shanty and extending his arms, he remarked, "Ladies, behold, you have the whole Country before you, your success in Monopolizing all the good works of this beautifully rising Country depends on your begin-ning. Let the World see your zeal and capacity — your fervor for God's glory."

The sisters' beginning in St. Paul was of necessity modest, but even early in 1852 their enthusiasm was evident as they

devoted themselves to building up the school made possible
by the grant from the Society for the Propagation of the
Faith.

As the letters of Sister Francis Joseph and Mother St. John
Fournier have told, St. Joseph's Academy was opened in the
second week of November 1851, only a few days after the
arrival of the four sisters. The vestry of the old log church
was used for a time as the classroom and then the school was
moved into the church proper. Toward the end of June 1852
Bishop Cretin revealed his plans for a new building to house
the school. In a report to the Society for the Propagation of
the Faith he said that the dwelling of the sisters was too
small to allow them to accept more than a few boarders and
they had been forced to refuse a good number. He was going
to borrow money and build a brick house for them large
enough to accommodate twenty boarders.

This building is clearly located on a map of the Bench

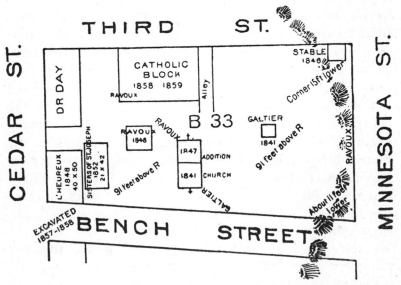

MINNESOTA HISTORICAL SOCIETY

Bench Street Properties (from a map prepared by
Father Augustin Ravoux)

Street properties prepared by Father Ravoux. It was one
story in height, forty-two feet in length, and twenty-one feet
in width. Years later John Ireland, first archbishop of St.
Paul, had this to say about it: "Mean of proportion and of
form this building seemed to eyes of the later generation that
doomed it to demolition; but in 1852 it was the wonder of
the village, and its construction was taken by the settlers as
an indubitable sign of rapidly-coming prosperity and civilization in the Northwest."

When school opened in the new brick building in the fall
of 1852 there were eighty-seven pupils including seventeen
boarders. Mother St. John Fournier was still in charge, and
she and two other sisters instructed the girls in reading, writing, arithmetic, grammar, geography, plain sewing, and all
kinds of needlework. They also gave lessons in sacred and
profane history, elements of astronomy, chemistry, botany,
literature, and music.

Long before this, however, in January 1852, the sisters,
few as they were, undertook also to staff the Long Prairie
Indian mission. Short-lived though this mission was, it is
more ably documented than any other of the undertakings
of the Sisters of St. Joseph during the century after they
came to Minnesota. The lack of material success and the
similarity to the usual situations in Indian schools of the
period have not in this instance obliterated the essential
charm in the old letters and official records concerning the
bizarre little venture. The fading documents have a reminiscent flavor from the earlier pages of American history
when devoted "Black Robes" endeared themselves to Christian Indians. Historians have lingered fondly over the details
from time to time and despite the lacunae left by them, the
Winnebago mission at Long Prairie retains a challenging
interest.

One of the reasons for the extensive documentation of
this venture was Bishop Cretin's deep interest in it. He
regarded it as an opening wedge in the struggle with the

government for a division of educational funds. This struggle, on several fronts, was to be one of his gravest concerns
during his term as bishop.

Cretin's interest in the Winnebago preceded his bishopric,
however. While he was still a priest in the Dubuque diocese,
he had worked among this tribe in the Fort Atkinson-Turkey
River region. He had great difficulties, for he was not allowed to establish a school and eventually Catholic missionaries were prohibited from appearing at the agency. He felt
keenly the preference shown to Protestant clergymen, and
he regarded as an injustice the appointment by the government of David Lowry, a Presbyterian minister, as Indian
subagent and superintendent of the school for the Winnebago at Turkey River.

When Bishop Cretin arrived in St. Paul to take over his
see, he found that the tribe had been transferred to Minnesota, and he at once sent his most promising young priest,
Father Francis de Vivaldi, to organize a mission at Long
Prairie. At the same time he wrote letters to every religious
order of men in the United States and Europe in an effort to
induce them to make a foundation among the Winnebago,
but, he complained, seventy orders refused to supply him
with their members. Fortunately the Sisters of St. Joseph
were at hand, and only two months after their arrival he
sent Sister Scholastica to the mission to begin religious
instructions among the "dear Indians."

Sister Francis Joseph, one of the most intrepid of the early
chroniclers of the Sisters of St. Joseph in Minnesota, wrote
of the adventure, "One of our colony Sister Scholastica Vasques, went alone up to the long prairie, amongst the [Win-
nebago] Indians, remained one Winter Instructing, aiding
an enthusiastic Italian Priest, Pere De Vevaldi, who afterwards became a fugitive from the Church. Poor Sister told
us thrilling tales about [the mission] — you know her School
was grown up men and women."

Sister Scholastica lived with a half-breed family named

Lequier while she was alone in Long Prairie. The oldest daughter of the family assisted her with her classes preparing the Indians for first communion.

Meanwhile Bishop Cretin had begun negotiations with officials in the territory and in Washington which he expected would result in government support for a Catholic school for the Indian children. He planned to use the Sisters of St. Joseph as teachers for the girls and small boys and he still hoped to persuade an order of men to come to Long Prairie to teach the older boys. But his efforts toward Indian education brought him troubles a plenty.

During all his years as bishop he carried on a complicated correspondence — in fretted English — with the purpose of securing fair play for Catholics from the commissioner of Indian affairs. His effort of February 24, 1852, set forth his ideas on the subject: "I am extremely pleased as a man as well as a Christian minister to see that the government of the United States think, at last, seriously to adopt efficacious measures to save from a prompt and unavoidable destruction the forlorn remainder of so many once powerful tribes. The World will applaud to this liberal, philant[h]ropic, though tardy course of policy, and by it, many prejudices very injurious to the glory of this great empire will be removed from the minds of Mil[l]ions."

The bishop went on to say that in spite of this advance he was pained to remark that only material means were considered in the report of the Bureau of Indian Affairs and no mention was made of the religious principles which must be the basis for any civilization. Men of zeal and great devotedness, "who can gain the confidence of the red men," were needed for this hard work. "Now it is an undeniable fact," wrote the bishop, "that all the indians tribes manifest a greater confidence in the ministers of the Catholic denomination. . . . The Catholic Worship is more calculated to make impression on their hearts and to convey to their minds ideas of the Christian Mysteries. Those among them who

have had chance to hear preachers of both side[s], call the
Catholic Religion, *the religion ready made,* and the Protestant religion, *the religion to be made,* or to be found from
the Big Book. Hard work indeed for these children of the
forests."

It was a duty of conscience, the bishop declared, to promote the spiritual and temporal welfare of the twenty-five
thousand Indians living within the territory entrusted to his
special care. He was convinced that Catholic missionaries
would have done a great deal for Indian civilization if they
had been helped by government money. He asked that part
of the fund set aside for the instruction of the Sioux and
Winnebago might be given for the establishment of a
Catholic school. This action, he was confident, would result
in a happy change in the tribes.

In May 1852 Bishop Cretin traveled to the East with the
dual purpose of attending a conference in Baltimore of all
the bishops of the United States, known as the First Plenary
Council of the Church and of making a personal appeal to
President Millard Fillmore for an Indian school appropriation. From Baltimore on May 20, he wrote to thank the
Society for the Propagation of the Faith for 7500 francs
(part of the grant of 37,500 francs promised in 1851) which
had reached St. Paul just two days before he set out for the
council. He said that he had been undecided about making
the long journey until he received the gift from the society.
His small resources made the trip difficult but he was sure
that the association would be gratified that he had been able
to attend so important a meeting.

It was, to be sure, fortunate that Bishop Cretin could be
present with his brother bishops for the initial discussion of
legislation for the church in America. Few of the prelates
had known more stirring encounters than he, and he was in
dire need of encouragement by his colleagues. As he wrote
in the same letter to the Propagation, he was engaged in a
continuous struggle against heresy and paganism. Catholics

were pouring into his diocese from every direction at the rate of two or three hundred a day. The work of saving the faith of the Catholics and trying to convert the thirty thousand savages presented many difficulties.

On the fifth of June he wrote again to the Propagation, this time from Washington. After reporting briefly on conditions in his diocese, including the work started by the Sisters of St. Joseph and the organization of four parishes (St. Paul, St. Anthony, Mendota, and Little Canada), he proceeded to explain his business with the government. He had come to Washington expressly to ask for a part of the $12,000 allowed for the education of the savages since the last treaties. The Indians prefer Catholic priests to all other instructors, he told the society, and "the Government avers that they have more influence and success than all the Protestants."

The problem was not as simple as that, however. The Protestants "have presented themselves for three days to the President to the number of 150 and they have reminded him that this country is *Protestant*. I have seen the President and I am convinced that he would like to oblige the Catholics, but he does not wish to displease the Protestants. So far he has given me only promises." The bishop was still hopeful, for, he said, "We can intimidate the President by giving publicity to the denial of justice to the savages. The Catholic vote is beginning to hold the balance in elections. They do not dare to disregard it."

In neither Washington nor Long Prairie did Bishop Cretin have the field to himself. Reverend Lowry, the superintendent of the Winnebago school at Turkey River, had encouraged one of his teachers, A. C. T. Pierson, to move to Minnesota with the tribe in order to take charge of the school there. Supported by the Indian agent, Major Fridley, Mr. Pierson had apparently proceeded to establish a manual labor school at Long Prairie. Both Mr. Pierson and Agent Fridley seemed to assume that the former would be ap-

pointed by the government as superintendent of education
for the Winnebago. They did not regard the claims of Bishop
Cretin as of much moment.

But they had evidently underestimated Bishop Cretin's
powers of persuasion — or the influence of his political pa
trono for in the summer of 1852 the government awarded
a five-year contract to the bishop for a Winnebago school
at Long Prairie. He was to be paid seventy-five dollars a
year for each child over five and under eighteen enrolled in
the school. In addition he received less conspicuous help for
the Pembina Sauteux. Bishop Cretin appointed Father de
Vivaldi superintendent and arrangements were made for the
school to open in the fall of 1852.

It must be regretted that Bishop Cretin experienced no
enduring satisfaction in the Long Prairie project. The
primary reason for this was the failure of officials in Wash·
ington and Minnesota to render him the moral support and
financial aid which had been promised. Agent Fridley's
opposition to the school was made very effective because of
the long delays of the Indian Bureau in answering letters
about any matter in dispute. Disagreements with the agent
about the ages and number of children enrolled dragged on
for months. The government was slow too in meeting its
financial obligations toward the school; again and again
Bishop Cretin was obliged to write to Washington begging
for the promised funds, and he was often forced to use
money from the Society for the Propagation of the Faith
(which had financed the founding of the mission at Long
Prairie) and other diocesan funds to support the school.

A second cause of his disappointment at times became so
embarrassing that it overshadowed, even in the bishop's consideration, the fundamental difficulty. That circumstance
was the emotional instability of the priest he had sent to
take charge of the mission.

Canon François de Vivaldi, brought from Europe by
Bishop Cretin after his consecration in 1851, had been a

member of the cathedral chapter of Ventimiglia, Savoy. The title of canon was an honorary one bestowed in European countries on the priests of a cathedral household. It was a distinction never used in this country, although there are some similarities to the honor bestowed here on a domestic prelate, where a monsignor has a distinctive purple vesture. The canon wore a special kind of collar with white tabs extending to the chest. Bishop Cretin was a canon in Ferney and we have a daguerreotype in which he wears the canon's collar.

François de Vivaldi, who was born in 1824, was the younger son of a noble Italian family. His older brother, Dominique, was a captain in the Seventeenth Savoyan Infantry. François was endowed with attractive physical qualities and a considerable amount of talent. He is credited with an excellent education. Bishop Cretin said that he was "at the head of a newspaper." As a scholar, however, his achievements seem to have been brilliant only in a shallow and superficial fashion. Although frontier statesmen cited his familiarity with languages as noteworthy, his letters in English are faulty in mechanics and florid in style. He also wrote execrable French, as he admitted to a friend in France in 1852. "I have not the courage to write in French as I have never applied myself to French literature and orthography: for me it is an insurmountable difficulty, as you see."

During the Italian Revolution of 1848, Canon de Vivaldi was expelled from Italy and sought refuge in France. Hence, he agreed readily to accompany Bishop Cretin to his new diocese in America. A mutual interchange of visits to relatives of bishop and priest took place before the departure and these continued by letter after they reached Minnesota. The bishop's sister, Clemence, and several of his nieces became well acquainted with the colorful young missionary. On the canon's side there was a cousin, the Countess de Vedaljer, to present. Later on when his father translated from Italian to French a long letter telling of the son's initial

experiences in Long Prairie and describing his missionary
methods, the canon's mother, Henriette de Vivaldi nee Ber-
nardi, sent the French translation to Mademoiselle Clemence
Cretin. The letter, with an account of the missionary's parley
with Descending Thunder, was dated August 3, 1852, at
Long Prairie.

"An Indian called 'Thunder which descends' said to me,"
wrote Father de Vivaldi in Italian, " 'Black Robe, we listened
to all that you told us until now, and we know that you speak
well and that what you say is true, but we cannot at all
believe that the Indians are of the same nature as the Whites.
See how black we are and how white you are. Therefore,
until now you spoke well, but we cannot believe you now
when you tell us that we are equal to the Whites.' "

The priest had answered elaborately that "the Indians, in
spite of their color, have a common nature with the white
man." He had gone back to Noah and his three sons Japheth,
Sem, and Cham. For his correspondents he explained that
the Indians would call Japheth's country the land of the
rising sun. This land was also his own, Father de Vivaldi had
told the Indians. Sem went to Egypt and dwelt there until
his descendants became so numerous that the land could not
support them all. The vanquished in the struggle which
ensued decided to go out in search of another country. "After
a long trip on the ocean," the missionary had said, "they
landed on the shores of America where they multiplied and
after having passed through many vicissitudes provided for
their living exclusively by hunting. They found in this
country all sorts of game, large and small, and this circumstance made them forget to cultivate the earth and caused
them to give themselves completely to hunting — a life which
exposes men to the inclemency of the seasons. Without commerce, without industry they became destitute of everything
and were obliged to clothe themselves in winter with the
skins of the animals they had killed in hunting and to go
naked in summer."

The instruction had been complete with a "so you see, Descending Thunder, that although your color is darker than mine nothing is opposed to your having the same nature as mine," except that the Italian had added a thought on the sons of Cham, who were changed from white to black by the burning sun in Africa. He told his European audience that the Indians understood the doctrine. With a pedantic flourish, he explained that the savages were called Oot-Ciangra in their own language, Winnebago in English, and in Italian Puzzulente.

Father de Vivaldi used the same newly acquired information in his first letter to Governor Alexander Ramsey, at the same time making clear to the governor the efforts he was expending in behalf of his charges. He described the needs of the mission beginning with, "The Sisters of St. Joseph that accompanied me here to teach these Indians and half-breeds, they have opened a school. The first day this school was opened we number 27 scholars and it is daily increasing. These teachers have a very bad and inconvenient lodgment and they do not yet get any assistance from the Indian Department. The principal object of my prayers to your Excellency is that you interest your goodness in favor of our scholars to obtain immediately from the Agent of the Winnebagoes provisions and clothing in same proportion that is issued to the other school among the tribe. Of this favor I always will feel under a great obligation to your Excellency."

Sister Appolonia, whose description of the convent in St. Paul has already been quoted, has left us a vivid picture of the sisters' "lodgment" at Long Prairie. "You might like to know how many stories high our house was at Long Prairie," she wrote. "Well: it was one Room; it had been used for keeping the salt meat in for the use of the Indians; it sufficed for Parlor, School Room, Kitchen, and in fact for everything. We had a little Room, upstairs, with hay on the floor to sleep on — that was the mattresses we had there."

Sister Appolonia had accompanied Mother Celestine Pom-

merel, the superior general of St. Louis, to St. Paul following
Mother Celestine's visitation in Philadelphia. Sister Francis
Joseph, writing in 1891, recalled their arrival:

"The first recruit we received was in July '52, when
Mother Celestine (of happy memory) came to visit us. She
was accompanied by Sister Appolonia from Philadelphia.
She is a native of Germantown Pa. and was one of the first
received in the Phil. mission . . . by Mother St. John be-
for[e] she was sent to St. Paul. . . . I returned with M. C.
to St. Louis, and thus bid a final farewell, to the beautiful
Prairies of Belle Minnesota. . . . Although I bad[e] farewell
to St. Paul, I have a most ardent desire to see again the old
Camping ground. . . . I do not forget anything about that
famous Mission — as it has been deeply set in my crucified
heart — It seems to me but yesterday — Just 40 years this
fall."

Mother Celestine seems to have taken the hundred-mile
journey north to Long Prairie with Sister Appolonia, the
latter to stay in the mission for eight weeks. In the meantime,
Mother St. John had gone to St. Louis for new recruits. Of
these, she left Sister Xavier in St. Paul and proceeded to
Long Prairie with Sister Cesarine, who was to spend the
school year there with Sister Scholastica. Sister Appolonia
returned to St. Paul with Mother St. John to remain until
both were recalled to Philadelphia in May 1853. Sister Appolonia was still living, and head of St. John's Asylum in
Philadelphia, in 1890 when Sister Francis Joseph was writing of the early years in Minnesota: "She is upwards of 70
years old — I saw her about 8 years ago. She was then [a]
very smart active woman, directing a very large and important institution."

Although the tenure of the sisters in the various early
works of the community seems brief, it is comparable with
the general turnover in professions and business at the same
period. Editors, lawyers, doctors, teachers, as well as grocers
and real estate men came and went with almost lightning

rapidity. Still other sisters, according to Sister Appolonia, came from St. Louis as the two were going east. They were Sister Victorine and Sister Simeon.

While the sisters at Long Prairie were preparing to open their school in the fall of 1852, Agent Fridley was writing to Governor Ramsey on the subject of Indian education in general and the Catholic school at Long Prairie in particular. Fridley did not "Your Excellency" the governor in every sentence as Father de Vivaldi had, but he flattered him more subtly and at even greater length.

His letter of September 9, 1852, opened with a description of the longing on the part of his charges for their new home and of their dissatisfaction and their "present vagrant life." He explained carefully that the former homes of the Winnebago had been "amongst the elevated prairies of Wisconsin and Iowa." The greater part of the present location, he said, was "covered with swamps and almost impenetrable thickets," in addition to which "Musquitoes" and other insects which swarmed here during the summer months to a degree unknown in other parts of the country "contribute to render a residence here disagreeable to these children of the prairies." The agent looked forward to an improvement in conditions if liquors were excluded "as appears probable from the operation of the stringent liquor law now in force in the Territory." This, of course, referred to the passage of the short-lived Maine liquor law by the Minnesota territorial legislature.

Agent Fridley went on to discuss the Manual Labor System of Education, a new plan proposed by the Bureau of Indian Affairs. Under this system "manual labor becomes the principal object of instruction and secondary to this is a reasonable devotion to litterary pursuits with a view to learning the scholars the English language, with moral and religious teachings as an auxiliary. Herein lies the difference," declared the agent, "between the new and old systems of instruction; while the latter makes religious teach-

ings and book learning its first and almost only aim, the new
plan ranks labor first and religious and litterary pursuits as
incidental though desirable features, but experience has
made it manifest that it is futile to begin civilization among
Indians by attempting to force upon there benighted understanding mysterios truths which no previos habits of there
minds or bodies has prepared them to receive or comprehend
aright."

Mr. Fridley managed to make the Manual Labor System
sound not a little like Mr. Squeer's celebrated educational
system as elaborated to Nicholas Nickleby.

"Now, then, where's the first boy?" said Squeers.

"Please, sir, he's cleaning the back parlor window."

"So he is, to be sure. C-l-e-a-n, clean, verb active, to make
bright, to scour. W-i-n-, win, d-e-r, der, winder, a casement.
When the boy knows this out of the book, he goes and does
it."

Having expanded his own ideas on schools for Indians,
Mr. Fridley continued in his letter to the governor to discuss
a subject close to Bishop Cretin's sensibilities for a long time,
namely, religious education among the Winnebago. This was
summarily disposed of by the agent, who ventured to tell the
governor that during the hundred and fifty years that Catholic missionaries had been laboring with the tribe they had
left "no monument of piety or civilization or belief to their
descendants." Impartially enough, he added that the whole
fruitage of fifty years of efforts by Protestant missionaries
was "a few dozen of the most indolent and worthless of the
tribe who can understand more or less perfectly the English
language with a little smattering of letters which not one of
them has ever put to any practical use."

To this lengthy exposition Mr. Fridley said he had been
aroused by the "proposition of the Catholic church of the
Territory to assume the entire direction of the school fund of
the Winnebago nation." The Indians were opposed to this.
Some time since, Mr. Fridley said, he had set aside a portion

of the school fund to aid the Catholic priest at Long Prairie in sustaining his school for half-breeds. At the same time he allowed the Indian children to go to that school if they wished. At first, he said, "about half dozen Indian scholars, probably for the novelty of the thing, attended the Half Breed school but these have since returned to the Manual Labor School. The other continues as pretty exclusively a school for half breeds only."

The present situation had its favorable features, the agent affirmed. "Indeed, I regard the separation of the Indian from the half breed children as beneficial to both. . . . Far less difficulty is experienced now in managing the Indian children than when the mixed and unmixed races were united in the same school." While earnestly deprecating a resort to the old system of mission schools for Indian children, Major Fridley did, nevertheless, recommend allowance for the support of a separate school for the Catholic half-breeds.

There is some doubt whether the Manual Labor School was ever in as flourishing a condition as this letter would indicate, but at any rate Major Fridley obviously did not regard the granting of a contract to Bishop Cretin as settling the issue of education for the Winnebago.

Mr. Fridley's ideas and activities were echoed in St. Paul, for on November 17, 1852, the *Democrat* carried a comment on Indian education which read, "In the late Council between the Winnebago chiefs and Gov. Ramsey, Big Bear said that he did not want to see any more schools among his people, because . . . education makes the young women bad and the young men too lazy to hunt and too much like some of the pale faces to speak the truth, keep sober, or behave themselves like honest Winnebagoes."

This was too much for the apostolic missionary at Long Prairie. The *Democrat* printed his reply on December 1.

Father de Vivaldi opened his letter with an ironical allusion to the "great philosopher of the Otchangras, a certain 'Big Bear' of the Winnebago tribe," who had arrived at the same conclusion as the Bear of Geneva, Jean Jacques Rousseau, that "the tendency of learning and of instruction is only to corrupt individuals and society; and that white men ought to live like Bears in the woods or 'like honest Winnebagoes.' There follows a sociological generalization by the canon which is not quite empirical: "Unfortunately, too many facts in our days seem to corroborate this sophism. Undeniable statistics show that the majority of those who fill our prisons and penitentiaries are not the ignorant and unlearned. The greater part of our rogues, robbers, drunkards, and murderers are able to read, write and calculate; their minds were formed or rather left unformed in our Public and Godless schools."

This type of faulty social inference was not a peculiarity indigenous alone with the loquacious missionary at Long Prairie, but characterized reform orations to the very end of the century. Even such a distinguished social reformer as Archbishop Ireland was guilty at times of ascribing all crime to a single cause — alcoholism. Moreover, he and many other advocates of total abstinence maintained that alcoholism was a crime rather than a disease.

Philosophically, Father de Vivaldi was on somewhat safer ground. By a series of rhetorical questions he arrived at the great error of the age — the separation of instruction from education. Learning and science are considered as everything, he said; education is disregarded or looked upon with distrust. "But," he declared, "no education can be conceived without religious principles."

This was sound enough Catholic teaching, but it is doubtful whether his readers followed his circumlocutions that far. It must have been a relief to them when, after a long section on President Fillmore and Indian affairs, he returned to Long Prairie. "The school now is, and has been during the last two months, under the direction of two Sisters of Charity [a term he sometimes used for the Sisters of St. Joseph]. The attendance was never before as numerous, the school was

never so orderly, and there is strong reason to hope that the
Indians will begin to know the true God and experience the
benefits of civilized life." The letter was signed, "A Looker-
on in Venice," which was doubtless a pedantry from Shakespeare's "My business in this state / Made me a looker on
here in Vienna."

On the other side, a letter went to President Fillmore from
Alexander Wilkin, then secretary of Minnesota Territory,
complaining that a good Whig had been displaced as superintendent of the Indian school at the Winnebago Agency by
the appointment of "an Italian priest (Catholic) who does
not speak the English language." Mr. Wilkin had learned
that the change was effected by Democratic influence and
the "whole influence of the Catholics, in return, was exerted
in favor of the Democratic candidate for the Legislature who
was defeated with a majority of three votes only, where
formerly nearly the entire vote had been given to the Whig
candidate."

The president replied that he was "somewhat surprised
that charges of so grave a character should have been presented against the Commissioner of Indian Affairs" and referred the whole matter to Governor Ramsey. The governor's
duties included the superintendency of Indian affairs in the
territory in addition to his regular administration, so that it
was nearly six months later before he penned his reply. Then
he enclosed two letters written by Father de Vivaldi in
order to indicate the missionary's acquaintance with the
English language. "It is true," wrote Governor Ramsey, "that
Mr. De V. is a priest — he is, however, a fine scholar, speaking with ease and fluency the English, and many of the
continental languages."

The governor also enclosed a copy of the contract into
which he as Indian superintendent had entered with Bishop
Cretin and an explanatory letter in which he said, "You will
see that I have allowed $75 per head, per annum, for educa-
tion, maintenance, &c. I am satisfied that this is the lowest

sum for which the service can be rendered. . . . It is the universal admission of every one, at all cognizant of affairs in the Winnebago school, that under its recent management [presumably referring to the Manual Labor School] it was doing no good. It is to be hoped that under the charge of Bishop Cretin a greater degree of usefulness will be attained. Should this not be the case, the Government can at any time annul the contract."

The protest of the displaced teacher, Mr. Pierson, contained in a letter to President Fillmore, is an illuminating little sidelight on the spoils system. He explained that he had gone to considerable expense in moving his family to Minnesota, feeling that he would not be disturbed during a Whig administration. To his chagrin, Governor Ramsey had turned the school and property over to a Catholic priest who had been only a few months in the country. The first act of the priest, he charged, was to assemble the French and half-breeds at his house to tell them that they must support the Democratic party at the coming election, because Bishop Cretin had succeeded in getting the school fund turned over to him by the influence of certain Democratic senators. Worst of all, "using the whole of his priestly influence, he told them that they must vote for a certain drunken, lazy, worthless loco-foco." And they came near electing him against the regular Whig candidate. Moreover, in St. Paul the Catholics under the lead of the bishop "elected four foreign Catholic loco-focos of the five to which St. Paul was entitled as members of the legislature."

As a threat at the end of his letter, Mr. Pierson added that the Indians were highly incensed at the change. "The chiefs," he said, "are going down in a body to see Governor Ramsey on the subject."

Father de Vivaldi had his own friends among the Indians and half-breeds down to see the governor in November. Their petition, presented with the marks of fourteen half-breeds and of twenty-one chiefs and braves, denied the false reports about their school and the Reverend Mr. de Vivaldi which had been made by two of the chiefs in a council at St. Paul. They begged that their school might remain in the hands of Roman Catholics and they declared that their young men, "instead of leaving the white man's dress for the blanket, leave the blanket for the coat and cap."

The exigencies of the situation thus forced Bishop Cretin into the role of religious competitor, but his business and political acumen was not highly developed. It was not long before he perceived the unreliability of his difficult missionary. To Mother St. John, who had returned to Philadelphia after a year and a half in St. Paul, he wrote on April 6, 1853, "I still do not know what to make of M. de Vivaldi. He takes power to himself without authority." Again on September 21, 1853, the bishop told Mother St. John news of her old mission field, including the canon. "I may send M. de Vivaldi to make a collecting tour although he is a pretty bad preacher in English. He wants it intensely. One is obliged on certain occasions to close his eyes tight on things and pray. That remedy is often more useful than all the counsels. Sometimes small honors are not less vaunted than great — since he is a superior in a little distant savage place he feels he is an important personage. So far he has done nothing really serious."

One effect of the dispute over the superintendency of the Winnebago school was to delay the payments due Bishop Cretin under his contract. Months passed after Father de Vivaldi's dramatic appeal to Governor Ramsey and still no funds were forthcoming. On August 17, 1853, the new governor, Willis A. Gorman, wrote to the commissioner of Indian affairs to ask for a settlement. By this time also Major Fridley had been replaced by Jonathan Fletcher as agent at Long Prairie.

To Father H. P. Donelan, who was acting in a semiofficial capacity in Catholic Indian affairs in Washington, Bishop Cretin entrusted his own appeal to the commissioner with this explanation: "This affair has caused me a great trouble & some pecuniary embarrassment. I am obliged to recall the teachers from this Mission. Many Catholics have suffered cruelly by the dishonesty of the Agent Fridley. If I cannot obtain justice I'll address myself to the Senate, and to the public by way of the Newspapers. Such fact would not do much honour to the government."

The delay in payments he mentioned in a letter to Mother St. John a week later. "I shall have to withdraw the Sisters from Long Prairie as not a sou has arrived for them yet." The bishop hesitated to lose his foothold at Long Prairie by actually withdrawing the sisters, however, and he continued to dip into diocesan funds to support the school.

Early in November 1853 Father de Vivaldi sent his annual report to Agent Fletcher. The style is identical with his earlier and later expressions, yet there is more than a grain of truth in his complaints. He cited the fact that official negligence had allowed the introduction of great quantities of liquor into the neighborhood resulting in quarrels between the Chippewa and the Winnebago. Notwithstanding the difficulties, the average daily attendance in the school was sixty-two, and there was marked progress in reading, writing, spelling, arithmetic, and geography. The missionary said that the pupils were remarkable for their capacity, application, and docility, and he added:

"The little girls especially have acquitted themselves in a manner worthy of praise. Nearly all . . . frequenting the schools have succeeded in learning to read and write and to sing. A great number of them have embraced the Christian Religion and make rapid progress in civilization; this is especially owing to the zeal and untiring care of the Sisters of Charity. The boys and girls have been employed also in manual labor. During winter the boys were engaged in cutting wood for the school — in the spring they were placed under the direction of a skilful farmer and were occupied in tilling and cultivating the School Farm. The occupation of the girls was to make their own dresses and the clothes for the boys."

Since Bishop Cretin had not been successful in his attempts to persuade an order of men to send teachers to Long Prairie, Father de Vivaldi had found it necessary to use nearby farmers as teachers for the older boys. The younger boys were taught by the sisters.

Sister Ursula Murphy, who lived at Long Prairie for a time, has presented the more important aspects of the work there as well as an entertaining recital of her first trip to the mission. Her matter-of-fact relation sketches many aspects of frontier life that are all but incomprehensible today. With her stirring portrayal touching up the foreground, it is possible to fill in the bizarre details of this fascinating chapter in the history of the sisters.

"I was sent to Long Prairie Jan. 3, 1854. Sister Scholastica was recalled to St. Paul. I found Sister Cesarine and Simeon there. . . . Sr. C. was put in Sr. Scholastica's place as Superior, I remained there until the Indians were removed to Blue Earth. . . . The children [stayed at home] with their parents and attended the schools. According to their Treaty, each pupil received a certain amount of flour, pork, blankets, and everything needed for food and raiment. Each of us received $40. per month, the Superintendent recd. $60. per month — besides there was a farmer, who had to take the boys a certain number of hours in the week to teach them how to work — he recd. $50. per month. All of which came out of the school funds. There were horses and all farming implements. Also a store-house for their provisions. You know everything had to be bought in St. Paul and hauled in wagons to the Mission. It was in one of those trips that I was hauled up there. . . .

"You know dear Bishop Cretin was fond of sending Sisters off alone — so I had to go alone." This, of course (for the benefit of the sister to whom she was writing), was a reference to the traditional rule of companionship in all convents. Obviously, with the limited numbers available, it was necessary for the bishop to dispense at times from the strict observance of that regulation.

"As I have said," Sister Ursula went on, "the teams had to go to St. Paul for provision, *etc.* for the school. They came after Christmas so I was sent with them. They were driven by young men (Half Breeds). The weather was extremely severe, and I was not well provided for such a journey in an open wagon, loaded with barrels of flour & pork, *etc.* After riding all day we arrived late in the evening at a little log house, occupied by an old couple & their son. They had no accommodations — however we were glad to get shelter for the night. The horses were worse off — they had to stay in an open shed all night. The old woman fell in love with me — she tried every way she could think of to have me stay with her. She seemed almost heartbroken next morning when I was leaving her.

"The next day we were overtaken by a man by the name of Moran, with a team loaded with provisions going to the pineries above Long Prairie. We put up at Waatab for the night. Mr. Moran came to me and asked where I was going, how I came to be alone — he said: I see those men have no judgement or no care for your safety — you will never get there alive travelling in this way. I will take you in my sleigh and try to get you there safe. You will perish if you remain as you are. I asked if he were going the same way — he said yes — I will keep right along with them — I want to take care of you. I consented to travel in his sleigh — he deprived himself of his Buffalo robes, blankets, &c, for my comfort. At night wherever we put up the best accommodations had to be for me, the rest might be satisfied with anything they could get."

There is a little relish in Sister Ursula's recital of the awkward moment when she reached the mission. "When we arrived at Long Prairie, Rev. de Vivaldi met us. After Mr. Moran had left he showed some displeasure and asked me

why I was with that Orangeman. I told him how and why.
I had been sent out without robes or blankets and the men
had kept theirs for themselves & I was very cold, when that
man took me and gave me his robes and took good care of
me all the way. It seemed to satisfy Rev. F. de V. He said
'that is an orangeman of the worst kind.' But I did not think
so."

Sister Ursula added a cheery note, "I never forget my
early life in St. Paul — it seems to be the only life I ever
lived. . . . I left St. Paul 21 of Sept. 1861."

The essentially supernatural character of the way of life of
a Sister of St. Joseph is perhaps less clearly manifest in all the
pious literature than in this and other fragmentary remains
from the Long Prairie experience. The utter unconsciousness
of human considerations of competence and stability and
visible achievement gives new meaning to the shield of faith
and the helmet of salvation, to say nothing of feet shod with
the preparation of the gospel of peace.

Sister Ursula's letter about the tumultuous times was
written to Sister Ignatius Cox, a stately Bostonian who had
entered the convent in St. Paul in 1855, so that she remembered the circumstance that Sister Ursula, Irish and im-
petuous, had been dismissed from the community in St. Paul
at the beginning of the Civil War for her too open expression
of southern sympathies, on account of which the work of the
mission was threatened. She went to Wheeling, West
Virginia, and was received by the Sisters of St. Joseph, then
an independent foundation under the direction of the bishop
of Wheeling. After a short period of poor adjustment to that
group, she finally settled down to a peaceful life with the
Sisters of St. Joseph in Buffalo, New York, where she died
in 1916.

It is amusing to note that Sister Ursula, according to her
annalist, often related that Archbishop Ireland was a student
in her class in St. Paul, although in fact he went to study in
France shortly after she came to St. Paul and had not yet

returned for ordination when she left. And he came home to St. Paul such an ardent partisan of the northern cause that without a close examination of the dates, one is tempted to think he had something to do with Sister Ursula's departure from St. Paul. As it is, there is but the reflection that she clung desperately to the veil and habit and cincture — to the sword of the spirit in her rosary. At long last they helped her to face in patience even her own human failures.

Sister Ursula seems to have caused no uneasiness to Bishop Cretin, which was fortunate, for almost everything else connected with Long Prairie brought him problems. He had commented in a letter to Mother St. John, before Sister Ursula's arrival, "It appears that the harmony [at the school] is not perfect. The religious who have not learned to obey and to conquer their humors are poor religious. I hope, however, that all will go better. Pray hard for your dear companions."

The bishop kept on appealing for the $2000 owed him on his contract. Partial payments were made from time to time, but the long delay had created new needs and there was never any sense of security, such as was experienced upon the receipt of money from the Society for the Propagation of the Faith. In July 1854 Father de Vivaldi petitioned the secretary of the interior to establish boarding schools for the Winnebago and to allocate the whole fund to him. The letter seems to have been sent without Bishop Cretin's knowledge while the canon was making an eastern tour.

Among the many schemes of the Italian which added to Bishop Cretin's worries was the building up of a religious order called the Sisters of the Love of God, who were largely recruited from half-breed girls living near Little Canada. Vivaldi maintained that the sisters under his direction lived a more perfect life of prayer than the Sisters of St. Joseph and that the Sisters of St. Joseph of Carondelet were not fully approved by the church. The plan seems to have been to establish a self-sustaining and independent community —

like the Jesuit Reductions in Paraguay perhaps — of which
Father de Vivaldi would be in complete spiritual and financial control.

Toward the end of October, Father de Vivaldi returned
from his tour of the East and presented his annual report to
the Indian agent. Father Daniel Fisher had been stationed
at the mission during Father de Vivaldi's absence and the
school had continued with an average attendance of forty-
three. The report said that the pupils had been "instructed
in the different branches of a plain English education with
constancy, zeal, patience, and a true devotedness by the
religious ladies known as the Sisters of St. Joseph. . . . A
part of each day was employed by the Sisters in teaching the
girls certain branches pertaining to housewifery such as
sewing &c."

Agent Fletcher's report to Governor Gorman for 1854
stated that "the Very Rev. Canon Francis De Vivaldi, Apostolic Missionary among the Winnebago Indians . . . has
manifested great interest in the welfare of these Indians by
his efforts in their behalf. Two Sisters of Charity [Sisters
of St. Joseph] have been employed as teachers." He noted
the fire which had destroyed their dwelling house in the
previous winter and said that by it they had sustained a
loss and been put to much inconvenience.

At about the same time Bishop Cretin was again occupied
with claims on the contract. He estimated that he had sustained a loss of $1500 when many of the Indians had wan-
dered away and remained for nearly twenty months, in
anticipation of the treaty-making at Crow Wing; the number
of pupils enrolled in the school during this period had sharply
declined but the expenses had gone on. His claims had not
been paid for a year and the delay had been the occasion of
additional loss. Now he had a new debt of $200 for the de-
struction of the house of the sisters, which had burned
down, along with all their personal effects and the clothing
the bishop had sent for the children a few days before. He

had replenished the supplies for the sisters and the children and had been resigned to bear the loss without claim, although the fire was caused by the negligent use of worn-out stove pipes, until he heard that a Protestant missionary at Pembina had recently been granted payment of a similar claim. Therefore, Bishop Cretin expected that he too would be reimbursed.

A sidelight on what the well-dressed Indian child wore is revealed in a little sheet of paper, preserved among the official papers of the school, wherein Sister Cesarine and Sister Ursula attest that they distributed "to the boys, each one of them: 1 pair of satinet Pantaloons, 1 shirt of muslin. To each of the girls: 1 Calico dress, 1 chemise, or in place of it two pairs of Pantalettes. To both sexes: 75 Pairs of Shoes."

For some time the Winnebago had not been content at Long Prairie. The Crow Wing Treaty of February 27, 1855, acceded to their wish to change their residence to Blue Earth, Minnesota.

Agent Fletcher then wrote to Governor Gorman recommending a change to district schools similar to the system in New England. Since Bishop Cretin had indicated that he would bear no further expense on account of the school after January 10, 1855, the agent considered that he had defaulted on his five-year contract and that the agreement with the government could therefore be considered void.

Governor Gorman answered that Bishop Cretin wished to turn the school over to Father de Vivaldi's sole charge, and the governor regarded the priest as eminently qualified for the duties involved.

This did not settle the matter, however. Arguments over the monthly payments continued, especially for March and April 1855. Even before the removal to Blue Earth in May, the agent and Father de Vivaldi were in controversy over allowances in supplies and the age of the children attending the school, and such disputes continued after the move. Numerous documents were filed by both sides, including an

interesting if not particularly informative report in Father
Fisher's hand of a conversation between Father de Vivaldi
and a Winnebago chief, Hoono-Krat-aka. The conversation
related to the Indian's comprehension of the questions asked
him concerning Father de Vivaldi's conduct of the school
and distribution of supplies. The principal contribution of
the Winnebago brave was to reiterate that he always knew
what he was doing when he took up the pen. That is, when
he made his mark opposite his name he understood the
content of the paper.

The governor finally forwarded all pertinent papers to
Washington with the recommendation that the bills be paid
up to the departure from Long Prairie and that a new contract be made with Bishop Cretin for Blue Earth, whatever
Agent Fletcher's objections might be.

No new contract was made, however, and the old one was
terminated by mutual consent after the removal to Blue
Earth. Father de Vivaldi was appointed superintendent of
the Blue Earth school under a verbal agreement with the
government; he had not waited for the official appointment
but had opened the school in May 1855.

The Sisters of St. Joseph did not accompany Father de
Vivaldi to Blue Earth. In a report on December 5, 1855, the
priest praised highly their work at Long Prairie: "The Sisters
of St. Joseph from St. Louis, Mo., have been the teachers
of this school for the past three years . . . their zeal,
charity, and constancy in the work of civil and Christian
instruction of these Indians will never be forgotten, and will
one day produce fruits of benediction for this tribe."

The teachers at Blue Earth included both men and women
lay teachers, Brother Ernest of the Order of the Holy Family,
and the Sisters of the Love of God, the order founded by
Father de Vivaldi and headed by a former Sister of St.
Joseph, Sister Cesarine Mulvy. Mother St. John Fournier
had also been invited to join the new order, but she had
refused. The only other Sisters of the Love of God whose

names are known were Sister Victoria Lequier and Sister Anselm McCourt.

Father de Vivaldi's report mentioned specifically three lay teachers, Misses Darthula H. and Fannie J. P. Smyth and Mr. Robertson C. Smyth. The Smyths were the children of the late Colonel Harold Smyth of Wytheville, Virginia, a distinguished officer of the United States in the War of 1812. His children were "highly educated," giving instruction to their savage pupils in all the branches of a common English education, and also giving lessons on the piano and guitar.

In the same report Father de Vivaldi gave an attendance average of 210 for his school. In order to refute the charge that the school was a source of great pecuniary profit and that the Catholics in taking it did so for the purpose of making money, Father de Vivaldi cited current prices. Pork was selling at $40 per barrel, whereas it had been only $12 when the school was at Turkey River, Iowa. Flour was $20 per barrel, while formerly it had sold for $3.50. Each scholar received 22 pounds of flour and 15½ pounds of pork every month, which at current prices cost $15.50.

Agent Fletcher and Father de Vivaldi had nothing good to say of each other during 1855, but the agent included a favorable statement about "Mother" Cesarine in his letter of January 21, 1856, to Governor Gorman: "Mother Cesarine, who has been for a long time engaged as a teacher in the school, is an intelligent woman, well educated and is held in high esteem by the Indians, and generally esteemed by all, would, I am satisfied, if permitted, do all in her power to carry into effect the stipulations of the contract with Bishop Cretin [there was still some confusion about the status of the original contract], and the stipulations of the Treaty of 1832 relative to instructing the scholars of the school in the several branches of housewivery, etc."

Although Bishop Cretin's official responsibility to the government had ended with the removal of the school to Blue Earth, his problems in connection with the school did not cease. As Father de Vivaldi's superior in the church, he continued to regard himself as responsible for the priest's debts and behavior. And there were still the unpaid claims for the Long Prairie period to be settled.

On January 21, 1856, Bishop Cretin wrote to Mother St. John in Philadelphia, "Perhaps you already know the difficulties with deserters to which your old community has been subjected here. Oh, how inspired you were not to yield to the temptation which the Rev. M. de Vivaldi suggested to you! Or have you heard from here? He has led astray Sister Cesarine who left the house on his counsel, in spite of my order and that of her superior. I have had to excommunicate her. M. de Vivaldi has appealed to the Pope, saying that his Order is ten times more perfect than that of St. Joseph of which he says all imaginable evil. He hopes that the successor of Monseigneur Kenrick [the bishop of St. Louis] will suppress it. He has accumulated debts up to $3,000. There was a question of arresting him. He appealed to me on his knees with tears to permit him to go out collecting for the mission to save him from the embarrassment of being arrested and of thus heaping maledictions on the church. I had to yield to his insistence. Did it make him more grateful and docile? I doubt it. He is vanity and frivolity personified, joined nevertheless with excellent qualities. Sister Augustine [Spencer] was on the point of deserting also. Pray then for your former companions that they will all become saints."

Governor Gorman informed Commissioner Manypenny of the Office of Indian Affairs on February 18, 1856, that he had suspended Father de Vivaldi with Bishop Cretin's concurrence.

To the Propagation of the Faith, Bishop Cretin wrote the distressing story on June 7. "Would to God that only his head was bad!" he exclaimed. "He is a very dangerous priest, for he has written to Rome against me and even to the Propagation of the Faith. He was driven from Rome in 1848 — he could become a second Gavazzi. I have often warned him to dread a like misfortune." (This was a reference to the apostate priest who instigated the mobs against Cardinal Bedini when he made a visit of courtesy to the president of the United States in 1853.) The bishop went on to warn the society that his missionary, "who has compromised the existence of all our missions," would probably try to make collections in Paris if not intercepted. He should be deterred, for "it would be throwing money into a whirlpool."

In another worried letter written four days later, Bishop Cretin named Cardinal Franzoni as the dignitary at Rome whose letters Father de Vivaldi had made public to prove that his mission was from the pope directly and that he had to receive no order from the bishop.

Also in June, Agent Fletcher was trying to have Father Ravoux appointed as principal teacher (or superintendent, if he must) of the Blue Earth school, with Sister Cesarine as assistant teacher. In view of Mr. Fletcher's earlier vacillation in regard to Father de Vivaldi, it is difficult to place trust in his remarks about Sister Cesarine, who, as far as we know, was not then in good standing with the diocesan authority in St. Paul. However, Mr. Fletcher may not have been aware that Sister Cesarine had left the Sisters of St. Joseph and become the superior of the Sisters of the Love of God at Blue Earth. At any rate, the agent wrote to the new superintendent of the Minnesota district, Francis Huebschmann, that he had spoken to Sister Cesarine and that she expressed a willingness to continue to teach in the school in case Father Ravoux was engaged as principal. Of Father Ravoux he wrote, "He is favorably known to me and I have wanted the man particularly, hoping that he would accept the appointment."

The bishop replied that Father Ravoux "would have resided among the Indians this long while, if his health permitted him to do it. General Fletcher is free to make another choice."

Finally the Winnebago school at Blue Earth passed into

non-Catholic hands. The Sisters of the Love of God dispersed soon after Father de Vivaldi left, several of them joining other orders. The needs of the Catholics among the Indians at Blue Earth were then served by the priest at Mankato, who journeyed to Blue Earth at rare intervals.

Nevertheless, financial cares continued to harass Bishop Cretin. As he had said, there seemed to be no way to stop the trouble about the claims. As late as the middle of December he was trying to get money to pay Canon de Vivaldi's debts. This was very late, indeed, for two months later the bishop himself was dead.

As for Father de Vivaldi, he was not dead, but he was far away. In the diocese of Milwaukee he seems to have been given charge of parishes in Platteville and Green Bay. He left the priesthood, married a wealthy widow named Meade, a trader's daughter of mixed blood, and disappeared from Wisconsin in June 1858. He went to Manhattan, Kansas, became the editor of the *Western Kansas Express* and mayor of the village. During the presidential campaign, his paper was credited with being an influential Republican organ working for Lincoln's election. As a consequence, many politicians recommended his appointment to the consular service in a European or South American port. He was briefed for several posts, but was actually appointed only to Santos, in São Paulo, Brazil, where not more than three or four American vessels called during the year.

He left Manhattan, Kansas, in 1861 and had taken his post by the end of the year. With the exception of a visit to Washington and New York in the spring of 1866, he remained at Santos until 1869. Then he moved to Rio de Janeiro to engage in business, leaving his stepson, Edward L. Meade, in charge of the consulate. Within the same year, his stepson died, and Vivaldi closed the consulate in April 1870.

On May 1, 1882, Francis de Vivaldi left his family, consisting of his wife, Mary Frances Lawe Meade de Vivaldi, and his only daughter, Corinna, in Rio de Janeiro to make a trip to the southern boundary of Brazil. He was never again heard from by them, and after seven years had elapsed, it was presumed that he was dead. His wife died in 1885 and his daughter married the undersecretary of war under Dom Pedro, José Visconti de Coaracy.

In January 1883 Vivaldi was in Buenos Aires requesting to be readmitted to the sacred ministry. The ecclesiastical authorities imposed upon him the condition that he should first live for a year in some religious house. He was admitted by the Salesians, the order founded by John Bosco, the worker with Turin delinquents who died in 1888 and was canonized by Pius XI in 1934.

After fourteen months, the archbishop of Buenos Aires restored his priestly faculties to Father de Vivaldi for one year and he was sent to Chubut in Patagonia, as a sort of missionary-at-large to the scattered population, with the Salesian Fathers conducting the settled parishes. His faculties were renewed annually until October 1890, when he went to Europe with the idea of being made the vicar apostolic of Chubut by the Holy See. The archbishop of Buenos Aires favored this promotion and a gift of 100,000 hectares of land by the government seemed to hinge on his elevation.

Reminiscent of his days in Minnesota, the records show the former canon "intriguing in Rome to become Vicar Apostolic of the Chubut region in Patagonia." He succeeded in getting a decree to that effect from Cardinal Simeoni and he seems to have worked up some clerical following in South America. This was a threat to the Salesian Fathers, until Dom Rua, the successor to Dom Bosco, was told by Pope Leo XIII in January 1892 that Patagonia was not going to be split up, for Father de Vivaldi's record was not worthy.

In that same year Archbishop Ireland met Father de Vivaldi in Rome and told him about a land litigation in St. Cloud in which the missionary had an interest. In turn, Father de Vivaldi gave to the archbishop some old letters of Bishop Cretin which he had been treasuring all those years.

This detail is recorded by Dr. William Watts Folwell, to whom the archbishop gave an account of the meeting. Father de Vivaldi at once set out for St. Cloud to establish his claim to a forty-acre tract near the St. Cloud Reformatory which he had acquired by patent entry in 1856.

The spicier aspects of the guest from Chubut, Patagonia, registered at the St. Cloud hotel were not lost on the St. Paul, Minneapolis, and St. Cloud reporters. The tags were: "Like a Novel," "Patagonian Prelate," "The Dead Come to Life," and "Ireland in Favor." The latter caption referred to Archbishop Ireland's progress at Rome in the Faribault-Stillwater school controversy, about which Father de Vivaldi expressed himself freely. Amusing variants in the spelling of the traveler's name by the newspapers do not obscure the fact that he was about sixty-eight years old and that he was a heavy, round-headed, well-kept old gentleman, with pure white hair.

The judge in St. Cloud decided adversely on Father de Vivaldi's suit. The claimant departed from Minnesota and was next heard from in Paris.

In 1911, when Father William Busch was a student at Louvain, a fellow student from Paris told him of meeting an aged priest who had once been a missionary in Minnesota. It was in the course of St. Vincent de Paul work in Paris that the young man had encountered Father de Vivaldi and because he was living in poverty a letter was sent in his behalf to Archbishop Ireland, who responded with a cordial reply and a bank deposit. Some years later, Father Busch heard the archbishop relating the story of Father de Vivaldi to the faculty at the St. Paul Seminary, including a mention of the letter from Father Busch's associate in Louvain.

In 1934, during a research project Father Busch wrote to his friend l'Abbé Joseph Courtade and asked for information regarding the last days of Father de Vivaldi. The reply stated that for some years the old missionary had celebrated his daily private Mass in a convent in Paris. Eventually, he entered an institution conducted by the Sisters of Charity of St. Vincent de Paul, where he died and was buried in a well-recorded grave. In 1951, the Abbé Courtade recalled that Father de Vivaldi had translated into Spanish the works of Louis Veuillot, a Catholic writer, for which service he was decorated by the Spanish government. He died in the hospice of the Sisters of Charity of St. Vincent de Paul in 1902.

Sister Cesarine's story is not recorded as fully as Father de Vivaldi's, but she too seems to have settled down to a peaceful life with the Sisters of St. Joseph. Born in County Tipperary, Ireland, Margaret Mulvy had received the habit in Carondelet when she was seventeen years old, on April 19, 1849, so that she was barely twenty-one when she came to Minnesota. That she was a person of some spirit and intelligence is evidenced by the record in other fashion than through Father de Vivaldi's high praise. The annals of the Buffalo, New York, Sisters of St. Joseph tell that four sisters from Carondelet under Mother Julia Littenecker opened St. Louis parochial school in Buffalo in the autumn of 1858. The other sisters were Sister Anselm McCourt, Sister Victoria Lequier, and Sister Cesarine.

It seems something more than a coincidence that the names McCourt and Lequier appear repeatedly in the half-breed lists from Long Prairie and Blue Earth and that Sister Cesarine mentioned Sister Victoria in a letter she wrote to Bishop Cretin shortly after Father de Vivaldi left the mission. Moreover, it was a Miss Lequier who assisted Sister Scholastica Vasques in her first season at Long Prairie.

There was considerable shifting about to the different missions in various parts of the country during that decade and it is quite possible that the Sister "Cecerine" who went with a group to St. Ann's Academy at Corsica, Pennsylvania, in 1860, was the former Mother Cesarine of the Sisters of the Love of God. The records of the diocese of Erie may some day bring forth a burial record as much on the side of the angels as Father de Vivaldi's.

Miss Fannie Smyth, one of the teachers of the Indian school at Blue Earth, entered the Sisters of St. Joseph at Wheeling, West Virginia, in 1859, and became Sister Vincent. During the Civil War she was one of the army nurses at the Wheeling hospital. In 1883, she became the superior general of the sisters in Wheeling, so that her life too shows the keen desire for living in a community of religious which the rugged experiences of frontier Minnesota could not dispel.

✗ III ✗

They That Dwell Within

Catholiques: 5,000 — hérétiques: 7,000 — infidèles: 30,000.
THIS neat statistic in the *Tableau* of the Society for the Propagation of the Faith for 1853 comprised Bishop Cretin's population report. Presumably the infidels were the *sauvages*,
but it is altogether too depressing for any researcher at this
date to account for thirty thousand scattered souls. A round
with Mr. Webster on definitions reveals that the vocabulary
of our forefathers was far richer than ours in what to call
those who thought otherwise, especially about God. Distinctions in classification are not quite so clear today. Thus the
difference between infidel and heretic seems to be merely
more of the same.

From Bishop Cretin's correspondence it appears that he
found it difficult to distinguish between Protestant opposition to Catholics and political objection to foreigners and
Rome. And in the matter of schools, of course, there was a
united front by all non-Catholics against giving financial aid
to Catholic institutions.

The battle for a share of educational funds from the government had not been limited to the Indian school at Long
Prairie. The campaign in St. Paul was long and bitterly con-
tested. Bishop Cretin's comment on the situation there appeared as a note in the *Catholic Directory* for 1854: "The
New Englanders, pretty numerous in St. Paul, have imported
from their former home their narrow eastern prejudices

against liberty of conscience and the freedom of education. In the name of liberty, as understood by them, they disregarded last year numerous petitions on that subject and defeated a bill claiming that each denomination should be authorized to have schools of their own supported by the public funds, provided these schools be well conducted and although religious instruction be given there. They thought proper to compel parents to pay taxes for schools that their consciences and their pastors forbid them to profit by. There is no hope to obtain anything this year from our Legislature, neither from the School Commissioners, for our numerous schools. These gentlemen would do well to take some lessons of liberality from their neighbors in Dubuque and Galena."

The school controversy had been raging in the newspapers of St. Paul for some time. The editor of the *Minnesota Pioneer* had expressed his views on July 29, 1852, when he had written that St. Paul was "an opulent town, swarming with children, little untaught brats . . . along the streets and along the levee in utter idleness, like wharf rats. All this in a town that boasts half a dozen steepled churches. If St. Paul is not a priest-ridden town, it is in a fair way to be." This was not so much an objection to religious schools as a booster's desire for quick results, which he felt the churches had failed to produce.

There were other facets to the controversy. Various religious publications in the East had copied the remarks of the Reverend Lyman Palmer, a Baptist minister of St. Anthony, from the New York *Baptist Register* pointing out that "the elite of St. Paul Protestants send their daughters to the Catholic School. In Galena, Illinois, they elect a Catholic mayor and rule the Bible out of the public schools, the Catholics are so strong."

But it was the doings in St. Paul that really scandalized Mr. Palmer. "While the Man of Sin is making . . . rapid strides," he continued, "a Protestant, Presbyterian N.S. [New School] minister in Saint Paul, calls the Bible a sectarian book and thinks it should not be tolerated in the schools. How is this? Is it intolerance to use the Protestant version of the Scriptures in schools contrary to the wishes of the Catholics?"

Mr. Neill, whose friends called his attention to this publicity, promptly replied to the charge in the *Minnesotian* and the *Pioneer*, the two leading St. Paul papers. He characterized Mr. Palmer as a "mild, gentlemanly, and useful member of a small Baptist church at St. Anthony," while he himself was the only New School Presbyterian minister in St. Paul. He said that he loved the Bible, but he did think "the Douay and new Baptist versions of it" gave it a "sectarian aspect." On the other hand, he could readily suppose that a Roman Catholic could be sincere in his assertion that he believes "the translation made by the divines and laymen of the Church of England (a translation which I prefer) is a translation that has a sectarian coloring." Therefore, since these versions of the Bible could each be opposed as sectarian by one or another religious group, Mr. Neill did not believe the Bible should be used at all in the public schools. Further on he suggested that if Mr. Palmer were living in Italy, he would "consider it high-handed tyranny if the Tuscan officers should say, you shall read the Scriptures only as they are translated in the breviary."

(This erroneous notion that the breviary, the office book of priests and religious orders, is simply a translation of the Scriptures passed unchallenged. The breviary is an arrangement of psalms, canticles, hymns, and lessons, taken partly from the Old and New Testaments and partly from the writings of classical Catholic authors. It is doubtful that Mr. Neill had ever seen any vernacular translation of the breviary, since the first English translation was made in 1879 by the Marquis of Bute, who was only converted to Catholicism in 1868, well after Mr. Neill's letter of 1853. There are no evidences of earlier translations in Continental languages.)

Mr. Palmer — mild as he was reputed to be — defied the minister of the "large brick church in St. Paul" to produce a

"Bapist version" of the Scriptures, and a second exchange of letters made it clear that Mr. Neill's actions as superintendent of schools in the territory were not motivated by any love for Catholics.

This little skirmish ran into columns of print after the introduction into the territorial legislature on February 25, 1853, of the bill authorizing the public support of denominational schools to which Bishop Cretin alluded in the *Catholic Directory*. The bill, drawn by Father Daniel Fisher, a native New Yorker who spent a few years in the St. Paul diocese, was sponsored by William Pitt Murray, a well-known Methodist and lawyer. The newspapers assumed the responsibility of killing it, and discussion on the floor of the legislature after the first two readings of the bill seem to have been purely perfunctory. There was no third reading.

In answering a letter which protested the exclusion of Catholic teachers from the public schools, Mr. Neill took occasion to discuss various aspects of the "bill of abominations" as the *Pioneer* called it. His objections to the bill were largely economic, for, he said, "In the district where I reside, the tax, last year, for the hire of teachers, amounted to about $650, and though I have not the list before me, I do not think that more than $65 was collected from those who would send [their children] to a Roman Catholic school." The inference that St. Paul Catholics were poor, was, of course, accurate.

Mr. Neill's report for the Minnesota Bible Society informed the public through the *Minnesotian* of July 23, 1853, that "though there had been no action upon the part of the Trustees of the Public Schools, the Bible had been read as a devotional exercise in the majority of them, and [this] has been agreeable to those directly concerned." Not quite agreeable to one correspondent in the *St. Anthony Express* was the discussion held by the Lyceum in the schoolhouse on "The Republic More in Danger of Catholicism Than Slavery."

In October, the papers were once more filled with discussions of the division of school money. Mr. Neill gave the editors the complete text of the sermon he preached in the First Presbyterian Church on September 25, 1853, on "The Nature and Importance of the American System of Public Instruction." The printing was prefaced by a letter from a group of citizens requesting its publication.

After an opening section on the interest of the ancient Hebrews in popular education, Mr. Neill said that "since the assembling of an ecclesiastical council in Baltimore in the spring of 1852 [the meeting which Bishop Cretin had journeyed east to attend] a number of foreign prelates, who acknowledge allegiance to a foreign power, have incited the priesthood which they control to make a ruthless and concerted attack, from the pulpit, upon the educational system of the United States; and have urged their people to petition the Legislature of many of the States, and of this Territory, to pass a law for the encouragement of sectarian schools, the enactment of which would result in crippling the State in her efforts to instruct the whole people."

Although Mr. Neill's statements seem to betray deep-seated prejudice, the basic consideration in all his discussions appears to be economic rather than religious. The value of the district school, he felt, was that it helped to repress vice and crime and secondly, that it increased the wealth of every community. "Among the heaviest burdens," he said, "upon a populous State, is the support of paupers and criminals. . . . Where the State instructs her people, the long lines of beggars that are seen on some of the highways that lead to the large cities of Italy and Ireland . . . are missing.

"Public Instruction is important," he gave as a third point, "because it creates a national sentiment. At all periods America has been a land of refuge. . . . Here the cultivated and polished Lord Baltimore, cramped by the exactions of the British Government, found a place on the shore of the broad and beautiful Chesapeake, where he could say his Ave Maria and Pater Noster, with all the freedom and fervor of any devout Papist at Rome. . . ."

The sermon flowed on. "The dark-eyed Italian, the blue-eyed Hibernian, the mercurial Frenchman, the high-spirited Hungarian, the contemplative German, the hardy Norwegian, the brawny Highlander, and the reserved Englishman, are all found living together upon the prairies of the far west, who, only a few months ago, were dwellers in European capitals, and accustomed to the sight of royalty and its many appendages." The idea probably was that as beggars they saw the king ride by.

"These new comers are people of strong prejudices," Mr. Neill continued. "Many yet love their fatherland. . . . Others . . . have no real love for the form of government to obtain which our forefathers sacrificed their lives and fortunes. Without a system of popular instruction, the offspring of the emigrant would grow up with all the peculiar prejudices their parents had imbibed in European countries. . . . Fourthly, Public Instruction is essential to the preservation of our civil and religious liberties. . . .

"If the bill introduced to our Legislature last winter, by the influence of the Roman Catholic 'Bishop of St. Paul,' had passed, any school numbering twenty-five children and giving religious instruction would have been allowed all the rights and privileges of a regular district school, and been free from the inspection of the civil authorities. A Presbyterian minister would then have been allowed to go into a community where there were twenty-five Protestant and ten Roman Catholic children . . . to teach that the Roman Church worships the Virgin Mary as the Romans worshipped Venus, as a divine being, and that the members of the Roman church at this day bow before a statue which was once a representation of a heathen deity, and that the priests of the Pope had always opposed the general diffusion of intelligence. The ten children of Popish preferences must [then] either go to this Presbyterian school, or they must grow up ignorant of the rudiments of learning, for the state cannot give money to support a school of ten.

"On the other hand, if a great majority of the children were under the influence of the Roman church, as in the district which adjoins this town [Little Canada], under the law that the friends of the Bishop desired to have passed by the last Legislative Assembly, the Protestant children then would have been obliged to have gone to the Papal school, and to be taught that none but Romanists are safe from hell, or remained at home in ignorance."

In his inscrutable manner, Mr. Neill declared that "judging from the past" the pupils under the influence of a Roman priesthood would "chiefly receive oral instruction." He believed that the Catholics did not base their support of the bill on a regard for the spiritual welfare of their children, but rather on the belief that public instruction "trains the pupil to exercise the right of private judgement and even think and do as Rome does not on many subjects." He exhorted his congregation not for one moment to "give ear to the clamor of Roman Catholic priests, who, if their assertions are to be credited, never have any children, do not pay one cent into the treasury and without exception acknowledge allegiance to a temporal power in Italy."

Letters to the papers for and against this sermon of Mr. Neill continued through all of December. One signed "American" said that the bishop of St. Paul felt that Mr. Neill had destroyed the effect he had hoped to produce by calling Catholics popish, papists, Romanists. The superintendent speaks, commented "American," like a true nativist, for he lavishes contempt upon foreigners — "those newcomers, people of strong prejudices."

Bishop Cretin's letters to Mother St. John during 1853 merely mention the school controversy, asking for her prayers and saying, "in spite of the recrudescence of antipathies, of the malice of prejudices which our Protestants manifest at

the instigation of their wicked leaders some good may yet
be done." But for the greater part they were concerned with
less momentous doings.

In April he thanked Mother St. John and Sister Appolonia
for their prayers and begged a continuance. He told Mother
St. John he suspected she was the kind donor of three copies
of the Catholic Almanac, for which he was particularly grateful since the ones he had paid for when he was in Baltimore
had not arrived. The bishop said he had not the least disa-
greement with the sisters in St. Paul, although others (doubtless in Long Prairie) had given him some embarrassment.
Sister Scholastica seemed to be in better health. (Apparently
she had already developed the tuberculosis which was to be
the cause of her death six years later.) He knew the bishop
of Philadelphia, Monseigneur Neumann, had found Mother
St. John a tremendous help. The priests of the St. Paul
household begged to be remembered to her. The winter had
been magnificent and they expected a great increase of population in St. Paul that spring.

During the week of Mr. Neill's celebrated sermon the
bishop wrote of the opening of school. Everything was going
well. There were only six boarders, but more were expected
during the winter. The general enrollment was up to the
same mark as the previous year — eighty-seven. All the sisters
— eight and two postulants — had been present for their
eight-day retreat.

Late in 1853 the Sisters of St. Joseph opened a private
school in St. Anthony, which was known for a time as St.
Mary's Convent. When this school was merged with the
parish school across the street some years later and was
called St. Anthony's, like the church, the convent, which
provided a home for the first parochial teachers in Minneapolis, continued to be known as St. Mary's for many years.

Sister Ursula Murphy recalled that the "St. Anthony Mission opened Nov. 5, 1853, with Sister Philomene Superior,
Sister Ursula, teacher, cook & house-maid in general with a

young lady to assist me; as well as I remember her name was Bridget Maloney. She was from Dubuque. The Bishop thought a great deal of her, and insisted on her being received. She had only one arm; however, he gave her the habit, but Mother Celestine in St. Louis was informed of it and she would not consent to her making any vows or remaining in the Community at all. She was sent home."

Discrimination against a physical handicap was not characteristic of frontier religious, for in that very year of 1853, a Grey Nun — Sister Mary Xavier Dunn — passed through St. Anthony. She had only one arm, but her biographer says that "she was known far and wide in the old days. She lived forty-two years in St. Boniface."

Miss Maloney appears again in the annals of the Sisters of St. Joseph for the reason that young John Ireland was sent to escort her from the boat upon her arrival to the Bench Street convent. It is recorded that, having deposited her at the step, he pounded upon the door and took to his heels without waiting for the awesome greeting of the sister who would open it.

The sisters' new school must have flourished, because on June 3, 1854, the *St. Anthony Express* carried an announcement by the Reverend Denis Ledon, the pastor of St. Anthony's Church, of the "erection of a large building for a Female Academy in this place." The *Pioneer* of St. Paul said on November 25 that the "St. Anthony Seminary" had opened under the management of "Mother Abbess Scholastica Nasquer [Vasques]," who had replaced Sister Philomena, and that it had between thirty and forty boarding scholars. The building was said to be capable of holding one hundred scholars and since the "Abbess" had called to her aid three sisters, there was no difficulty in regard to a sufficient number of teachers. French, Latin, and music, together with the English branches, were taught in the institution.

Colonel John H. Stevens, one of the founding fathers of St. Anthony, made it clear that Catholics were no more popular by the falls than in St. Paul. In an address in which he reviewed local history, he managed to leave out the Catholic church from his account, justifying himself with the observation that when he spoke of a church he meant a Protestant church. At about the same time a lecturer before the Minneapolis Moral Reform Society pleaded for the support of true piety without priest or pope.

The fact that the falls had been discovered and named by Father Hennepin in honor of his patron saint was always something of a bother to these historians of the place. The Reverend John A. Merrick, for example, gave a footnote to the saint: "Antonius de Padua, a Portuguese Franciscan friar, noted for his oratory and profundity in Theology. He was called to Rome and received special marks of honor from Popes and Cardinals. . . . Notwithstanding his erudition, he was a weak man and his expositions very clumsy." No wonder the falls disappeared!

The hospital which Bishop Cretin had listed, together with a sisters' school, a school for Indians, and an orphanage, as a need of his new diocese in his appeal to the Society for the Propagation of the Faith in 1851 finally became a reality in 1854.

The hospital was planned in 1852, and by the early months of 1853 a huge building was under construction. But Bishop Cretin was finding it hard to decide whether to use this building for a hospital or for a college. He was waiting for teachers and priests from Europe, the bishop said in a letter written in the spring to Mother St. John in Philadelphia, but he had also told Mother Celestine Pommerel to have some sisters ready for the hospital. If he changed his plans, the sisters could be used otherwise.

He soon definitely decided on a hospital, and by June 30 the delay in hearing from Mother Celestine about sisters to staff it was taxing Bishop Cretin's patience. He thought, he wrote to Mother St. John, that Mother Celestine should realize how important it was to avoid any pretext for criticism in a new venture by taking care to have everything run smoothly.

At the beginning of the winter of 1853–54 the bishop was able to inform Mother St. John that the building was roofed and enclosed. "Of wonderful strength and size," it would afford room enough for a hospital, an orphan asylum, and an entirely separate and independent novitiate for the sisters. This first unit of St. Joseph's Hospital, torn down in 1890, was built on the precise location of the central administrative unit of the present institution at Ninth and Exchange streets in St. Paul.

The *Pioneer* listed the hospital among St. Paul's public buildings at the end of the year. An arrangement by which the city's poor might be accommodated there as soon as the hospital was in operation was mentioned in the *Minnesotian* for June 3, 1854. As things turned out, however, it was not possible for either the sisters or the city to wait for St. Joseph's Hospital.

By June, the newspapers were no longer able to conceal the fact that there was cholera in St. Paul. They kept on insisting that the victims were brought by the boats from unhealthful places where they had contracted the dreaded disease. But there was no denying that people were dying of cholera in St. Paul and no one was caring for them — no one, that is, except Bishop Cretin and the Sisters of St. Joseph, who had hastily converted the old log chapel on Bench Street into a makeshift hospital and were doing all they could to relieve the sufferings of the victims.

There was no lack of appreciative comment, especially in the *Democrat*, on the "truly Christian and self-sacrificing ladies" for the "humanity and Christian benevolence" they had demonstrated at the "appearance of the scourge." This glowing sentiment was some check to Know-Nothingism, for the *Democrat* scored political religionists who would unite Protestants and infidels against Catholics and thus "attack some of our best citizens and represent them as criminals of the deepest dye."

It was Bishop Cretin and Father Marcellin Peyragrosse who had been thus stigmatized because the young priest, with the knowledge and consent of the bishop, had filed on a claim of a quarter section of the Sioux purchases. The claim was "pleasant and sightly" and a jumper had decided that because the land would be used for the purposes of education and charity and not as a family farm, the filer had no right to protection under the pre-emption laws. He seized the claim forthwith, including Father Peyragrosse's lumber and improvements.

A group of the neighbors in Dakota County invited the jumper to leave and when he refused, they removed him and tore apart the shanty he had built with stolen lumber. This "claim mob" scandalized the Know-Nothing party and evoked columns of newsprint. The *Minnesotian* was sure that Bishop Cretin had ordered on the mob, while the *Democrat* insisted that he had "here taught Jesus and Him crucified long before the wily politicians of Minnesota learned to court popularity by heaping abuse upon the pious."

On August 30, 1854, the *Democrat* quoted a eulogy of a "Sister of Charity" from the Philadelphia *Gazette*. The particular sisters described were the Daughters of Mother Seton, an American convert, who were shortly to be amalgamated with the French Sisters of Charity of St. Vincent de Paul. Their works of charity were well known on Chestnut Street in Philadelphia, but the St. Paul editor obviously hoped that the same ideas would run through the minds of his readers when they encountered the Sisters of St. Joseph in Minnesota. By a coincidence the Sisters of St. Joseph of Philadelphia under Mother St. John Fournier established their motherhouse on the same street and both the institution and the sisters are known as of Chestnut Hill to this day. The newspaper piece abounded in contrasts of black dress and dashing throng, of poverty and affliction with gossiping promenade, gaunt-cheeked children and glittering human butterflies. The unrealistic article finally came to an end on a moral note: "Never sneer at the quaint aspect of one of the self-sacrificing Sisters as seen among a fashionable crowd."

It was not alone that writing was different a century ago. It might be that neighborly charity was still a personal responsibility and the sight of human distress still excited men to effective pity. The hospitals of the 1850s bore little resemblance to modern institutions. They were almost exclusively for the care of the poor and those who had no homes. This is apparent in the *Democrat*'s story about the opening of St. Joseph's Hospital on September 20, 1854.

The account made clear that the old chapel on Bench Street which had been used as a hospital during the previous summer had "scarcely sufficed for the wants of the neediest among the sick and the generous labors of the Sisters of Charity were restricted." There was no suggestion that any but the poor or strangers would find their way to the more ample quarters of the new hospital. The division of the sick into classes related merely to the nature of their diseases and not to their social or economic status.

A pensive reverie marked the *Democrat*'s Christmas offering that year. The editor wondered why the day set apart to commemorate the birth of Christ was observed only by Catholic and Episcopal congregations in St. Paul. This matter had been puzzling him ever since as a child in school he and other Presbyterians had failed to receive presents and enjoy the Christmas holiday which their school fellows of the Episcopal church enjoyed. That brought the writer to the matter of charity. He thought it somewhat singular that all denominations of Christians in this country seemed by common consent to have given up to the Catholics or the local authorities that relief which a sick and distressed stranger required. Catholics built hospitals with Sisters of Charity in attendance and every patient without regard to his religion was carefully nursed. Readers were reminded that many examples of this kind had occurred during the cholera siege of the past summer, when local authorities had done little and Catholics had done much, silently and without ostentation, to relieve the victim strangers.

"So it is all along the Mississippi River," the writer rhapsodized; "many a man has cause to bless these Sisters of Charity for a life which without their assistance would have been lost."

The *Democrat*'s editor added a small apologia, lest any misinterpret his eloquence. He did not mean to censure other denominations, he said, but just here Catholics deserved praise. "We are no believers in the Catholic religion," he protested, "but are willing to do them justice."

The *Pioneer* emulated this charitable flight on January 26, 1855, in an account of the "Catholic Hospital." Father Fisher had conducted the editor through the building where there were ten patients. The sufferings incident to poverty and the pain of sickness were removed by the tender solicitude of sisterly affection extended to them by "those Angels of Mercy, the Sisters of St. Joseph, to whom the care of the distressed is a joyful trouble." Mother Seraphine Coughlin was reported to be in control of the internal policy of the establishment, which exhibited to the visitor neatness, orderly arrangement, and an air of comfort.

It was well on into February before the editor of the *Democrat* got around to make his tour of inspection, but then he was thorough about his observations. He noted, for example, that a beautiful pure stream of spring water ran near the building. This was the rivulet drawn in certain early sketches of St. Paul which trickled through the present Seven Corners into the river near where the public library now stands. The spring water, according to the paper, was carried by a force-pump into every story of the hospital. A force-pump sounds like an automatic, labor-saving device, but one of the sisters has left a description of a similar arrangement at St. Joseph's Academy which dispels all such

illusions. Four sisters had to operate the pump together to
draw water.

The *Democrat* called attention to the bathrooms in each
story of the building and the constant and healthy cleanliness throughout. The galleries surrounding the house gave
convalescents an opportunity of taking restorative exercise
and enjoying pure air.

The cost to patients in private rooms was eight dollars per
week, a moderate charge the editor thought. No funds had
been provided by public or private donations locally, but
the institution was one which the editor was sure reflected
credit upon the whole community. He understood that a
bill for its incorporation was to be introduced into the legislature. That technicality, however, was not achieved for
another thirty-five years.

The whole establishment was "under the supervision of
the Sisters of St. Joseph," wrote the kindly editor, "a religious
order well known for more than two hundred years for their
kind and attentive care of the sick, of orphans, and the
instruction of youth."

There were thirty orphan children enjoying the devoted
attention of the sisters at St. Joseph's Hospital, the editor
told his readers. Orphans were cared for in every establishment of the Sisters of St. Joseph, but this group at the
hospital was the largest. Part of the original grant from the
Society for the Propagation of the Faith was used to support
them, and this was supplemented by an annual Orphans'
Fair.

A free school for girls, the second of the schools to be
established by the Sisters of St. Joseph in St. Paul, had been
opened on the first of January in a brick building near the
southwest corner of the property. Sister Margaret Senselmeyer taught a class of twenty to thirty girls there.

At the conclusion of his article, the editor of the *Democrat*
could not resist repeating his "meed of praise to these devoted sisters, who, secluding themselves from the world, its

allurements and pleasures, devote their lives to the most
arduous and trying duties that can devolve upon a woman."
Some people could see no good in this because it was done
by Catholics, said the editor. For men calling themselves
Christians often endeavored to prescribe and afflict those of
other faith than themselves; especially did they have a holy
horror of Catholics.

The bishop's letters to the Propagation of the Faith in 1854
indicate his awareness of hostility in the community. "We
have to struggle," he wrote, "against Protestant propaganda
which gets possession of the children through the schools."
He said that Minnesota was very attractive to emigrants
from Europe, but Americans from New England were still
in the majority and "they are Protestants with great prejudices." Protestants perverted many isolated Catholic families,
since the children were taken free in Protestant schools at
the expense of the government and the Bible societies. Their
pupils were inspired with such a horror of Catholicism that
it was difficult for them to return to the church later on.

To indicate how important the work of establishing
Catholic schools seemed to him, Bishop Cretin told of the
large subscriptions already collected with the avowed purpose of stopping the progress of papism in the state of
Minnesota. He said that the Presbyterians had built a college
which would cost 500,000 francs, just a quarter of an hour
from St. Paul. Forty miles away, the Methodists had built
another which would cost 600,000. The Methodist institution
established at Red Wing in 1854 was the forerunner of
Hamline University. The Presbyterian college was the Bald-
win School, which was later to be named Macalester College.
This school had been incorporated by the territorial legislature on January 27, 1853, three weeks to the day before
Mr. Murray introduced the bill for aid to schools teaching
religion. Mr. Neill was the founder and it was he who discovered a benefactor in Philadelphia to bear the initial
expense.

In February 1855 the *Democrat* discussed the religious persecution of Catholics by the Know-Nothings. These expounders of American principles had a program which, according to the newspaper, ran something like this: "We, the majority who are Protestant, declare that they, the minority, who are Catholic, are ineligible to vote, shall not hold civil office, and their children must read our Bible, or lose the benefit of the common schools, to the support of which nevertheless, they (the Papists) *must* contribute." There were others, whom the editor called slightly quixotic, who said that belief in the dogma of the Roman church "unfits a man to eat Uncle Sam's pork and beans, and be shot at at the rate of eight dollars per month."

Citing contemporary and historical examples of anti-Catholic prejudice, the *Democrat* carefully defined its editorial position. "We are not and never have been a believer in the Catholic Church, its doctrine or plan of Church government. We are willing to allow Pius IX credit for all his good intentions, while at the same time we award him a hearty hatred and detestation for his misdeeds."

The four schools of the Sisters of St. Joseph — two in St. Paul, one in St. Anthony, and one in Long Prairie — and their one hospital, which was self-supporting, were the gratifying entries in Bishop Cretin's French reports to the Society for the Propagation of the Faith for March 1855. The Protestant colleges still worried him and there was the additional distress of the state university at the Falls of St. Anthony, "endowed by the government with a parcel of land worth more than ten millions." But the bishop told his benefactors it astonished him that with so much money they were doing so little; at the university they had not a student, but only some sinecures.

The celebration of St. Patrick's Day was virtually the only occasion on which territorial Catholics received any public attention as a group. It is true that in 1852 the Irish and French-Canadian temperance societies had been tentatively permitted to demonstrate for the Maine liquor law with the other societies, but the law had been declared unconstitutional so soon that the fervor of the other societies burned out. A surprising amount of respect was accorded to the parade and the banquet by the newspapers on March 17 and each year the temperance features were carefully noticed. The parades always stopped for speeches at the bishop's house and at the residence of the Sisters of St. Joseph. Civic officials spoke at the hot coffee and cold water banquets.

Perhaps because of the outbreak of Know-Nothing sentiment throughout the country, an effort was made to have the celebration of 1855 surpass those of earlier years. Governor Gorman eulogized Bishop Cretin in a speech which was fully reported in the *Boston Pilot*, except that his remarks on the treatment of foreigners in the United States, heartily approved by the *Democrat*, were not quoted in any of the papers.

Father Peyragrosse died that spring at the age of twenty-seven. A native of Puy-de-Dome, France, he had pursued two years of seminary study under Bishop Cretin, and the bishop was saddened by the death of his gentle young Benjamin. Shortly before his death Father Peyragrosse had written a letter to Mother St. John about some songs for which she had asked. He told her that they all regretted they could count on her no more for the "instruction and organization of savage Minnesota." She had left the territory, as it were, bankrupt. They should have been more clever than to let her escape from Minnesota. He was glad to hear that all her dear orphan children were well, and the novices too. "The dear Master accompanies you, doubtless," he wrote, "for all the difficulties you have had to endure to extend His glory and to execute His will during your too short sojourn in this ungrateful Minnesota."

He told her that good was done very slowly in St. Paul. But the "gatherings at nightfall" on Sundays in honor of

Mary continued to produce excellent fruit in souls. The Holy Virgin would not forget, for "she knows well that it is the zeal of Mother St. John which has occasioned these pious reunions weekly."

Bishop Cretin died on February 22, 1857. All the people irrespective of class or creed manifested grief. Protestant ministers asked the privilege of attending his funeral. After Mass the funeral procession moved down Wabasha Street to Third, thence west to the present cemetery, Calvary, at Como and Lexington, a distance of about two miles. The ministers of the Mass wore their vestments and the rest of the clergy cassocks and surplices. Catholics walked to the graveyard, non-Catholics following in carriages. The varied representation in the long procession to and from the graveyard included the Sisters of St. Joseph and the children of the schools. The last spoken and written words of the bishop breathed his sincere desire to do only the will of God and to bear patiently whatever trials might be sent him.

A brief description of church affairs in Minnesota at this time is provided in a letter written to France (after Bishop Cretin's death and before his successor had been appointed) by Father John Fayolle, who was then pastor at Little Canada and later at St. Anthony. Naturally, his thoughts were centered on the conditions in the diocese. He said that there were 50,000 Catholics dispersed through the vast territory and only twenty-seven priests, some of whom were getting old and others leaving the country. Nothing had been done toward building a seminary and the outlook was not very bright in that respect. As a consequence, the new bishop would have a great deal to occupy him.

The episcopal sees in the United States were anything but sinecures, wrote Father Fayolle, and the inclination of those appointed was rather to refuse the miter than to accept it. The life of a priest, too, was one of labor, privation, and sacrifice, since he was not always sure of subsistence. Some priests received too much compensation, whereas others had

nothing. Altogether, Father Fayolle considered the priest's
work here much more burdensome than in Le Puy, where his
brother was a vicar.

What gives the letter real interest is its treatment of the
problems created by diverse nationalities, each having its
"own ideas, manners, prejudices." Self-command was needed
to adopt other habits than those to which one was accustomed and beyond that, there was still the difficult matter
of establishing peace among the various peoples, especially
between Irish, Canadians, and Germans. Father Fayolle
observed that the prejudices of race were very strong and
seldom gave way to reason. (*Race* was the term then applied
to any national group, such as the *Irish race*.) The national
spirit opened the way to many difficulties, the solution of
which depended on experience. Irish would like an Irish
priest, Germans a German, and it was manifestly impossible
to please all of them. The French could not bear an Irish
priest, Father Fayolle added.

The rigors of the climate were a second source of difficulty. Thirty to forty degrees below zero was not a pleasant
experience when traveling about visiting the sick. Sometimes
one's face was frozen in three minutes. On the other hand,
the burning heat of summer made the atmosphere like an
oven. One extreme was replaced by the other.

The constitution in Minnesota was democratic, with officers elective and no rank of nobility, commented Father
Fayolle. All religions were strangers to the law and state
funds could not be appropriated to a religious purpose. Men
of every race except Negroes were citizens and enjoyed the
privileges of citizenship. In all Minnesota there was not a
soldier and the police could do little to quiet the roaring
lumbermen when they rushed into town.

Between the picturesque angels which the newspapers
would have made of the Catholic sisters and the clashing
multitude of the noisy, busy West, it is still possible to
distinguish a handful of quiet persons who were neither

leaving the country nor setting it on fire. They were the plain, unpretentious Sisters of St. Joseph at St. Joseph's Academy, St. Joseph's Hospital, the St. Anthony school. All that can be said of them is that they were folk of His pasturing. But it is enough.

⚜ IV ⚜

The Gate of the Corner

ALTHOUGH Bishop Cretin died without knowing whether his fatherly interest in the Sisters of St. Joseph would bear fruit in permanent and stable institutions, his imprint remained on the struggling community through his influence upon the vocations of two of its most promising candidates.

Ellen Ireland and her cousin, Ellen Howard, were the first graduates of St. Joseph's Academy in St. Paul to become Sisters of St. Joseph. They had come to live in St. Paul six months after the first sisters had established their school in November 1851. Between May 1852 and June 1858 the two Ellens had completed all the prescribed studies and had graduated from the academy, with the distinction of being the first graduates, but without a formal commencement. They were sixteen years old and they were convinced that God had called them to enter the convent. This purpose they accomplished by going a few blocks from their home on September 8, 1858, to St. Joseph's Hospital, where the novitiate was housed.

Not only to the two young girls, but to the sisters and priests and indeed to the whole cathedral parish, the step they took was a momentous occasion which recalled Minnesota territorial history in a vivid fashion. For even then the Ireland family had come to typify not only the story of the frontier church but of the young state as well.

All six of Richard Ireland's children had been born in the

County Kilkenny, in the parish of Danesfort, near the village of Burnchurch. There John, the future archbishop of St. Paul, was born on September 11, 1838, and baptized on the same day. Ellen, who was destined to be the provincial superior of the St. Paul Sisters of St. Joseph, was born in the same plain little stone house and baptized on July 1, 1842. The other children were Mary Ann, a half sister; Eliza, later Sister St. John; Richard, who died in childhood; and Julia, who became Mrs. C. I. McCarthy.

Just when the potato famine was at its height, Richard Ireland's sister Anastasia and her husband, James Howard, died, leaving four young children. Richard and his un-married sister Nancy assumed the care of these children and set out for America to find a location for the family. Richard found work as a carpenter in Burlington, Vermont, and within a year he was able to send for his wife, Judith Naughton Ireland, their children, and the Howards.

The five terrifying weeks on the ocean were softened by the mother's characteristic faith and courage. John was ten and the two Ellens were six. These little girls — Ellen Howard, one of the orphan cousins, and Ellen Ireland — were to be lifelong companions. The boat from Liverpool — like all boats that year — was crowded with sick and discouraged families fleeing from the distress of the famine. For the children it left for all their lives a vivid memory of the effects of persecution and poverty on the Irish.

The boat put in at Boston Harbor and there was a joyful reunion with their father and their Aunt Nancy. Richard's interest in many subjects came into play as he tried to make them good Americans without delay. He told them stories of the Revolution as he showed them Bunker Hill and Concord Bridge. These stories were but the beginning of four years of American history, panorama style, to which the eager children were to be exposed.

After a year in Burlington, they left New England by covered wagon for Chicago. There John went to St. Mary's

Catholic school for boys, and the girls attended the Academy of the Sisters of Mercy. The westward movement was surging all about them, but it was a chance meeting with John O'Gorman, a former Kilkenny schoolmate, on a Chicago street that made Richard Ireland decide to take his family to far-off Minnesota, then being advertised as a health resort as well as an agricultural paradise. Four prairie schooners were hired to accommodate the party of travelers bound for Galena, where they could take the boat for St. Paul. By that time John Ireland was fourteen years old, Thomas O'Gorman was ten, as were Ellen Ireland and Ellen Howard.

They steamed into St. Paul on the *Nominee* on May 20, 1852. A rude shack was thrown up at once at Fifth and St. Peter streets to shelter the two families. Its one long room was partitioned with sheets to separate the apartments of the O'Gormans and the Irelands. As soon as possible, lots were bought for more permanent homes. Mr. Ireland built a five-room dwelling that summer on West Fifth Street between Market and Washington. On the first floor were a kitchen, bedroom, and parlor, and there were two bedrooms upstairs. The O'Gormans were located nearby on Sixth Street.

Richard Ireland worked as a carpenter on all the Catholic building projects in St. Paul. His advertisement was carried in the city directories and the newspapers recorded that he did the "carpentering" on the three-story Catholic block built for store rental space between Bench Street and Third in 1859. At times he seems to have been an entrepreneur with a place of business and a partner. Certainly, all the early St. Paul historians characterized him as a builder in a symbolic as well as a literal sense. In later years Monsignor Joseph Guillot, then the oldest living priest in the diocese, remembered that Richard Ireland went to Waverly each year to contract for the wood to heat the Cathedral.

Stray notices indicate that he also took some interest in politics. In 1854 he was a defeated candidate for alderman in his ward. His name heads the list of signers defending

Henry M. Rice from a charge of Know-Nothingism in a statement in English and German carried in the papers through September and October 1855. Patrick Quain denounced Richard Ireland in the newspapers in 1858 for espousing the cause of the railroads, a thing no Irishman or Democrat should do.

The Irelands had soon become acquainted with Bishop Cretin. When low water in the river caused an epidemic of typhoid fever not long after they arrived and little Richard, eight years old, was a victim, Bishop Cretin went every day to instruct him for his first holy communion.

On one such visit the bishop said to the two little girls, Ellen Ireland and Ellen Howard, "You *must* be sisters. The Lord has need of you." And they never forgot his advice.

Books and papers were rare in the pioneer town, but Ellen Ireland developed an ardent love for reading as her brother John had done earlier. Father Daniel Fisher gave her three additional volumes of Butler's *Lives of the Saints* because she could repeat verbatim the lives of St. Eulalia and St. Agatha, which she had read in the first volume. Often, when she found a new paper in the house where she went for milk, she forgot entirely that her mother was waiting to make baking-powder biscuits.

Her love for books and her eagerness to learn were encouraged at St. Joseph's Academy. For the two Ellens, as for all the other girls, the sisters' school was an absorbing interest and the teachers were their models for holiness and culture. They took it as a matter of course that they must be bilingual. All the elementary branches were taught in both English and French. As they went on, they studied sacred and profane history, Latin, vocal and instrumental music, mathematics, rhetoric, and natural sciences, which included botany, physics, chemistry, and astronomy.

Bishop Cretin often visited the school and he conducted the "exhibitions." He used to smile at the Irish brogue with which many of the children pronounced French words, but he listened patiently to endless conjugations. His love for singing made all his visits lively — the children were heartily in accord with his desire for congregational singing at all services in the Cathedral. They were not aware that it was sometimes trying for the sisters when the bishop insisted that they must be present at every service to give good example and to lead the singing.

Information about the everyday life of the schoolgirls attending St. Joseph's Academy in the early years is not as extensive as we might wish. But the reminiscences of at least one of the first pupils of the Sisters of St. Joseph when they opened their school in 1851, Mary Mehegan (later Mrs. James J. Hill), have been set down by her daughter, Mrs. Clara Hill Lindley. Mrs. Hill recalled, for example, a dramatic performance, the trial scene from *The Merchant of Venice*, for which the costumes were the best white muslins and a black velvet bodice with Van Dyke points to distinguish the male characters.

Mrs. Lindley quotes Ellen Ireland as saying to her, "I remember your grandfather very well. He lived next door to what even then was grandiloquently called St. Joseph's Academy, and the Sisters regarded him as a devoted friend to whom they could look for help and advice. Although so young I gathered that he was more refined than the average man in our small town, and his manners were dubbed by the envious 'Mehegan's airs'."

Tim Mehegan, Mrs. Hill's father, died on Christmas Eve 1854 and was buried in the Catholic cemetery at Marshall Avenue and Western where St. Joseph's Academy now stands. His wife found that a frontier town was not an easy place for an unprotected young woman to live, but there were "simple childish pleasures" for her two little daughters in their convent school and in the neighborhood around their home. The riverbank was covered with wild flowers in the spring. Children met in the quiet streets on summer evenings to play. The shops began early to carry fine goods and for

Mary Mehegan the great occasion was the "French Mass" at the Cathedral when the Canadian families showed their taste for pretty clothes.

The clear, dry air of Minnesota was already becoming well known, and many of the early settlers came to live there as a cure for consumption. Mrs. Hill would remember the delicious fragrance of wood smoke rising like incense from every chimney when this air was still and cold.

The Mehegan children used to go to the courthouse nearby for the mail. A small pigeon-holed cabinet where the letters were sorted alphabetically constituted the post office of those days. One late afternoon when on this errand a "grewsome sight met their eyes — a gallows where swung the body of a woman hung that morning. Was she left there as a terrible warning?"

These memories were similar to those which Ellen Ireland and Ellen Howard carried into the convent with them. Perhaps they remembered more about the Mass and less about what the people who attended it wore than Mrs. Hill did. But in old age, Ellen Ireland told how envious she and her cousin, Ellen Howard, were when Rose Cox came from Boston to glide up the center aisle of the Cathedral in a white shawl and a fashionable bonnet. Even long years of seeing her as Sister Ignatius in a plain black veil and white linen headdress like their own did not cause them to forget the impression her finery had made upon them.

The Ellens were tall, healthy girls. Ellen Ireland was energetic and enthusiastic, impulsive and unsparing of effort. Ellen Howard was more stately and proper, more deliberate and careful of appearances. Each had a strongly marked individuality and ambition to overcome obstacles and organize enterprises. The frontier environment and their rugged health had filled them with powers of accomplishment which wearied those less well endowed with ideal designs. They tended to be impatient with slower ways, but again, their good health brought the graces and charms of laughter and conversation which captivated everyone. Their religion was deeply imbedded in them, but it was simple and unquestioning and as a result it caused them little struggle to contemplate the austerities of convent life.

Upon entering the convent the Ellens had become postulants. This meant literally that they were asking to be sisters. Postulants wore secular clothes "of a modest color" and lived in the novitiate where they had the example of the novices (who had already received the habit) to follow in performing the unfamiliar spiritual exercises.

The discipline of the novitiate was to the Ellens no great change from their own well-ordered home, where prayer and work were the normal preoccupation of everyone in the family group. The ardor which accompanied their desire to dedicate their lives to the service of God and their neighbor in the convent helped them to listen with docility to the initial instructions. The mistress of novices told them that in the convent everything was always in order because the sisters were ever asking direction even in the minute details of their lives. To the proud such an observation would be a mere incentive to conjure up new and original ways of doing things. To the Ellens it was a challenge to bend their wills to conform to the pattern so venerable from use. They did not try to make themselves think that this was the most artistic or the cleverest plan — it was simply that "their design was known to them" and they prayed that God might strengthen it.

So they did not occupy themselves with interesting and unusual arrangements for their desks or their cells. A little rebellion from Ellen Ireland — who had such marked powers of leadership and who later in life was to be entrusted with great authority — might have been expected to precede the acceptance of this traditional idea, but her struggle was rather with her own nature as she put forth every effort to conform to the principle. The spidery handwriting in the fading notebooks which contained the rules for the novitiate

seems doubly prim and quaint when considered as her training manual.

"Rise, dress, undress, and wash, modestly, quickly, and
always in the most retired place. . . . Do not leave anything
around your bed during the day, except what is necessary
for the night; however, during the winter your shawl may be
kept there sometimes, but neatly folded and put under the
pillow in such a manner as not to be perceived. . . . The
beds must be neatly made, the ticks well shaken, the husks
picked up and replaced in the tick, the clothes neatly
arranged, the beds square and presenting a good appearance. . . .

"You must be very exact and diligent in dischargement of
your employments, conforming yourself always to the orders
you receive from those who have the direction of the different charges in which you are employed and whenever you
are found in fault or receive an admonition never excuse
yourself nor accuse another, but say, 'I thank you, I will try
to be more careful or to do better.' . . . Novices and Postulants are earnestly to take care of the articles used in their
charges: brooms, brushes, dusters, pails, &c, and when you
have finished using them be exact in returning them to their
proper place. . . . "

This minute ordering of their lives did not seem repressive
to the two determined postulants. If this was the way the
other Sisters of St. Joseph had learned to follow their rule,
they wanted the same training. They struggled with no
doubts and it seemed a paradox that the convent world was
filled with a long succession of things which inspired them
with an uncontrollable desire to laugh — generally at quite
the wrong time. The daily program was absorbing. At five
in the morning, a loud bell awakened them. They did not
shudder at its jangling clang. No headache ever told them
they needed to sleep ten minutes longer. They sprang out of
bed with an overwhelming sense of privilege that there was
another day in the house of the Lord. The bell had sounded

the old monastic greeting *Benedicamus Domino,* to which
they answered heartily aloud, *Deo Gratias.* In twenty
minutes they were dressed and hurrying downstairs to the
chapel. As the youngest, they took the pew in front of the
other sisters.

Every instant of this morning hour was exciting. It was
the living fountain of grace which gave meaning to their new
life. Here they received the fire of "part and fellowship"
which made the idea of "community" such a creative force
in their lives. Here was where they became free Christian
souls, not merely part of a system that tied them through
custom to hidebound observances, but spirits living danger-
ously in hot pursuit of an ideal.

First a bell tapped — one tiny tinkle. That was a signal for
morning prayer to begin at twenty-five minutes past five.
One of the Ellens intoned the prayers and all the sisters
answered according to custom. They were brief, fervent
devotions to ask God's blessing on the work of the day. The
sense of the refrain to the Ellens was always, "O how good
and pleasant for brethren to dwell together in unity." Different as they were in disposition and with their diverse
human limitations, they were, nevertheless, all their lives
distinguished by their grasp of the idea of community.

Following the five minutes of prayers aloud together, one
of the postulants read from a book the points of the morning's meditation. These were short considerations of the
mystery or truth proposed for thought and prayer, generally
based upon the portion of the Gospel which was to be used
in that day's Mass. There was an almost inescapable incentive to live the Christian way with that daily half hour of
uninterrupted contemplation about the practical application
to their own lives of the great truths in the life of Christ so
soon to be enacted on the altar. What might have become
merely habits of neatness in replacing brooms and pails in
less imaginative souls became in the Ellens dramatic gestures
of tremendous responsibility. To them these acts meant

something very profound in union with Christ's own poverty and charity.

Mass followed meditation. It was offered by Father Demetrius Marogna, a Benedictine Father from the nearby Assumption Church. Always it was the central value of the day, each day more filled with meaning than the last. It was the drama of the life of Christ re-enacted for them, in which they lovingly participated with all the Sisters of St. Joseph and with all mankind. Every Mass recalled a new aspect of Christ's beauty. The preceding meditation had deepened their understanding of the treasures set forth in the great Christian text from day to day.

Ellen Ireland, particularly, was gifted with great simplicity. It was she who could point out to Ellen Howard with no embarrassment precisely what the words of St. Paul in the Epistle or St. Luke in the Gospel meant in relation to two would-be Sisters of St. Joseph. "If God clothe in this manner" could mean only that the clothing of the Sisters of St. Joseph was precious. "Having your loins girt" referred to the cincture which bound them to God. Sometimes the "breastplate of justice" was the cross of wood and brass and sometimes their white linen guimpe. Now the "helmet of truth" was the whole headdress and again it was the veil. The vestments the priest wore at Mass and their symbolism came to clarify the significance of their own religious garments.

But it was not instruction alone that they gained from the Mass. There in a real sense they lived charity. At the offering of bread they were giving themselves in love and service as eagerly as the early Christians had offered the blessed bread to the needy. They prayed not only for themselves but for all faithful Christians, living and dead. The very charity with which they prayed for the whole community in the widest sense flowed back upon themselves in strong and courageous love. The joyous moment when they could partake of the banquet of the Lord was a time of solemn exaltation that meant the receiving of the spirit of charity so that they might

no longer live their own lives but the life of Christ, seeing
only Christ in all the members of His Mystical Body. At
communion time, the sisters lowered their veils over their
faces and walked reverently to the railing. They moved
silently in regular order according to the time of their admission into the community. It was fascinating to the postulants to be part of the orderly procession. The sameness of
the routine never bothered them. This was the house of the
Lord and they wished ardently to belong to it forever, for
its willing poverty and its humble submission as well as its
walking in love.

Breakfast was a short and silent meal. Mother Seraphine
Coughlin stood at the head of a long table until all were at
their places. The reader bowed and grace was said in Latin.
Silently, the benches were moved out and all were seated.
The younger sisters took turns reading and waiting upon the
table. The service was plain and simple, the food adequate,
but not appealing to a fastidious appetite. The care which all
took to be attentive to the wants of others and to make their
own desires inconspicuous made a ceremony of meals
beyond the demands of a polite education. Graces and
appetites increased together.

Work in the refectory and kitchen occupied the postulants
after breakfast. Then they made their beds and tidied their
cells and proceeded to their "charge"—an employment
changed monthly to give them an opportunity to discover all
the work possibilities. "The postulancy, my dear sisters,"
Mother Seraphine Coughlin would say, "is a time when you
may discern whether or not you like us; the novitiate is the
time when we determine whether or not we like you." With
all that the charges had their maintenance features; whatever they were, the house had to be kept in order. The
common denominator of all was sweeping and dusting and
scrubbing. The difference was only in location.

Studies were interspersed through the day and there were
prayers to learn and books to read. At eleven-thirty the bell

rang for examination of conscience in the chapel. After the brief scrutiny, the sisters went to dinner. On Sundays there was recreation during the meal, but on other days a spiritual book was read. The Ellens were always possessed of hard common sense, for all their deep religiosity. No one ever had to tell them that a fervent nun eats her meals and thanks God for the strength derived therefrom. After dinner, the sisters gathered in the Community Room for recreation until one o'clock when the Litany of the Blessed Virgin was recited and one sister read for fifteen minutes from a spiritual book as the others sewed.

In silence the sisters returned to their occupations until the bell at five brought them to the chapel for a half hour of meditation — a review of the day in the light of the action they had planned at the morning Mass — and five decades of the Rosary during which they reflected on the mysteries in the life of Christ. After supper, there was recreation until seven-thirty. Studies followed until time for night prayers at nine. The principal prayer was the Litany of the Saints, after which they went to bed in silence.

The evening recreation was enlivened by simple games — except for checkers, most of them were of ordinary, hand-made materials. Some were guessing games in which several could participate with quick, easy answers. Now and then Mother Seraphine Coughlin would read a story. But the conversation was the most interesting. There was a good deal of sameness and repetition and "What's that you said, Sister?" about it, but this did not appear so to the new members of the family.

The constant topic was the early history of the Sisters of St. Joseph in France, in Carondelet and St. Louis, and in St. Paul. The older sisters savored all they had heard or remembered as if it were an integral part of them and it was natural that the Ellens should soon know by heart all the anecdotes about the living and dead sisters of St. Joseph.

There was Mother St. John Fontbonne of Lyons, the

wonderful reverend mother who had sent Sister Philomena
and Sister Protais with the other sisters to America in 1836.
Both postulants knew well these two sisters who had lived
first in Carondelet, the motherhouse, where all the young
sisters who had never been in St. Louis hoped to go some
day.

When Mother St. John Fontbonne was old and had been
the superior general for a long time, the archbishop of
Lyons told her to resign, even though the chapter sisters
had just re-elected her. She obeyed humbly and she lived as
a simple sister all the rest of her life. But she was so cheerful
that no one would have guessed that she was aware of the
harsh manner in which she had been treated. It was only
long afterward when her room was being changed that one
of the sisters discovered a formal letter from the pope making her superior general of the order for life. She had never
told anyone about it.

Such heroic relations were the food upon which the Ellens
nourished their own fine dignity, that sense of worth which
was not pride but an appreciation of their value as Christians. Once Ellen Ireland asked Sister Protais if she thought
Mother St. John Fontbonne was a saint.

"Une sainte? Peut-être. Je ne sais pas . . . mais, une
bonne femme."

The Ellens could understand how it was that Mother St.
John Fontbonne became more devoted to the community
through her trials. This was doubtless the origin of one of
Ellen Ireland's own mannerisms which gave matter to
slightly irreverent mimics decades later. For there was a
sense of possession and grandeur in the way she said "community" which fell on some ears like "l'Etat c'est moi" and
on others like "omnis Gallia." Those who tried to imitate
ended on a -*tay* which they assumed was a bit of brogue,
but was more probably a remembered *communauté*. The
attempts caused laughter at recreation, but even the actors
never felt they had been successful in portraying what the

word meant as she said it. They did better with her. "My, my" and "Well, well."

In their novitiate days, the Ellens were not so enthusiastic about the older sisters' stories of Mother St. John Fontbonne's personal practice of community virtues as about her more dramatic exploits, but they listened attentively all the same. There were the stories the French sisters had heard the reverend mother tell about the mortification and charity of the first Sisters of St. Joseph as she had known them after the French Revolution from 1807 on. In those days a sister who used the smallest object without permission, who carelessly misplaced things, or who lost something, reproached herself as if she had committed a grave offense.

"The sisters now," the older sisters remembered Mother St. John Fontbonne would say, "consider anything as belonging to them. Nowadays we have quite a number of objects for our use. There is indeed written in the books — 'Obedience permits the use of this book to Sister So-and-So' — but if someone should take it from that sister, who is not poor since she wants for nothing, I doubt not that she would cry out 'Stop thief!' No one should be able to steal anything from a Sister of St. Joseph, since she owns nothing. We should remember that whatever we receive as food and clothing is given to us through charity. Other people may make provision for future needs, but we must live from day to day."

One Saturday, the rememberers said, a sister who was passing out the clean linens gave Mother St. John Fontbonne a cornet with only one string. Mother St. John made a sign for the sister to give her another headdress with two strings. Later, at the conference, when all the sisters were assembled, Mother St. John asked pardon as if she had committed a great fault. The superior told her that she had done no wrong — she could not wear linens with only one string. But Mother St. John said, "If I thought myself poor, I would have been happy that they gave it to me. I should have taken it as it was and later put a string on it."

But when the sisters spoke of the reverend mother's words on the graces God showers on model religious who are generous in His service, Ellen Ireland felt as if Mother St. John Fontbonne were right there in the Community Room speaking to her. Mother St. John had said that the first Sisters of St. Joseph had great ease in uniting together in prayer and it was not rare to see them bathed in tears when they spoke to God. They had a special gift for touching hearts and, above all, their work with the children in their classes and with the sick in the hospital bore much fruit. "There is no reason for astonishment," she used to say, "God is always the same. His arm is never shortened. He never lets himself be outdone in generosity. Rather we have changed. We would like to live comfortably and yet receive the same graces as they did. Instead of submitting to God's Will, we expect God to submit to ours."

Whenever Mother St. John Fontbonne's name was mentioned, the Ellens always thought of Mother St. John Fournier, who had been their teacher when they first came to St. Paul. Nearly all the sisters knew her too and they often recalled stories she had told them. When anyone said "Mother St. John Fournier" they all smiled, because it was generally an amusing story if she had any part in it. But the Ellens discovered there was also a very serious side to their former teacher.

Everyone remembered that Mother St. John Fournier used to say, "A Sister of St. Joseph should not show herself — she should love to remain in her little corner." It was like litany the way the sisters told it. Mother Seraphine Coughlin might suddenly say, "How Mother St. John Fournier always said we should love to keep in our little corner!" That was the cue for Sister Protais and Sister Philomena to chime in together, "Oui, ma Mère, la soeur de saint-Joseph, disait-elle, çà ne se montre pas; çà reste dans un coin, dans un coin!"

It was from Mother St. John Fournier that all the sisters had heard about the arrival of the Ireland family in St. Paul.

Thus the Ellens came themselves to be part of community tradition. More exciting to hear, however, was the story of Mother St. John Fournier when she was as young as they were now. Although she had been selected to accompany the first sisters from Lyons to St. Louis in 1836, she had been held back for a year to be trained at St. Etienne as a teacher for the deaf. Her companion was Sister Celestine Pommerel, her cousin, by whose family she had been reared. This similarity to their own condition interested the Ellens exceedingly.

When Sister St. John Fournier and Sister Celestine Pommerel crossed the Atlantic in the summer of 1837, they had remained seventeen days in Havana, for yellow fever was raging in New Orleans and the French consul who was to conduct them on that lap of the journey considered it unsafe to proceed. The commandant, too, feared to have the sisters leave the boat and he exercised great vigilance in caring for them. "Every morning," Mother St. John had said in telling the story, "he sent two officers in uniform to conduct us to Mass and at five o'clock in the evening he took us in his rowboat to the home of the consul or some other of his French friends. He brought us back at ten or eleven o'clock. A beautiful life for a *religieuse*! But we were saved from the sickness he had feared for us."

A sharp contrast to that sojourn awaited the two young sisters in Carondelet. On leaving them with the sisters who had come down the road to meet them, Bishop Rosati had pleasantly cautioned them not to lose their rosy cheeks. He neglected to mention, however, that the little convent was having a story added to the one with which it was provided, and just then it was without a roof. No sooner had the travelers opened their baggage to distribute the souvenirs they had brought with them than a torrent of rain drenched everything.

"The reverend mother," Mother St. John Fournier related, "had forseen that and she had rented a little cabin not far from our garden which had been abandoned for three years. We ran to it, but with the mud up to our knees, we could not make much headway. We carried some mattresses there which we put on the floor and we tried to take a little rest in our soaked habits, but, alas! who could sleep with the rats, mice, and a thousand other little insects not only for companions, but walking back and forth over us all night for ten or twelve nights. The convent was finally roofed and we left our famished companions to maintain themselves in any way they could."

Two years later, Sister Celestine Pommerel, who had come from France with Mother St. John Fournier, was named superior of Carondelet by Bishop Rosati. Misery upon misery filled the next five years.

Of all the ordeals, the Ellens liked best to have repeated the racial episode. "In 1843 or 1844," Mother St. John was quoted as saying, "the first mission was opened at St. Louis as a school for free Negroes. Obedience sent me there with two sisters. We also prepared slaves for the reception of the sacraments, which vexed many of the whites. After a time, they threatened to drive us away by main force. Threats came every day. Finally, one morning a number of people called me out of the church and told me that the next night they would come to drive us from the house. I said nothing to the sisters and I had no fear — I had so much confidence in the holy Virgin! At eleven o'clock, we heard a great noise which aroused the sisters with a start. A crowd of people in the street were shouting and blaspheming. We recited together the *Memorare* and other prayers. All at once, a patrol of armed police dispersed the demons who were trying to force the door. They came back three times that same night, but our good mother protected us, and they were not able either to open the door or to break through from the outside.

"We had about eighty children, all good and docile (a score of them were little boys) and we had already made progress. I believe that we stayed there a year and a half or two years. The morning after our adventure, the mayor of St. Louis advised Monseigneur Kenrick [the brother of the bishop of Philadelphia, who had succeeded as bishop of St. Louis upon the death of Bishop Rosati] to close the school for a time, which he did."

Close as the time was to the Civil War, this story moved the Ellens deeply. The antislavery cause was already as righteous as the temperance crusade and as religious in its bearing on their interests. They had no prejudices against Negroes, for they had been privileged to live in the same neighborhood with them since they had come to St. Paul. Every census after their arrival shows that the next house and others near the Ireland home were occupied by persons designated as "black" or "mulatto" by the color-conscious census taker.

Another of Mother St. John Fournier's stories belonged to the time when the Sisters of St. Joseph were struggling to maintain the St. Louis school for Negroes. The superiors of the Sisters of Charity of St. Vincent de Paul had recalled their sisters from service in asylums for boys and the bishop asked Mother Celestine Pommerel to send Sisters of St. Joseph to maintain the St. Louis asylum. There they found seventy-five little boys covered with vermin. They had been without proper care for six months, since there was only one sister in the asylum and she had had to depend too much on servants. "The Holy Virgin helped us," said Mother St. John Fournier, "the vermin departed and, still better, the children became tractable and pious."

The St. Paul sisters often recalled that in 1847 Mother St. John Fournier had been sent from St. Louis to Philadelphia to take charge of the male orphanage, where "ladies and servants" had been taking their salary and troubling themselves little about the orphans, "judging from the style" in which they found them. A parish school was opened in Pottsville, Pennsylvania, in 1848, which furnished useful training for similar work to come in St. Paul, but it was the opening of a hospital dedicated to St. Joseph in Philadelphia in 1849 which had proved the most fruitful background for the sisters' Minnesota experience. The institution opened under the bishop's patronage, with a lay board responsible for the finances. Five sisters constituted the staff.

"Three sick persons entered with us," Mother St. John had often related. "We had only five beds; we gave them three, and during nearly three weeks two of us had a bed and the other three slept crosswise on a mattress. Our sisters had such fear of the dying that I was obliged to stay up with them during the night. If there was a wound to dress, the nearest sister fainted. Little by little, the sisters — poor children — became accustomed to work for the sick and the dying."

The more the Ellens learned about the life of the sisters, the more they yearned for their own Reception Day, when they would be clothed with the habit and veil of the Sisters of St. Joseph. The date was set for December 8, 1858, and since no one had yet been appointed in Bishop Cretin's place, Father Ravoux, the administrator of the vacant see, would officiate at the ceremony. It was two years since anyone had been received into the community in St. Paul. Sister Peter Richard Grace had been the last; Sister Ignatius Loyola Cox had entered in 1855.

Ellen Ireland was all eagerness for the experience of wearing the habit — it was like a seal upon her dedication. She thirsted for the adventure of the new life. It seemed to her that she could never be her real self — never anything but an ordinary Christian — unless she could wear the religious dress which told her that she could in very truth live as a bride of Christ. She wanted the new family ties, the new relationships, closer in reality of love than blood relationships, nearer to the Head of the family, Christ.

She was at first less inclined to wear the wedding dress and the bridal veil which she knew were part of the great occasion. It seemed a little foolish to wear so much finery for such a little while. She and her cousin had looked just like fashionable brides when they had fitted on the apparel. Her imagination was fired, however, when Mother Seraphine Coughlin said solemnly, "Nothing is too dear for our Lord, my dear postulants. These garments are a symbol of the gifts of heart and soul the bride of Christ brings to her mystical espousal."

For ten days before, the Ellens were in retreat, praying fervently for the graces they would need all their lives. Days and hours slipped by and in no time at all they were in the back of the chapel on December 8, the feast of the Immaculate Conception. Sister Philomena was whispering to them in French to walk slowly. Sister Xavier was smoothing out their white veils and satin trains — they had held them up coming down the two flights of stairs from the dormitory. The chapel looked unfamiliar with so many people in it. They were to sit in the first pew on the Blessed Virgin's side and Mother Seraphine Coughlin and Sister Xavier, her assistant, in the first pew on St. Joseph's side. The other sisters would sit behind them, four in a pew. Then the Ireland family and all their friends from St. Paul and St. Anthony.

Now the last verse of "Jerusalem, My Happy Home" was finished. It had been Bishop Cretin's favorite hymn, and everyone in the chapel had been singing. The bishop had always insisted on congregational singing and so they all knew the hymns. But the Ellens could hear Sister Victorine's voice on the high notes. Sister would be embarrassed if she knew that. They remembered well the first time Sister Victorine sang in the church when everybody stopped to listen. She had the loveliest voice they had ever heard. Singing was such an important part of church services.

Father Ravoux was intoning the *Magnificat* — My soul doth magnify the Lord. That was a signal to walk slowly, ever so slowly, down the aisle. The sisters on the Blessed Virgin's side sang the second verse, on St. Joseph's side the third. How beautiful the chapel was. The altar was covered with white feather flowers and waxed lilies. The sisters had been making them during recreation for months. Sisters from France knew how to make everything. The sanctuary was filled with priests. They were all there — Father Ledon, Father Tissot, Father Caillet, Father Oster — with Father Ravoux in the center like a patriarch.

Presently the Ellens were kneeling in their pew. Sister Xavier had handed the basket containing their habits to one of the priests at the altar railing. Father Ravoux intoned, *Veni, Creator Spiritus* — Come, Holy Spirit — and priests and sisters sang to the end of the hymn. When it was finished, Father Ravoux said the Latin prayers of blessing and sprinkled the habits with holy water. The Ellens rose and walked slowly to the altar steps. Father Ravoux meanwhile had seated himself at the altar facing the two aspirants who advanced and knelt before him.

Holding the ceremonial book, Father Ravoux read, "What do you ask, my children?"

"Very Reverend Father, I ask for the Habit of the Sisters of St. Joseph of Carondelet." Their voices shook a little in the quiet chapel, but they pronounced the words distinctly.

"Are you fully resolved to wear it with devotion and to live and die in the exact observance of the rules prescribed for the Sisters who wear this Habit?"   .

"Yes, Very Reverend Father, I am fully resolved on it." Their voices were steady now and clear.

"In order to become true Sisters of St. Joseph, you should, my children, die to the world, to your parents, to your friends, to yourselves, and live alone for Jesus Christ."

"This is what I desire with all my heart — that the world be nothing more for me, and Jesus be my only possession." Their hearts were in the words. The tones were vibrant with sincerity. Added to the joy they experienced every morning in offering their hearts to Christ in the Mass, there was now an assurance that they were being accepted into the unity of fellowship with the Sisters of St. Joseph.

"Do you desire at once to renounce the world, its vanities,

and its pomps, and to take the poor Habit of the Sisters of St. Joseph?"

"I have long and ardently desired it, and I beg of you, Very Reverend Father, not to defer any longer the granting of my request." Ellen Ireland could smile inwardly at the insistence of this question — she had never cared for dressing up. The common stuff of the habit was the raiment of Solomon in all his glory to her.

"I am satisfied to grant your request, my children, and wish Mother Superior to receive you into the Congregation, to divest you of your hair and of your worldly dress, in order to clothe you with the Habit for which you long with such ardor, and I beg that at the same time you may be clothed with Jesus Christ. Go then, my children, to receive this holy Habit."

With great dignity the two girls rose from their knees and turned to walk slowly, with downcast eyes and folded hands, down the center aisle. They were not embarrassed, as they might have been in a pageant, for this to them was a vital change to a new existence, which, although accomplished in a ceremony, went deeper than any mere external representation could portray. Their whole unconscious demeanor spoke of holy things. Mother Seraphine Coughlin and Sister Xavier — with the habits which had been blessed — had slipped quietly out the side aisle, so that when the postulants reached the Community Room the superior and her assistant were ready to clothe them in their habits.

In a moment the white satin slippers and the white silk stockings were changed to black. "The shoes shall be black and plain," the Holy Rule specified. Someone whisked the white dresses upstairs. Mother took up the big shears. "Braids are a help," she smiled, "there is not much left after they come off. These frizzy bangs are the most troublesome — that will do for now."

The Ellens were unconscious of what was happening to them. They wanted only to dwell in the house of the Lord forever, to be the poorest of the poor. They were slipping the habits over their heads, hooking the waists, brushing down the pleats in the front of the billowing skirts. Then the starched white linen cornet, tight around the face, the white linen band close to the head, the underveil — then the veil. "The dress of the Sisters shall be simple and modest as becomes virgins consecrated to God. The Habit shall be of black serge, and shall be made quite plain." They remembered the words of the Holy Rule. They wondered how they looked. They felt queer enough.

At last the wide white linen guimpe. "Be careful not to twist around much until you are accustomed to it. The guimpe crushes easily and looks untidy." The cincture and beads — large, rattling beads with a big cross attached. "There — you look like real sisters. Start to walk up the aisle at the *Laudate pueri*. Don't forget to keep your hands in your sleeves."

At the altar steps once more, Father Ravoux was saying solemnly, "Now you are dead to the world, my children. Are you satisfied?"

"Yes, Very Reverend Father, I am satisfied."

"You have reason to be satisfied, as at this moment, by a special favor of God, you have in a particular manner, St. Joseph for your father, the most Blessed Virgin for your Mother, and Jesus Christ for your Spouse."

"I value this favor above all the goods of the world. These glorious advantages enable me to leave my parents, my friends, and all the vanities of the world. I implore of God the grace of persevering unto death in the life of the Sisters of St. Joseph, which I have so long desired, and which I on this day embrace in receiving this holy Habit."

There was a breathless pause. "Miss Ellen Ireland, you will be known in religion by the name of Sister Mary Seraphine. Miss Ellen Howard, you will henceforth be known by the name of Sister Mary Celestine. May God be praised, Sisters, for the good sentiments He gives you, and I beg that He may accompany them with His gracious benedictions. In the name of the Father, and of the Son, and of the Holy Ghost. Amen."

The new novices rose and returned to their pew. Facing the altar, Father Ravoux sang *Te Deum laudamus* which was caught up heartily. The Ellens sang too. They were Sisters of St. Joseph at last.

Their Little Corner

IN THE YEARS OF BISHOP GRACE

V

One in Fellowship

DURING the long interregnum before the appointment of a new bishop, Father Ravoux acted as administrator for the diocese, *sede vacante*. He was also the spiritual director of the Sisters of St. Joseph, to which office he called attention in an inscription opposite the frontispiece of the *Reminiscences, Memoirs, and Lectures*, published in 1890. He wrote that he had had his photograph taken at the urgent request of the Sisters of St. Joseph, St. Paul, whose spiritual director he had been for thirty years at least, and he gave it to them as a souvenir — "that we should often think and reflect on the love of Jesus Christ."

During this time between bishops, Father Ravoux was busy with the temporalities of the diocese, which meant that he tried to complete all of Bishop Cretin's plans. It was then, too, that the Sisters of St. Joseph became people with distinguishable personalities. Thus, on February 17, 1859, a three-column article in the *Weekly Pioneer and Democrat* was especially friendly.

"These sisters who," the writer affirmed, "from their attention to and care of the sick in St. Paul — when no one else would take care of them — have become familiar to the kindest sentiments of the people of all denominations, were established in this diocese in 1851, simultaneously with the formation of the diocese itself. They now number 18 members and several candidates. They are devoted to the education of children and care of the sick — sweet woman's work the wide world over. They have charge of the two female academies of St. Joseph, on Bench Street, St. Paul, Sister Blanche, Directress, and St. Mary's . . . [at] St. Anthony, Sister Xavier, Directress. They have also charge of a Free School for girls at St. Paul."

The article continued with more particular mention of the hospital. "But their principal theatre is St. Joseph's Hospital on Ninth street, of which Sister Seraphine [Coughlin] is superior. This Hospital is selected on a fine plateau planted with trees, the grounds having been donated by the Hon. H. M. Rice. It is a three story stone building, with balconies around each story, affording airy promenades and pleasant prospects for invalids. The interior arrangements are those of the best conducted Hospitals. Besides the wards and private rooms devoted to Hospital purposes, a portion of the building is occupied for a novitiate for the Sisters."

The same account said that the church in the diocese embraced fifty thousand souls; ninety missions or stations; thirty-one churches or chapels built, and seventeen more in course of construction or in immediate contemplation; twenty-seven clergymen, many of whom had been ordained at St. Paul. Mr. Neill was quoted on "Early Catholic Missions" to the effect that the Catholic church had derived an immense accession from the increase of population in late years, including in its pale nearly all the foreign increase except a portion of the Germans. At the Cathedral the morning congregation at the English service alone numbered more than the congregations of all the other churches in St. Paul together.

St. Anthony, too, was reported in May 1859 to be engaged in building a most "elegant and imposing" edifice which contemplated a tower 175 feet in height. The body of the building was of "handsome cut limestone" with a front of granite.

Then, on July 29, 1859, the new bishop finally arrived. The

long delay had been due to the customary difficulty in filling a frontier see. Father Anthony Pelamourgues, one of Bishop Cretin's colleagues at Dubuque, had been offered the bishopric and had refused. When Thomas Langdon Grace, a Dominican Father from Memphis, Tennessee, also declined the honor, his request went unheeded and he was enjoined to accept.

What may be called an interpretation of the Bishop's arrival was written for the *Boston Pilot* by Lawrence P. Cotter, whose son Joseph was to be the first bishop of Winona. Six or seven thousand persons — Americans, Irish, German, and French — assembled in the cathedral to welcome the new bishop. It was peculiarly pleasing, said Mr. Cotter, to the Irish portion of the congregation (for they were, as usual, the vast majority) that now at least they could be understood and appreciated as they deserved and that their offerings would be accepted with a spirit that would do justice to the Irish heart. (Bishop Grace's parents had been Irish immigrants.)

This was the beginning of a new era, Mr. Cotter thought. Indeed, there was much to be done. He included in the good works "teachers to be provided who are competent to educate our youth in the English language and in the truths of Christianity, as well as secular knowledge." A little farther on he remarked, "In this connection I take occasion to speak of the annual examination at the [academy] of the Sisters of St. Joseph, which took place some two weeks ago, when the scholars, to the number of 60 or 70, acquitted themselves creditably in the several branches of learning, and in the various exercises quite entertaining to their parents and friends, assembled in large numbers. But the building of the good Sisters is already too small and we look forward hopefully for the completion of their new House, ere another anniversary rolls round."

It is not this historical picture, however, but Mr. Cotter's final sentence which has a curious interest for reasons other than its length. Ninety years later his prophecies leave a disquieting feeling of unfulfilled promises. "When we look back a brief period and contemplate the wonderful change in our midst, we are tempted to doubt that but a dozen short years ago, the aboriginal red men of the forest, the 'Sioux' and the 'Chippewa,' contended for dominion and supremacy on the very grounds where a large commercial emporium now stands, which is destined to become not only the great metropolis and artery for the commerce of the Northwest, but also the great centre of Catholic unity, from whence will flow to the interior and to the far North the countless blessings of religious truth, and the practice of the great domestic virtues, so sadly neglected in our generation."

In his first pastoral of November 9, 1859, Bishop Grace said that the diversity of nationalities in the population of the state gave beautiful prominence to the unity of the faith. He also said that his hearers were living in the midst of those who were prejudiced against the Catholic church, not maliciously, but ignorantly; not willfully, but in spite of themselves. Their birth, their education, their habits of thought and judgment (formed from the erroneous sources of information alone accessible to them), their unfavorable impressions derived from the external appearances of things, had built up in their minds defenses against the Catholic religion, strong and impenetrable almost as those which of old required the power of miracles to break down and lay open.

"The witness to holy principles," Bishop Grace told his new flock, "is their active influence upon our outward lives." A portion of the Catholic people had been sources of scandal through evil lives and bad habits and he urged priests to correct these wrongs wherever they could. He singled out for special rebuke those who trafficked in liquor since they preyed upon the infirmities of their brethren. The Catholic press, the poor, Catholic education, and citizenship were other topics which the bishop brought to the attention of the laity.

An interesting survey of the bishop's impressions from his new field is given in a letter he wrote to the Society for the Propagation of the Faith on December 12, 1859. "The Church in Minnesota," he explained to the Paris council, "is peculiarly situated. Only so far back as the year 1854 the Catholic population of the State did not amount to more than eight or ten thousand; in 1857 it amounted to fifty thousand. This enormous increase was owing to the sudden influx of immigrants into the new territory, induced by the prospect of obtaining government lands at a nominal price. These immigrants were mostly direct from Europe, and brought with them very little more than was requisite to defray their travelling expenses. Settled upon the lands, they have had to struggle hard to obtain a sufficiency to sustain life, and large numbers of them have suffered for the want of the most common necessaries.

"These privations and sufferings seem to have made them feel most sensibly their need of the consolations and encouragement of religion, and wherever it has been possible they have by sacrifices — great to them — and by contributing of their labor endeavored to erect churches and to provide a small pittance to support a missionary among them, or enable one to visit them occasionally. . . ."

Once more the bishop tried to clarify the true situation as he went on, "The financial crisis of 1857-8 weighed very heavily upon this new State, and it has not yet recovered from the ruinous effects. With the return of better times, the condition of the settlers will be proportionably improved. With this large Catholic population covering wide districts and holding the proprietorship of the soil, we have the foundation of one of the most flourishing Catholic States in the confederation."

Bishop Grace soon had the opportunity to minister to one

of the less fortunate of the Catholic population of Minnesota, a Mrs. Bilanski. According to a manuscript account by W. P. Murray, "the fourth wife of [Stanislaus] Bilanski was hung in St. Paul, March 23, 1860, for having poisoned her husband,— the first and last woman ever executed in Minnesota." The same passion for souls which animated Bishop Grace in his attendance upon the hapless woman also brought the Sisters of St. Joseph to the hanging.

To the newspapers, the event was a most rewarding experience and they made the most of it. They earned, as a consequence, a death-day lecture from the condemned woman on the injustice of declaring guilt in the paper in advance of court decision. Her words were as fully reported as all the other sordid details.

In their six columns or so on the Bilanski murder the papers for March 24, 1860, laid special stress on "The Last Day of Life." Minute recording told that the prisoner had passed nearly the whole of the preceding night in religious exercises which continued until three in the morning, when she lay down to sleep. She was awakened by her attendants at five o'clock. "Father Caillet of the Catholic church remained with her nearly all the time, with several of the Sisters, and one or two other ladies, besides some of the officers of the prison."

The previous day the papers had announced that Mass had been celebrated in the jail and "the solemn rite of confirmation was administered to Mrs. Bilansky by the Right Rev. Bishop Grace." The assisting clergy were Reverend Messrs. Caillet and Oster. The accounts said that an altar was erected between the inner and outer walls at the east corner and the ceremonies were witnessed by about fifty persons, a portion of whom were ladies, including several of the Sisters of St. Joseph. Some of the cells were opened and the prisoners had an opportunity of joining in the services. The writer concluded, "the solemn and imposing rites of the Church were rendered doubly impressive by the circumstances surrounding them. The condemned woman seemed composed and well aware of their significance."

On the last morning Mrs. Bilanski presented her jailer with a little book entitled *The Most Important Tenets of the Catholic Church Explained*. About nine o'clock, in company with Reverend Mr. Caillet, she went around to each cell to bid farewell to the prisoners. The substance of her word for each was, "Be prepared for death."

Bishop Grace called and spoke consoling words to the prisoner. Next the black robe which she was to wear for the gallows was brought in. The sheriff told her that he would request the sisters to put it on her. Two Sisters of St. Joseph and a lady "who stood god-mother to her at her baptism" accompanied the prisoner from her cell to the gallows. Fathers Caillet and Oster were also present. All knelt and prayed aloud for several minutes. After the execution, the reporters noted that the priests stepped back and "with the females kneeled down facing from her towards the engine house" and remained kneeling for twenty minutes in prayer.

A crowd of 125 persons had filled the enclosure to witness the hanging. Some were carrying infants who cried in unison with their mothers. The papers noted that in the curious crowd they had observed no native American, but mostly persons of German and Irish birth and half a dozen Sioux women with their babies. Some came in carriages from St. Anthony. The affair was "hardly private, as the heads of those on the scaffold were visible from the street."

The papers accepted a correction of their version of the condemned woman's last remarks. Father Caillet said he had not heard her say that she was innocent of the crime, that it was committed by another. In their apology the editors deprecated the confusion caused by the presence of the curious spectators. Yet in all the acrid comments there was not a word to suggest that the sisters or priests were out of order in the jail or at the execution or that they were behaving in any other way than might have been expected of them.

Even before the Bilanski case, Bishop Grace had won public attention for his charitable activities. On February 17, 1860, both St. Paul dailies carried a letter signed by a committee of the Conference of St. Vincent de Paul, identified as William Henry Forbes, A. L. Larpenteur, and William Markoe. The letter was addressed to Bishop Grace and it requested him to deliver a lecture under the auspices of the St. Vincent de Paul Society, the proceeds of which would be devoted to the society's works of charity. The lecture on the subject of "Human Rights" was delivered on February 23, and favorably commented upon by the papers thereafter.

Early in March the papers printed another sequence of letters. This time the letter to Bishop Grace was signed by J. M. Gilman, John S. Prince, E. D. Neill, and others, who declared that they had listened with great pleasure and attention to the very learned and interesting lecture on "Human Rights." They earnestly requested that the speaker would give another lecture containing the illustration and application of the principles so ably enunciated in the first. In a gracious acceptance, Bishop Grace announced his subject as "Civil Government and Human Laws Considered as External Defenses of Human Rights."

In due course it was announced that the proceeds of the lecture would be devoted to the aid of "the free hospital under the charge of the ladies of the Rev. Dr. Patterson's [St. Paul's Episcopal] congregation, in acknowledgement of the relief extended by these ladies during the past winter to many Catholic poor of our city." This lecture, delivered at the Capitol, drew even more favorable notices than the first. Moreover, on April 4, 1860, the *Pioneer* noted the establishment of the "St. Paul Free Hospital by the ladies of Dr. Patterson's society for the poor."

Such activities brought Bishop Grace considerable prestige. The journalists spoke of his high abilities, gracious manners, and unaffected piety — those qualities which had won for him the confidence and respect of all the citizens of St. Paul without regard to nation, party, or sect.

This was gratifying, no doubt, but less pleasant sentiments also came to the surface from time to time. Thus in June at a Sabbath School Convention Mr. Eggleston of the Market Street Methodist Church, in speaking of the Roman Catholic opposition to the circulation of the Bible, said that the greater portion of Bishop Grace's sermon on St. Patrick's Day was in abuse of God's word — that the bishop had told his people that St. Patrick did not go up and down the land circulating Bibles. "If St. Patrick had gone into Ireland," Mr. Eggleston declared, "with a pocket full of Bibles, Bishop Grace would not have such a set of deluded hearers." All during June and July the papers carried the debate on the relative amount of delusion of the auditors of Bishop Grace and Mr. Eggleston.

On the Catholic side the argument was handled by the remarkably able William Markoe, a Catholic convert who had been an Episcopalian minister. His response to the toast "To the Sisters of Charity, ministering angels sent by Providence to afflicted humanity: may their worth be always appreciated" at the St. Patrick's Day entertainment was declared by the *Pioneer and Democrat* to be the best speech of the evening. It was said to be a "warm eulogium of the true charity springing from a sense of duty which animates these devoted women."

In 1862, Bishop Grace secured the services of Mr. Markoe as the principal teacher in his seminary for training priests, a post Markoe filled with distinction for five years, until he resigned for a two-year sojourn in Europe. During all of Mr. Markoe's long life he was so active in scholarly and civic pursuits that too little notice has been taken of an achievement which must have outweighed his erudition in making him an attractive teacher. That was his successful ascensions in his own balloon which he demonstrated first at the St. Paul Fair on October 8, 1857.

The new rectory which Bishop Grace had erected in the spring of 1860 came in for its share of unfavorable comments. Some clergymen with less pretentious dwellings were petitioning for tax exemption on their residences and they were irked that Bishop Grace did not murmur about paying taxes on his $15,000 rectory. (Thirty-five years later W. P. Murray, in mentioning the criticisms, said that the bishop had built on such a large scale to give employment to as many men as possible in hard times. In any case, Mr. Murray said, the house did not seem as pretentious in 1895 as it had when it was built.)

The press was kinder in its treatment of the new rectory. In a Sunday feature on November 25, 1860, the *Pioneer and Democrat* commented, "Bishop Grace's new residence on Sixth street is now completed and in all the essential elements of durability, convenience and architectural finish it is, perhaps, ahead of any other building in Minnesota and will compare favorably with the palatial residences of our Merchant Princes in the Atlantic Cities." True or false, the description of architectural features is captivating. The stone was cut in "Draft rustic range" style and the architecture was of the Corinthian order. Everything from the cupola and the cornices to the imitation of English oak graining and the gaslights was considered not only to add beauty and grace to "our utilitarian city," but also to convey to strangers an exalted idea of the architectural taste and refinement of our citizens.

Despite the minor clashes, the first year of Grace's bishopric was largely satisfying in terms of his relations with the community at large; he was widely regarded as a leading citizen of St. Paul. The Catholic population too was well pleased with their new spiritual leader. They found him a learned and eloquent preacher. And the bishop's adherence to the religious life as a Dominican Father made him an especially understanding guide for the Sisters of St. Joseph in his diocese.

The bishop had no sooner arrived than he took in hand the matter of a new "house," or convent home, for the sisters. This had been a subject of general parish concern for some time, because the two-story brick building and its frame additions on Bench Street could no longer accommodate all the applicants for St. Joseph's Academy. To aid in the erection of a new building the proceeds of the St. Patrick's Day supper in 1859 (Captain John O'Gorman presiding) had been turned over to the sisters. Bishop Grace began laying plans for building at a site "above the city." This property, at Nelson (now Marshall) and Western, had been purchased by Bishop Cretin for a cemetery, but it had not been used after the growth of the city had forced the removal of the burial ground to Como and Lexington. The building for the sisters was commenced in 1861 and completed in 1863.

Meanwhile Bishop Grace transferred the school from Bench Street to the hospital on Ninth Street and moved the patients into the brick building on Bench. There were fewer patients then than students and by repairing the hospital building the bishop was able to announce the reopening on the first Monday of September 1859 of St. Joseph's Academy for Young Ladies, a boarding school. There were sixteen boarders and forty day pupils at the academy that fall. The novitiate and the orphans remained in one part of the hospital building on Ninth Street until the new academy building was completed. Then the novitiate was moved with the school to the new location.

Attention was called to the hospital by an item in the *Pioneer and Democrat* for July 12, 1860, since an impression was abroad that the institution was closed. The public was assured that it was still open for "invalids of every nation and faith" and that the Sisters of St. Joseph were devoting themselves as usual to the care of "those who may be taken sick or become the victim of casualties away from home."

The hospital, said the paper, was located near the head of Bench Street in "an airy and healthy" situation overlooking the river.

Within the sisters' community during this time there was a great deal of discussion of the relative merits of local government by the bishop of a diocese where sisters were working and general government of all the sisters in the United States according to a constitution approved at Rome. The latter form resembled the general structure of ecclesiastical hierarchy within the church and the federal principle in the American system. Especially under frontier conditions, bishops were inclined to feel hampered when a far-off mother superior recalled sisters for whom the bishop believed he had the most urgent need. On the other hand, the sisters thought that only they could direct the ordinary course of life in their houses with complete understanding of the ends and means of their institute. Many, for example, anticipated that bishops might make changes in customs and dress for local conditions which would destroy the unity of spirit which must characterize their little design.

Mother Celestine Pommerel, before her death in June 1857, had been working to establish a central government for all the Sisters of St. Joseph in the different dioceses to which they had gone. When she died, Mother Seraphine Coughlin of St. Paul had been elected her successor as superior general at Carondelet. She had begged to be excused from accepting the office, partly because of diffidence and partly for reasons of health. Also Father Ravoux had objected to her leaving St. Paul at least until the new bishop was appointed. Mother St. John Facemaz had then been chosen superior general, and she had continued Mother Celestine's efforts on behalf of a central government.

A meeting was called in 1859 and the constitutional procedure was established tentatively, but of the later provinces only the bishops of St. Paul and Albany, New York, permitted the sisters within their jurisdiction to enter into the new agreement. There is no evidence that either Bishop Cretin or Bishop Grace sought independence for the sisters of St. Paul. It may be that they were aware of the difficulties of securing an adequate supply of sisters without outside assistance or they may have been moved by a sense of gratitude for early aid. For whatever reason, the pronounced independence and self-reliance which came to be characteristic of the St. Paul community never caused any movement toward autonomy. There were, of course, no further exchanges of sisters between the numerous foundations in independent groups as in Philadelphia, Wheeling, Buffalo, Toronto, Rochester, and Brooklyn.

In the new constitution St. Paul was designated the center of the territorial area called a province, and St. Joseph's Academy became the Provincial House instead of "our House of St. Paul." Mother Seraphine Coughlin was named the first provincial superior. The new constitution required much negotiation with the officials in Rome and several trips to Europe, for it was necessary for Rome to determine whether the Congregation of the American Sisters of St. Joseph was sufficiently stable and well organized to permit an autonomous government outside the jurisdiction of the local bishops.

Not only the bishops, but some of the sisters preferred diocesan government or, for personal reasons, did not wish to be governed by an authority established at Carondelet. Naturally, the whole problem was a source of unrest.

All this meant little to the novices Sister Seraphine Ireland and Sister Celestine Howard beyond their desire to understand and accept the form of government which was finally to be adopted. They thought more of their Profession Day, December 8, 1860, than of any other event.

On December 15, 1858, Sister Celestine Howard had left the novitiate at St. Joseph's Hospital for a post at the St. Anthony Falls school. Sister Cyril, one of the teachers there, was ill and had to be replaced.

Sister Seraphine Ireland had helped in the free school on the hospital grounds while she was a postulant, but on December 15, 1858, she was sent to teach in St. Joseph's Academy, where she soon became one of the principal teachers. Sister Seraphine had retained her fun-loving disposition — her intense desire to be perfect had not tended to make her sedate. Within the community her humor was proverbial. There was a custom among the Sisters of St. Joseph that on the feast of the Holy Innocents, the youngest novice in the house should sit in the superior's place and grant all the permissions. When Sister Seraphine's turn came, she ordered out the dried raspberries and there was such a feast of pies that day that the more serious minded questioned the wisdom of the custom.

Sister Seraphine was a gifted teacher. With her industry and enthusiasm she mastered astronomy and natural philosophy and fine needlework. The children loved her for her friendliness and for the fascinating digressions which accompanied her classes in history and literature. Since the day when a Sister of Mercy in Chicago had cast her story of Jack and the Beanstalk into the fire, she had loved extracurricular reading. Now it enriched her teaching to a degree beyond the unimaginative methods usual at that time.

Their new work as teachers, absorbing as it was, did not separate Sister Seraphine and Sister Celestine from a realization of the presence of God in the way of life they desired to adopt. While the solemnity of being received into the community temporarily had its dramatic appeal for those outside the convent, to the novices it was but a step toward the goal of the more permanent dedication of themselves by the three vows of poverty, chastity, and obedience.

The promises they were to make on Profession Day came to seem to them like the three nails by which they would be fastened to the cross of Christ. In human affections they would renounce everything for the love of God and their neighbor. By the vow of poverty they would promise not to dispose of any temporal thing without the permission of their superior. The vow of chastity would bind them to a life of celibacy and the vow of obedience would be their obligation to observe the rules and constitutions of the Congregation of the Sisters of St Joseph. To them the solemn tone of finality in the promises conveyed merely their intention to do natural things in a supernatural way. When asked to carry bread to the poor, they would do so for the love of God, in whose image the needy person was made, and who therefore deserved more than mere human pity for misfortune.

They did not consider that their vocation to be religious should be taken on by every woman or that they were superior beings because they were willing to live as sisters. The sanctity of Mrs. Ireland alone — to say nothing of all the other good mothers in St. Paul — kept them from thinking that holiness could not be achieved in the married state or even that such goodness was not ordinarily a concomitant of Christian marriage. Rather, they humbly thanked God that convent life appealed to them, that they liked it so much that they felt they could not be sure of saving their souls in any other state of life.

The ceremony of December 8, 1860, when three postulants received the habit and two novices made their vows, was impressive to all. The Ellens' part of the service came after the postulants had left the chapel to be dressed in the habit. Together as on their Reception Day, Sister Seraphine Ireland and Sister Celestine Howard begged to make their profession in the Congregation of the Sisters of St. Joseph in order to devote their whole lives to the service of God and their neighbor. They knew now that this devotion meant a warm, personal love surpassing the love of friends and relatives. It was a tender and willing attachment to all God's human creatures, as deeply revolutionary in its possibilities as was the going forth of the twelve apostles into a hostile world.

They had learned in their two years of novitiate how slowly perfection is acquired and with what strenuous effort

human weakness is overcome. They knew that in the Holy
City there are many mansions and that in the church there
are many religious institutes in which religious persons serve
God. But they were fixed in resolve to follow the design
marked out for the Sisters of St. Joseph. They had studied
the letter which the founder had written more than two
hundred years before in October 1650, and they wished to
work in his "annihilated institute." To be nothing in the eyes
of the world was to them the natural response for the Lord's
invitation to "Come, follow Me." They were proud of the
fact that when the cult of St. Joseph had not yet attained its
full development in the church, his virtues of humility and
charity had commended themselves to their pious founder,
Father Medaille, as the proper model for his little design.

Slowly and reverently, in the formal ceremony, each in
turn pronounced her public promises. "My God, All-powerful
and Eternal Being, I, Sister Mary Seraphine, Thy most un-
worthy daughter and servant, desirous of living entirely for
Thee, and of being altogether subject to Thy grace, in the
presence of Jesus Christ, Thy Eternal Son, of His glorious
Virgin Mother Mary, of our holy patriarch, St. Joseph, and
of the whole court of Heaven, make to Thy Divine Majesty,
the vows of poverty, chastity, and obedience, according to
the Constitutions of the Institute of the Sisters of St. Joseph
of Carondelet."

The special badge which sealed their profession was the
cross which they received during the ceremony. At the foot
of the altar, kneeling before the bishop, they bowed their
heads as he placed about their necks the woolen cord upon
which they were to wear the cross. To each in turn he said,
"Receive, my child, the cross of our Lord Jesus Christ, to
which you are affixed with Him by the three vows, as by so
many nails. Wear it openly on your breast as a most sure
defense against all the attacks of the enemy. Especially
endeavor to carry it faithfully in your heart, by loving it
tenderly and by bearing with delight and humility, this

sweet burden; that, faithfully living and dying in the love of the cross with Jesus, you may also triumph with Him in glory."

Te Deum laudamus, the bishop intoned. How many times the Ellens had sung the *Te Deum* on great occasions. Every notable day in their lives had closed with it, but there was a new grandeur in its rhythm today. Their own particular verse sang out clear and strong, "To Thee the Cherubim and Seraphim continually do cry: Holy, Holy, Holy, Lord God of Sabaoth."

There is never much time in a convent to bask in the sweet sentiments engendered by a beautiful ceremony, but the profession of Sister Seraphine Ireland and Sister Celestine Howard partook perhaps more than usual of the haste of a wartime wedding. For the hard times of the financial depression of 1857 had brought forth the even more heart-rending days of approaching war.

Bishop Grace wrote to the Propagation of the Faith on February 9, 1861, that "owing to political troubles the favorable reversion in the financial affairs of the State and country which we so confidently expected last spring and summer has not taken place, but on the contrary things at the present writing present a more gloomy and discouraging aspect than probably at any previous period of our country's history. The Republic is fast drifting into a Civil war between its Northern and Southern Sections the end or issue of which God alone can know."

The visitation of the remote parts of his diocese Bishop Grace undertook in August and September 1861. He kept a diary of his trip to St. Boniface via the Red River steamboat, with detailed descriptions of people and things encountered along the way. At Breckenridge when the coach halted to deliver the mail and change horses, the bishop and Father Ravoux hurried to the bank of the river to gaze upon the great Red River of the North. The bishop observed that it was "great from its associations and relatively only, as it is in reality not more than 60 yards in width; the deep narrow current is sluggish and crooked, the water is turbid & of a whitish color from the washing of the low clay banks."

Certainly the most interesting personage encountered on the journey was Father Joseph Goiffon whose experiences during and after a blizzard on November 3 to 8, 1860, have been told again and again with many variations. Losing sight during a blizzard of the caravan he was traveling to Pembina with, Father Goiffon, according to one account, disembowled his horse, which had frozen to death, and crawled inside the body of the animal. His feet protruded and although they were frozen, he still retained strength enough to call out so that after five days his party, which had been searching for him, heard his voice.

Upon arriving at Pembina, Father Goiffon was found to be in a serious condition and he was sent by sledge to the doctor. At the bishop's house in St. Boniface, Sister Gosselin, the Grey Nun who was the housekeeper, took care of him. The surgeon cut off his gangrenous right leg and he improved.

Eight days later it was thought he was bleeding to death. He was anointed and they began to melt grease for the candles to be used at his funeral. The pot overflowed and set the kitchen on fire. When the whole place was ablaze, they remembered the dying priest. He tried to persuade them to save something else since he would die anyway if put out into the cold, but over his protests, Father Goiffon was carried out and laid in the snow. Instead of dying, however, the priest recovered; the cold had stopped the hemorrhage. Then his left foot was partially amputated. He made himself a wooden leg and a wooden foot which he refused to replace with more professional ones throughout his long life. When he died on May 6, 1910, he was eighty-six years old.

Bishop Grace was deeply affected at meeting this zealous

missionary stumping about from settlement to settlement attending to his duties and he prevailed upon him to return to Little Canada near St. Paul where life would be less arduous. It was a great satisfaction to the bishop to go on to St. Boniface to meet the kind benefactors who had cared for Father Goiffon in what seemed a superhuman fashion.

Bishop Grace made entries in his diary relating to his visit at the school of the Grey Nuns in St. Boniface and no doubt he took greetings from them to the Sisters of St. Joseph in St. Paul, for the relations between the two sisterhoods were most friendly. Sister McMullen had written to Montreal after her arrival in St. Boniface in November 1859, "About 11 o'clock we arrived at St. Paul where the Sisters of St. Joseph received us very cordially, sparing nothing to make us forget the fatigues of our journey. They even left their occupations to hasten our preparations for reaching the caravan which had left a short while before with two of our Sisters whom we were anxious to rejoin."

Upon his return trip Bishop Grace received the profession of four Sisters of St. Benedict in St. Cloud and gave the habit to two postulants. The bishop was delighted with the piety and spiritual happiness of these sisters. His account of his visit with the Benedictine Sisters was welcome news to the Sisters of St. Joseph in St. Paul, for the founding sisters of the St. Cloud convent had spent several days at St. Joseph's Hospital when they arrived from Pennsylvania in 1857.

On December 21, 1861, the briefest possible notice in the papers announced an event which had been eagerly awaited — the ordination of John Ireland by Bishop Grace in the St. Paul Cathedral. The ceremony, which occurred at the 10:30 Mass on Sunday, was considered a historic occasion and it freshened memories of pioneer days and all that lay behind them. To the young priest's own family, it marked the fulfillment of a lifetime of hope.

It probably reminded them too of an equally memorable

day before, soon after the Irelands had arrived in St. Paul. Bishop Cretin had called John Ireland and Thomas O'Gorman to him that day and had asked them if they would like to be priests. When they replied in the affirmative, it is related that he said, "Kneel down and I will create a seminary to the Lord."

This made as deep an impression on the two boys as the oddly similar experience had made on Ellen Ireland and Ellen Howard. Thomas O'Gorman once publicly declared that this was the real beginning of the St. Paul Seminary, although it was many years before the seminary became an actuality.

John Ireland and Thomas O'Gorman had soon become as fast friends as the Ellens. They went to school together in the basement of the three-story second Cathedral of St. Paul, where Father Peyragrosse was their teacher. Long afterward Thomas O'Gorman recalled their school days. He said that John Ireland's "most unusual characteristic — and one which has doubtless been his greatest practical asset in life — is the faculty of being mentally quick and mentally deep at the same time. I recall in the little parish school in St. Paul, as well as through the years we spent together at school in France at Meximieux, he stood at the head of his classes with apparently none of the effort expended by the other boys merely in keeping a foothold. For him, seemingly, to want to learn a thing was to learn it. The usual rule is that quick acquisition and shallowness go together, as do thoroughness and plodding. But he has been an exception to that rule all through his life. His grasp is both instant and deep."

Bishop Cretin had been responsible for sending the two boys to Meximieux where he had made his own seminary studies. He had importuned the Society for the Propagation of the Faith in Lyons for traveling expenses, and the society had responded generously. The boys had left on September 20, 1853, under the care of Father Augustin Ravoux. John was full of life, walking up and down, making friends with everyone on the train. Monsignor Ravoux reproved him to no avail until he said, "If you do not sit down and keep still, I will take you back to St. Paul." That was the last thing John wanted and he subsided until they reached New York and the boat. Then he went about everywhere on the vessel talking to the mariners and the passengers. He was deaf to Father Ravoux and his pleadings for propriety. "Now you cannot take me back to St. Paul," said he, with the impulsive daring which often characterized his later years.

While the boys studied in France, they spent the vacations visiting Bishop Cretin's relatives and traveling as far as their funds permitted. John was a bright scholar, and he also displayed a winning personality, as the letters of Father Babad, Bishop Cretin's agent with the Propagation of the Faith, make clear. He loved French life and customs and he was able to win prizes even in French composition and literature. But there was in him a deep attachment to St. Paul and he was anxious to be back home. Letters and newspapers went back and forth and served to keep him informed of things social and political which were to be a predominant interest all his later life. Family devotion was strengthened by the long separation. One of Ellen Ireland's first letters to him began, "Dear Brother John: As pants the hart for living waters, so does my soul pant after thee."

John Ireland returned to America in the late fall of 1861. After his ordination he was stationed at the Cathedral and he was soon preaching sermons on patriotism and temperance and education that drew the attention of all Minnesota. The legends say that when he was applying for his passport in France, he declared that he was stanchly Unionist. Others aver that he returned home from Europe ahead of time to take his part in the war. Certainly he was as opposed to slavery and discrimination against Negroes as any abolitionist. A factor in this attitude may have been that the Ireland family had always had Negroes and mulattoes as close neighbors in St. Paul. Thus they had learned early that there was no essential difference between them and the immigrants who were then called the "Irish race" or the "German race."

The Irish took little interest in shouldering guns as directed by people who had spent a decade in mocking them as Paddies or Papists. On the other hand, church officials feared to stir up the old taunt that Catholics were under foreign domination and could not be American patriots. The *St. Paul Daily Press* spoke of the "manly, patriotic, and Christian admonitions" which Reverend Mr. Ireland at the request of Bishop Grace had addressed to Irish Catholics on the subject of resistance to the draft. The sermon was considered a stirring exhortation to loyal obedience to law and an appeal to sense of duty and patriotism enforced "by all the awful sanctions of the Catholic Faith." The writer felt that it would not fail to have a salutary influence.

Since the present American theory that ordained clergymen or those in training are acceptable conscientious objectors to war had not yet been thought of, Father Ireland virtually became a recruiting officer, preaching the call to arms Sunday after Sunday in the Cathedral with the entire approval of southern-born Bishop Grace. Credit was given to the young priest — too generously — for raising an Irish regiment. And his efforts soon won his appointment as a war chaplain.

Although he was forced to resign after a year because of poor health, that year of experience is said to have been a determinant of his character as a citizen. His own evaluation of the experience he wrote thirty years later to Father Peter Paul Cooney of Notre Dame when the latter was preparing a history of the Civil War chaplains. Ireland wrote in the third person and he indicated in the appended note that Father Cooney might sift, reject, retain, and polish what he had written in loose language and chaotic form. The manuscript, written while Ireland was crossing the Atlantic, January 24, 1892, is preserved in the archives at Notre Dame.

"In the early spring of 1862," wrote Ireland, "five regiments of infantry had left Minnesota for the seat of war, Catholics being represented in good proportion through all; Catholics were especially numerous in the Fifth, composing one-fifth of the regiment. All these regiments, with the exception of the first, were in the West. Rt. Rev. Thos. L. Grace, Bishop of St. Paul, proposed to attend as far as possible to the needs of Catholic soldiers. At his request Alexander Ramsey, then Governor of Minnesota, appointed Rev. John Ireland, State Chaplain for all Minnesota regiments. The appointment was peculiar. The chaplain's commission was from the State of Minnesota — not formally recognized by the U.S. Government. The duty of the State Chaplain was to go from one Minnesota regiment to another — the letters of the Governor securing for him the federal authorities' protection and liberty to travel."

Shortly after the battle of Pittsburg Landing, Father Ireland joined the Fifth Minnesota, he recalled, at Camp Clear Creek, Mississippi. It at once became plain to him that the plan of a general chaplaincy to Catholics in the various Minnesota regiments could not easily be carried out. When a vacancy occurred in the regimental chaplaincy of the Fifth one month after his arrival, the position was tendered to him and he accepted. He remained with the Fifth until the early summer of 1863, when ill health compelled him to resign. He left the regiment at Duckport, Louisiana, a few miles northwest of Vicksburg.

At the time of his appointment he was quite a youthful priest unused as yet to work and hardship. That explains why his health broke down so soon. His enthusiasm maintained itself at fever heat the whole time of his chaplaincy and he returned from the work with deepest regret. Trying to show that he had all the devotion his field of labor called for, he wrote of himself in the manuscript for Father Cooney, "Fresh from the lessons and inspirations of his French Seminary, he looked forward to the hospital tent and battlefield as a possible opportunity for martyrdom. He was, moreover, a strong sympathizer with the Union, ardent for its preservation."

John Ireland was convinced that a grand opportunity was opened to the Catholic church in America by the war, and his lasting impression was that the opportunity had been woefully neglected. Numberless thousands of Catholics scattered through the army never saw a priest during the war — no one was near them at the moment of death. A magnificent impression could have been made upon Protestant soldiers by the zeal and exemplary conduct of priests. Somewhat sententiously, Ireland declared that it would have been better for other priests to have left two parishes to be taken care of by one pastor and to have "followed to field the heroes of the country."

There is in the memoir an expression of another attitude which was even more typical of John Ireland than his well-known patriotism, for he said, "The uniform kindness which he experienced from officers and men during the time of his chaplaincy has never been forgotten and has tended largely to form in him the conviction which he holds so deeply that the American people are fair to the Catholic Church and that prejudices exist where Catholics give reason for them and seldom elsewhere."

When the penciled manuscript closes with the words, in the first person now, "My years of chaplaincy were the happiest and most fruitful years of my ministry," it seals half a dozen little stories of special graces accorded to the dying and of sweet memories of spiritual ministrations to the wounded which are difficult to place in the stock pictures of the great citizen-churchman of later years. The reminiscences do leave a pronounced impression of a sensitive interior spirit. However, it is not these stories of faith that are usually repeated. Rather we are told that at the battle of Corinth the chaplain ran to the front again and again, bringing cartridges to keep the soldiers supplied with ammunition.

Even William Watts Folwell, in the section of his four-volume *History of Minnesota* devoted to the Civil War, perpetuated this story: "In the battle of Corinth [Father Ireland] not only exercised the offices of his ministry but he also displayed a manly intrepidity on the firing line."

This bit of lore is now worked into the huge canvas in the governor's reception room at the state Capitol, where the artist's conception of the battle of Corinth put Father Ireland in a soldier's uniform in the line of battle. In later years an aged executive aide, William Williams, maintained, however, that John Ireland told him that he was not there at the battle. As a chaplain, he said, he had no place on the firing line. Granted that this tale is a legend, there is still no pacifist leaning in Ireland's own remembrance of "hardships, of course, but withal delightful time."

After the siege of Vicksburg, Father Ireland, on his way home wasted with fever, stopped in St. Louis to visit Sister Seraphine, his sister, who had been sent there to teach in St. Joseph's Academy at the Carondelet motherhouse in the summer of 1863. This assignment had been a surprise and a test of obedience to Sister Seraphine. It was also the result of a misunderstanding, for when she arrived, she was somewhat abashed to discover that she was not expected. Even in a convent it was difficult for a patriotic northerner to feel comfortable in the South during the war years. But she forgot her heartaches and made the most of her interesting surroundings in the suburb of St. Louis. The red cherry-wood desks she selected for the academy study hall are still in use in the classrooms there.

Young as he was, Father Ireland protested to the superiors against their taking his sister from St. Paul. Or perhaps the strange thing is that they listened to him. It is said that he predicted there would never be another sister from St. Paul if they took the St. Paul girls to St. Louis and kept on sending French sisters to St. Paul. Whether this was an effective plea is not known. In any case, Sister Seraphine was returned to

St. Paul in 1868, where she was made assistant to the provincial superior and directress of St. Joseph's Academy.

By that time the Rule for the houses under the general government of Carondelet had been approved in Rome and St. Paul was permanently made a separate province with its own novitiate and superior. Thus, Sister Seraphine Ireland, as an official of the community, signed the act of profession of her own sister, Eliza, Sister St. John, who was given the habit in St. Paul on December 8, 1868, and made her vows on December 8, 1870. Eliza had been teaching school in Cahill Settlement, west of Minneapolis, for a number of years after her graduation from St. Joseph's Academy in 1860 and she was twenty-four years old when she entered the convent.

The name given to Eliza Ireland on her Reception Day brings to mind Mother St. John Fontbonne, Mother St. John Fournier, and Mother St. John Facemaz, superior general at Carondelet. No explanation is available for the custom of repeating as names for the sisters the ones already in use, even locally. Unless it is a vestige of the same sentiment which inspired families of the period to have their children christened so that they had to be distinguished as "young Annie" and "old Annie" or as "big Mary" and "little Mary."

Sister St. John Ireland and Sister Celestine Howard were early directresses and superiors in St. Anthony and Minneapolis schools. With Sister Seraphine Ireland and Father John Ireland, who had returned to his pastorate at the St. Paul Cathedral, they formed an outstanding family group in the Catholic community of Minnesota.

The periodic appearance in Minnesota of ex-nuns and escapees who were willing to tell — for a consideration — all about the durance vile in which sisters are kept in convents provides a little comic relief in the face of the doubly voluntary character of the Sisters of St. Joseph in the 1860s. For each sister on July 2, 1868, had to decide whether she chose to renew her vows under the Carondelet Rule providing for general government. Bishop Grace and Father Ravoux were in favor of general government but they left the sisters free to decide for themselves. Mother George Bradley who had been the superior of the St. Paul house of the sisters from 1865 to 1868, chose the diocesan system as did Sisters Aurelia Bracken, Emelina Ellis, Madeleine Hipples, and Thomas Cuddy. They went to Meadville, Pennsylvania, to the Sisters of St. Joseph of Erie, and in 1872 to Paynesville to make a new foundation of the Sisters of St. Joseph in the Cleveland diocese.

A letter in the archives of the Sisters of St. Joseph of Cleveland from Sister Seraphine Ireland furnishes her interpretation of the situation on June 1, 1922, when she wrote, "I knew Sister George intimately both as a teacher and fellow religious and can therefore speak of her with authority. While with us, she was at all times most edifying and was highly esteemed by all who came in contact with her. . . . In 1867 when we received from Rome the 'Decree of Commendation of our Constitutions' — the last step toward final approval — Sister George, along with a number of other sisters, became dissatisfied with the new form of government. . . . Thus it seems that Almighty God in His wisdom and goodness draws good out of all things. He has drawn great glory to Himself and great good to souls by the zealous works of the excellent and edifying community of the Sisters of St. Joseph of Cleveland, founded by Mother George Bradley."

Sister Aurelia Bracken in 1902 was the founder of the Sisters of St. Joseph in Lewiston, Idaho, and the builder of St. Joseph's Hospital there. Since 1924, this community has been affiliated with the Sisters of St. Joseph of Carondelet. Sister Emelina Ellis became the mistress of novices of the Sisters of St. Joseph of Erie and died in that community.

Of the forty-three sisters listed before Sister St. John Ireland in the book of the acts of reception and profession in St. Paul, eighteen did not remain in the St. Paul province.

One of these is listed as "dispensed and left," six as "transferred." Two of the transferred went to the St. Louis province, two to the Cleveland diocesan Sisters of St. Joseph, one to the Erie diocesan Sisters of St. Joseph, and one is recorded only as "transferred to another community," which may mean another order than the Sisters of St. Joseph. The other eleven may have returned to secular life or entered other religious orders. There were, of course, many older sisters who had been received and had made their vows before they reached St. Paul. Mother George Bradley was one of these.

Of the ninety persons received or professed in St. Paul during the first twenty-five years — through 1877 — only twelve do not have complete records to death in a convent in St. Paul or elsewhere. These twelve were not professed members and presumably they were dismissed or left of their own accord during the trial period, the reason for leaving being considered unimportant in the record before taking vows.

Of more concern is the fact that, in addition to Mother Seraphine Coughlin's death at the age of thirty-six, seven sisters died in St. Paul before 1878 at an average age of 24.3. Of these the oldest was twenty-eight and the youngest two were twenty. Apparently, it was taken as a matter of course that people should die before they were thirty. Obituary notices in the papers indicate that many young women outside the convent of comparable ages died of "consumption" or in bearing their first child. The causes of the early deaths of the sisters are not determinable from the pious necrologies which remark either that the young woman was a victim of "the ravages of that dread [and nameless] disease" or that she "went into a decline."

With Father Ravoux it is a problem of longevity rather than early demise which is puzzling. Pope Pius IX named him titular bishop of Limyra and vicar apostolic of Montana on July 11, 1868, but Father Ravoux declined the honor because of his poor health, which he described for the Holy Father as follows:

"Many years ago, to my misfortune, I swallowed a pin, which for three or four months, remained fastened in my throat. From that time on, a marked debility and a strong susceptibility to disease have been present in my throat, and at times there has been danger of losing my voice. I am affected, at least at times, with deafness. As to my eyes, I am quite shortsighted. I am sometimes afflicted with gravel in the tonsils and also in the bladder. I suffer also from rheumatism, palpitation of the heart, from poor digestion, and not rarely, from weakness in all my members. Again, I am afflicted with a sickness, as a result of which comfort and health demand at intervals a certain surgical operation, namely bleeding. Also, I could not say Mass after 10:30 for many years because I could not fast till that time."

The Holy Father, upon receipt of this document, excused Father Ravoux from service in Montana. Yet the pioneer missionary remained active and enjoyed life (and presumably poor health) in St. Paul until his death at the age of ninety-one in 1906.

One of Father Ravoux's continuing concerns in Minnesota had been the Indians. In a letter to the Society for the Propagation of the Faith in 1863, Bishop Grace wrote that Father Ravoux had followed up the good work so auspiciously commenced in the conversion of twenty-four Sioux prisoners who were awaiting execution after an outbreak in 1862. Father Ravoux continued to visit the Indian encampment regularly with encouraging results. "He has already baptised one hundred & forty children and adults; and the whole encampment of near 2,000 souls manifest a deep interest in the instructions of the good priest,—& need only a more settled condition of affairs to be brought over in a body to the faith of Christ."

Bishop Grace too was concerned with the problems of the Indians, continuing the interest of his predecessor. In the same letter to the Propagation he mentioned, "I have had a correspondence with the President and the Indian Department . . . and assurance has been given me that the wishes of the Indians in respect to the Missionaries to be resident among them shall be consulted and respected." To Ignatius Donnelly, the active political reformer from Nininger, Minnesota, Bishop Grace wrote a testimonial on May 18, 1864, saying Donnelly's was "the first voice that has been raised against the iniquity of this Indian policy [that is, the confusion of administrative regulations which resulted in depriving the Indians of their rights] in the only place in which the evil can be corrected [Washington]."

That same year in a letter to the Society for the Propagation of the Faith the bishop told of accepting a commission from the government to examine and report the condition of the Indians and the manner of fulfillment of treaty stipulations. He also pointed out to the society that the children of the immigrants from all parts of Europe were growing up without opportunities of religious instruction, "whilst," he wrote, "Protestant missionaries are active in their efforts to pervert the minds and corrupt the faith of these unprotected people."

In the spring of 1867 Bishop Grace and Father Ravoux traveled to Rome and Ireland in search of recruits for the priesthood in Minnesota. The bishop also made his *ad limina* visit to the Vatican.

The newspapers made a great deal of their return on August 17, 1867. To the accompaniment of church bells and bands, they were met by marching units of Catholic societies and escorted home from the depot. From his front porch Bishop Grace reviewed his impressions of Europe, commenting especially on the growing interest in religion he had observed in France. Father Ravoux, on the other hand, dwelt on Ireland, where he found that the "people were rich, rich not in the world's goods, but rich in the sight of God who estimates the wealth of the soul, not of the pocket."

Father Ravoux might well have used the same words to describe a group even closer to his heart perhaps than the Irish — the Sisters of St. Joseph in St. Paul. The sisters were certainly not rich in the world's goods in the 1860s, but their wealth of soul showed itself in their acts of charity to all kinds of persons, daily increasing the facility with which the people of St. Paul could think of them as one in fellowship with themselves. And their poverty in pocket did not deter them from constantly extending their activities beyond St. Paul as they founded and staffed schools, convents, hospitals, and orphanages in surrounding communities. The sisters were indeed rich in the sight of God.

⚥ VI ⚥

Frontiers Beyond the Town

"Just as if women were not already scarce enough for wives and mothers out that way," wrote the *St. Paul Daily Press* on September 12, 1872, "the Roman Catholics are building a large nunnery at Detroit Lake, Becker County."

While this particular project did not belong to the Sisters of St. Joseph, they were equally careless about population problems as they began to widen their sphere in the 1870s. Growth was slow and repeated the St. Paul territorial experience on a westward-moving, tree-felling, land-breaking frontier. There was the same muscular output to wrest a living from the elements, the same unattractive houses where the women churned and baked and stewed in heat and cold, the same loneliness and yearning for the beauty and softness of things remembered from a youth spent in remote and more cultivated places. And the same goaheadativeness — that realization of the almost superhuman power which ambition could put into the human frame — matched itself against the infrequent visits of hard-working priests and needy Sisters of St. Joseph saying over and over, "What doth it profit a man if he gain the whole world and suffer the loss of his own soul?"

The visits of the sisters to outlying districts were trips made to their own homes to comfort their families when sickness or death harassed them or they were expeditions through the countryside at harvest time to beg the threshing crews for help for the orphans. To the farm women, rendered shapeless and uninteresting by their monotonous toil, the sisters were a vision of gracious, spacious living in ladylike daintiness and elegance. That their own daughters might be saved from their dour kind of life on the farm by learning convent refinement became an ideal to many. And more and more opportunities were opened for them as the Sisters of St. Joseph reached beyond St. Paul to establish convent homes, district schools, and parish, or parochial, schools.

Three sisters took charge of the district school within the venerable parish of St. Peter at Mendota in 1867 and they lived in the old home of General Sibley until 1879 when the sisters were withdrawn, according to Sister Ignatius Cox, because of lack of support. Mother Pauline LeMay, Sister Ignatius Cox, and Sister Columba Augé comprised the first staff.

The earlier settlers in Mendota were French Canadians, but through the 1850s the immigrants were largely Irish families who took farm land in Dakota County. The parish was thus made up of French, Irish, half-breeds, and native Sioux.

Mother Pauline, who spoke only French when she entered the community, was distinguished among all the sisters who knew her for the strange kind of English she acquired and also for her exceptional devotion to the poor. She took on the Indians as her special care in Mendota. The children of Mendota could remember on into their old age the privilege it had been to go with her to visit the Indians and bring them food and clothes and medicine.

As Ludmilla Augé, Sister Columba had attended the first session of the sisters' school in the old log chapel of St. Paul in 1851. On December 8, 1860, she received the habit, at the age of eighteen, in the same ceremony during which Sister Seraphine Ireland and Sister Celestine Howard made their vows. She taught the district school for boys across the street from the Sibley House, where Sister Ignatius taught the girls.

Sister Columba — whose name often became "Columbia" — was generally assigned to teach boys because she was a strict disciplinarian. Thomas Shields, a pupil from a nearby farm, described her in his book *The Dullard* as a strong, muscular woman. It was she who advised the parents of this future head of the department of education and the founder of Sisters' College at the Catholic University in Washington to take their son home when he was nine and set him to work on the farm because she thought he would never learn anything in school.

While *The Dullard* describes somewhat emotionally the mistakes Dr. Shields' teacher and parents made in his training, judging them by what are the now matter-of-course or somewhat outmoded educational theories he learned in later life, the book does present a unique picture of country life in Mendota and of school procedure there. The picturesqueness of the township made a lasting impression even on the retarded intellect of "Shields' omadhaun" and he speaks feelingly of the air, the soil, and the scenery.

One reads on eagerly to see how all these valuable natural surroundings were used to help teachers and students to love rural life and to prefer the farm to any other mode of existence. But the reward is just a series of memory pictures which, if anything, seem to have led the boy toward the invention of labor-saving machinery and the development of industrial processes to manufacture it. He learned his physics from the old oaken bucket which he recalled with romantic nostalgia.

Dr. Shields' account of his reading difficulties includes the titles of the books used and provides a fairly realistic picture of teaching methods then in vogue. Older Sisters of St. Joseph affirm that it is a true presentation of teaching in the country schools which they attended. Those who also attended St. Joseph's Academy say that certain teachers there were just as wooden — it depended entirely on individual difference if more elasticity was introduced. The unimaginative method had obvious defects even for a normal child.

"When I first went to school I could read fairly well for a boy of six," wrote the doctor, "that is, I could read the simple phrases of Wilson's [Willson's] First Reader. I was immediately promoted to Wilson's Second Reader, where, as far as I now remember, I also succeeded fairly well. But early in my eighth year, probably because the teacher did not want to have me in a class by myself, she made the mistake of putting me into class with children older than myself, who were reading in the National Third Reader.

"Nothing was done by the teacher to bring us to a realization of the content of the literature that we tried to read. The selections in the Third Reader were all classical and were chosen without any apparent regard to the limitations of a child's vocabulary. There was, consequently, little chance that the children would understand what they were reading. To be sure, we were required to memorize some of the words with their definitions; but all this was a meaningless memory drill for most of us, and . . . it was entirely beyond me. Many of the words I could not even pronounce, and whenever I was called upon to read, I stumbled hopelessly, felt humiliated before the whole school, was laughed at by the children and scolded by the teacher. I ended up with the conviction that I 'had no talent' for reading. . . .

"Before I was nine years old I knew my catechism by heart from cover to cover, and it will be admitted that the catechism holds its own, even with the National Readers, in its total disregard of the child's capacity to understand. There are few readers of any series that can produce such a splendid array of long, and to the child, unpronounceable words as are to be found in the catechism. I learned the catechism through by ear. . . . My sister 'heard my lesson' every evening. . . . She pronounced it for me, word for word. . . . But transubstantiation, indefectibility, sover-

eignty, etc., had no more meaning for me than transmagnifi-
candandubobanciality that was commonly used at that
time for practice in syllabification."

Thomas Shields' parents took Sister Columba's advice and
removed their son from school about this time, but when he
was thirteen he returned to prepare for his confirmation. He
found school methods no improved. "There were between
twenty and twenty-five children in my reading class. When
the bell rang for the lesson, we lined up according to the
place that we had held in the spelling exercise at the close of
the preceding lesson. The pupil at the head of the class read
the first paragraph of the two or three pages assigned for the
day's lesson. Straightway, each one of us counted the para-
graphs and calculated which one would fall to his turn. He
neither knew nor cared what went before nor what came
after his own paragraph. . . .

"During the three months of my stay at school I do not
remember that the teacher ever offered a word of explanation or of comment on the subject-matter of the reading
lesson. She taught us how long to pause for a comma, a
semicolon, a colon, and a period. She drilled us in the proper
pronunciation of the words, and in the correct inflection
before a period and before an interrogation point. . . . The
lesson consisted of two or three pages of an extract cut out
of the body of some classic; the reading book gave no synop-
sis of the text from which the lesson was taken, nor did it
give any account of the circumstances which called it forth."

No one would question the soundness of Dr. Shields'
criticism, but candor requires that we acknowledge a certain
quaint charm of matter and manner in the way Sister
Sebastian Cronin at eighty-two recalled the content of the
National Readers by ready quotation — with appropriate
gestures — of long selections in verse and prose.

Other students retained pleasanter recollections of the
Mendota school than did Dr. Shields. Two of the Halloran
girls became Sister Fabian and Sister Jerome of the Francis-

can Order in Rochester. They were nurses at St. Mary's Hospital there. Sister Fabian could remember the very spot on the stone wall outside the front window of the Sibley House where she used to sharpen her slate pencil. Mrs. Nellie Curran loved music as a child and remembered in later years that she took lessons on the melodeon from Sister Scholastica.

All the girls took sewing on Friday afternoon. They learned to make hair flowers, wool flowers, and to do canvas work (something like the hooked rugs of today, Sister Fabian said). When the Hallorans moved to Glencoe in 1880, they took with them a glass globe which contained birds of worsted they had made in the Mendota school. People used to come ten miles to see the birds. Mrs. P. F. Barry, another former pupil at Mendota, said that her mother saved the white goose feathers for the sisters, who used them to make lilies for the altar at Christmas. The girls also did knitting and tatting and crocheting. And they learned how to make lace curtains.

Bishop Timothy Corbett of Crookston was an alumnus of the Mendota school and Nancy Campbell, daughter of the Indian Duncan Campbell, was remembered by all the old pupils. Unimportant as the little school appears, it is worthy of note that twenty-five Sisters of St. Joseph have been born in Mendota and a number of them attended the Mendota school.

In 1872 Mother Seraphine Ireland, directress of St. Joseph's Academy, St. Paul, was sent to open the convent in Hastings. Seven sisters in all, including Mother Seraphine as superior, were sent to Hastings — two for the German parish of St. Boniface, two for the Guardian Angels' parish school, three for the academy boarding school.

The convent where all the sisters lived and which housed the academy was called St. Teresa's, but the academy was called either St. Boniface's or St. Teresa's. On July 9, 1873, in Teutonia Hall at Hastings, Father John Ireland conferred a medal on the one graduate of the academy that year, Miss Davie.

The German parish had bought a large building for a school for young ladies. As in other places, the people of the parish preferred to have German-speaking sisters and they asked the Sisters of St. Benedict to take their school including the academy within a few years, but the Sisters of St. Joseph continued to teach the grade school in the parish of the Guardian Angels. The Hastings house of the sisters in still called St. Teresa's Convent.

Ignatius Donnelly lived at Nininger, near Hastings, during this period. His daughters attended St. Teresa's Academy. In 1929, Mother Seraphine could recall an occasion on which he had presented her with a book. The sisters were spending the day at the Donnelly home—"the Feast of St. Aloysius, June 21, just after school closed." A box of books arrived from Ignatius' sister in Philadelphia, Eleanor C. Donnelly, then widely known as a Catholic "poetess." Upon being told by his daughters of "a box from Aunt Eleanor, Papa," the sage of Nininger, as he was called by many, retired to open it and presently returned with the new volume of his sister's poems which he presented to Mother Seraphine with "a great bow." She looked at the inscription. "To Mother Seraphim from Brother Cherubim," it read. Mother Seraphine laughed and then said to him, "Well, there are a few things you will have to do before you can be called Brother Cherubim."

The political explosiveness of Donnelly was undoubtedly a topic of conversation when Father Ireland visited his sister at the Hastings convent during 1874. While women did not vote, there was talk in farm homes about the relative merits of political issues and girls who entered the convent between 1860 and 1890 from Minnesota counties were interested in the political problems and personalities of the day. They had almost certainly heard such speakers as John Ireland and Ignatius Donnelly. Donnelly especially was a well-known figure in Minnesota in the late nineteenth century. One Minnesota priest, Monsignor John A. Ryan, included in his autobiography a description of the "sage" which may explain the fascination Donnelly had for his contemporaries.

Ryan described Donnelly as a "very remarkable man . . . statesman, politician, agitator, social reformer, and author. . . . As a political stump speaker, Donnelly was the most entertaining and effective of them all. . . . He excelled in quick thinking, wit, repartee, and a kind of sarcasm that was always effective and rarely biting or bitter."

Monsignor Ryan, widely known as the director of the Department of Social Action of the National Catholic Welfare Council, was born in 1869 on a farm in Dakota County, nine miles from Ignatius Donnelly's home. On that farm, ten miles from Hastings and twenty miles south of St. Paul, his mother bore eleven children, of whom one died shortly after birth. Of the other children, two became Sisters of St. Joseph, two priests of the diocese of St. Paul, and six married.

In his dry manner, Monsignor Ryan remarked that in view of the large proportion of the family who were celibates, "the fact that the other six produced thirty-nine children is a striking refutation of the assertation still made occasionally that religious celibacy diminishes or has diminished the birth rate."

Monsignor Ryan made some interesting comments in his autobiography on the Hastings area at the period when Mother Seraphine and the other sisters were opening their schools there. The economic burden of buying land is tersely revealed. The Ryan family owned two farms, encumbered by mortgages. For some twenty years the interest on one of the two mortgages was twelve per cent annually; on the other the rate was ten per cent for about twelve years. In the early nineties, Monsignor Ryan says, the rate was reduced to six per cent. He adds that the "dominant economic opinion and policies of the United States in those days were still those of *laissez-faire*."

Nationality prejudices were an inevitable factor in the rural areas as they were in the church and school division in the village of Hastings. "The members of the farm community where I was born and reared," Monsignor Ryan wrote, "were all Irish immigrants and all Catholics. In the district school which I attended there was at no time in my experience even one non-Catholic pupil.

"The adjoining community to the south was composed entirely of Germans, likewise all Catholic. With them the people of our Irish settlement got along very well. There were no quarrels, enmities or friction between the two groups, although we Irish regarded our German neighbors as somewhat inferior. As a matter of fact, they were superior to us in some respects. In those days, however, we shut our eyes to those qualities and kept our attention only on the characteristics we thought marked us as a superior race."

During this period another facet of the nationality problem commanded the attention of the Catholics in Hastings and the rest of Minnesota. Erik L. Petersen, a native of Norway, had come to St. Paul as a deacon in December 1872. He was ordained a priest by Bishop Grace on December 21. Early in January 1873 the *Northwestern Chronicle* announced that the newly ordained priest would preach at the Cathedral on the following Sunday morning in the Norwegian language. On February 22, a series of lectures in Norwegian was announced at St. Louis (French) Church. A biographical sketch from a New York paper pointed out that Father Petersen was the only Norwegian priest in the United States.

Within a year, Father Petersen married and became an Episcopal minister with headquarters at Faribault. He was named a missionary at large for Minnesota to preach to the Scandinavian people. Newspapers throughout the state carried accounts of his change of faith and of the various controversies in which he became entangled. Norwegian settlers in particular repudiated the young man and his life became a series of bitter experiences.

He had been led to the United States by the false rumor that there was a movement among Scandinavian-Americans to enter the Catholic church. In his autobiography, Father Petersen described his experience. "Having arrived there I soon found out, to my great dismay, that the idea of a tendency among the Norwegians towards Catholicism was a mere phantom arising from a misunderstanding of the actual state of things. The facts were that in the course of the discussions among the Scandinavian Lutherans in America the Synod had been charged with Catholic sympathies. . . . Catholics had been led to look upon the Synod as a connecting link between their Church and the Lutherans. I was not long in finding out the mistake and it was this discovery that perfectly dismayed me."

Petersen continued to be active in various literary and missionary pursuits until he took his own life in 1887. His daughter said that he left the Catholic church because he could not accept papal infallibility, which was defined by the church two years before he was admitted to major orders and made his promises of chastity and obedience. To his contemporaries, however, it was clear that it was the matter of celibacy which had cut him off. His own statement on his disappointment is significant in the light of the fact that Bishop Grace and Father Ireland and probably many priests and sisters were mistaken in their belief that Scandinavians in Minnesota had an interest in Catholicism.

The Sisters of St. Joseph undoubtedly were distressed at Father Petersen's defection and still more disturbed about the failure of Catholicism to gain a foothold among the Scandinavians in Minnesota, but they did not pause in their own efforts to expand the frontiers of the church in the state. In 1873 they founded St. Michael's parish school in Stillwater with Mother Stanislaus Saul in charge. And in 1877

Holy Angels' Academy in Minneapolis was established by the sisters.

The greater size of Minneapolis today tends to obscure the fact that for many years St. Paul was the great center of enterprise and population in the Northwest, while Minneapolis was but one of many smaller communities in the surrounding area. The Sisters of St. Joseph did not establish their first Catholic school in Minneapolis until 1866, when two sisters were sent to the parish of the Immaculate Conception. Every day the sisters went across the suspension bridge in a buggy with one horse from St. Anthony's Convent (then called St. Mary's). Sister Celestine Howard, who had been teaching at the St. Anthony school, was the first directress and her companion was Sister Ignatius Cox. Two months after the opening, Sister Cecelia Delaney was sent to help them, since the enrollment had reached 129. When Sister Celestine was made directress of St. Joseph's Academy in 1875, Sister St. John Ireland succeeded her. The parish with its school of the Immaculate Conception is now called the parish and school of the Basilica of St. Mary.

A report on the Minneapolis schools appeared in the *Minneapolis Tribune* on August 22, 1875. There is no mention of nearby St. Anthony, but only of the schools for boys and girls in the "West Division," including the Immaculate Conception school. Nevertheless, St. Anthony school was still in existence; it had continued without a break from 1853 except for a brief period in 1859–60, when Father Fayolle had to leave the parish on account of illness and the sisters were recalled to St. Paul. Mother Seraphine Ireland was sent there as superior in 1875.

Sister Bridget Bohan remembers Mother Seraphine's teaching at this time. She says that mathematics was not her forte but that the English and history periods were enlivened by travel reminiscences and accounts from books Mother Seraphine had read. She was full of life and energy and her good humor endeared her to the girls. Her six years there gave

her ample opportunity to display her gifts as a "born
teacher."

In 1877 a residence for the sisters teaching in Minneapolis
was opened on Third Street North in a rented house known
as the "White Convent." Thereafter the Minneapolis parochial school teachers no longer had to make the trip each
day from St. Anthony. Sister St. John Ireland, the directress
of the Immaculate Conception school, was named the superior of the convent. It was in that house that Holy Angels'
Academy was established. The convent, accompanied by the
academy, was moved through a series of houses until it was
finally settled at Fourth Street North in the Bassett property.
Mother St. John Ireland remained superior of the convent
and academy as well as Immaculate Conception school until
her death from consumption in 1897.

The Holy Angels was a large — and somewhat fashionable
— boarding school for girls in the grades and high school. Its
decline was attributed to the deterioration of the Fourth
Street neighborhood and in 1907 the high school, now a day
school, was transferred to a new location at Thirteenth and
Linden streets and called St. Margaret's Academy. The old
Holy Angels was closed in 1928; in the intervening years it
had been used as a grade school and the sisters from various
parish schools continued to reside there.

The next house to be opened in rural Minnesota was in the
western part of the state at Graceville, a town dear to John
Ireland's heart.

Father Ireland seems to have been the recognized voice of
authority from the day he was ordained. Complaints and
requests came to him oftener than to Bishop Grace. It is
recorded that he grubbed out stumps in the playground at
a St. Paul parish school; that he assembled the few colored
Catholics in St. Paul at an old brick school on Sixth and
Wabasha in 1863 and instructed them in the truths of religion; that he once rushed out on Sunday after Mass to help
a farmer save his crop before the rain came; that he organ-

ized a Catholic industrial school for boys and brought in the
Good Shepherd Sisters for girls (when discriminatory law
and practice in public reformatories caused Catholics concern); that he fostered a program for poor Irish immigrants
which encouraged self-help and land ownership.

Bishop Grace sent Father Ireland to Rome in his stead in
1869, to represent the diocese at the Ecumenical Council,
the important conclave which was to define the infallibility
of the pope. He took with him John Shanley, who had been
studying at St. John's College in Stearns County and who
was now deemed ready to enter Propaganda College in
Rome. They wrote back to the *Northwestern Chronicle,*
Bishop Grace's two-year-old paper, interesting accounts of
the voyage. Many of the passengers were bishops from
distant dioceses journeying to the Vatican Council. Their
stories made for the two young men a composite picture of
the work of the church in many lands.

Another of the Ireland legends grew up at the council,
where Cardinal Pecci, who was later to be Pope Leo XIII,
is supposed to have said of the young priest as he passed,
"Behold the future." St. Paul and Minneapolis newspapers
proudly recorded Father Ireland's departure and return with
the details of his travels through France, Italy, the Eternal
City, and "the Dear Old Land" of Ireland. They were careful
to point out also that he "returned with pleasure to St. Paul."

The *St. Paul Dispatch* of February 27, 1875, announced
the appointment of Reverend John Ireland as vicar apostolic
of Nebraska, Wyoming, Montana, and part of Dakota and
reported as well the creation of an apostolic vicariate for
northern Minnesota with the Right Reverend Abbot Rupert
Seidenbusch, O.S.B., in charge. Bishop Grace, who had felt
unequal to the burden of travel entailed in a trip to the
Vatican Council, took immediate action in this crisis. Twenty
years later, W. P. Murray, in an article in the *Pioneer Press,*
said that the climax of the career of Bishop Grace was his
trip to Rome without permission (Mr. Murray says know-

ingly "without permission" though what sanction was necessary for a bishop to visit Rome he does not reveal) to ask the pope to allow him to retain Father Ireland in St. Paul. Mr. Murray stated further that it was churchmen who were Americans like Bishop Grace and Bishop Ireland that St. Paul wanted — not those who were too much dominated by Rome.

Mr. Murray's conviction that fine people like Father Ireland and Bishop Grace had somehow cast off the awful occult domination of what was known as "the power of Rome" had been strengthened through the years by the very friendly relations which existed between Mr. Murray and the two priests. This relationship is exemplified by an exchange of letters in November 1866. Mr. Murray had called Father Ireland's attention to the political action of one of the diocesan priests. Father Ireland replied saying that he had advised the priest to be very careful about interfering in political questions, which "we generally consider foreign to our calling," adding the assurance to Mr. Murray that should the priest "have heretofore overstepped due limits, I have every confidence the thing will not occur again."

Bishop Grace succeeded in his Roman mission and on October 8, 1875, the *Dispatch* was able to inform its readers, after a careful perusal of the New York *Freeman's Journal*, that John Ireland, who had been bishop *in partibus infidelium*, was henceforth to be bishop coadjutor of St. Paul, *cum jure successionis*. This was something "our citizens of every religious denomination will rejoice to learn," commented the *Dispatch*, for the "gigantic services he has rendered in the cause of temperance and the immense good he has done among his own countrymen and others in this community . . . make this a fitting tribute to his great talents and his many private virtues." The occasion of the consecration was a splendid affair, for which the Sisters of St. Joseph presented Bishop Ireland with a miter, the bishop's ceremonial headdress.

It was shortly after he became bishop that Ireland founded Graceville, where the Sisters of St. Joseph were later to establish a house. In 1878 he erected a church near a trading post on the Fort Wadsworth trail on Toqua Lakes and located several hundred families in the vicinity through the Catholic Colonization Bureau. He named the settlement for Bishop Thomas L. Grace.

The colonizing work thus exemplified had originated with Bishops Loras and Cretin, who had used all available methods to publicize the rich farm lands of Minnesota in order to induce Catholic immigrants to locate in the territory. They had sent letters to such eastern papers as the *Boston Pilot* and the New York *Freeman's Journal* as well as to numerous journals in Ireland, Austria, Germany, France, and Belgium.

Bishop Grace had continued the work by organizing in 1864 the Minnesota Irish Emigration Society for the purpose of aiding distressed Irish settlers. Father Ireland was the president. No appreciable results in organized colonies are credited to this organization until 1876, when Bishop Ireland began to promote the Catholic Colonization Bureau of Minnesota.

Hand in hand with this bureau another worked closely. It was the Catholic Colonization Stock Company, which stood ready to set up a sober, industrious man with a farm and equipment "until he had taken off his second crop." Nothing came of the sale of shares and no projects were launched until Bishop Ireland secured the sale rights to all the railroad lands in Swift County. Similar arrangements were made for Big Stone County, where Graceville was located, and for the adjoining Traverse County. Ghent, Marshall, and Currie were towns that developed in a connecting area. Ghent was originally settled by Belgian farmers, and they were followed by Canadians, Hollanders, and Germans.

In 1925 Mother Seraphine gave her estimate of John Ireland's motives in his colonizing endeavors to an interviewer studying colonization in Minnesota.

"My brother received his inspiration for this great work," she said, "as he did for many of his other big deeds, from Monsignor James Nugent, his intimate friend from Liverpool, England. . . . My brother had the interests of Minnesota at heart in colonizing this state. Next to his Church he loved America, and then came his native land. The Bishop had no thought of organizing an Irish state in the West. Had not the state given official encouragement to immigration long years before the Bishop started? . . . No, he had no thought of doing anything more than helping his Church, his nation, and his people."

The importance of these colonizing endeavors is revealed in an incident which determined the Canadian investor Donald Smith and the English capitalist George Stephen to join with Hill and Kittson to take over the bankrupt St. Paul and Pacific. The incident was attested by Mrs. Clara Hill Lindley, daughter of James J. Hill, in extracts from her father's diary.

"In early September, 1877, George Stephen was called to Chicago on business. With him were R. B. Angus of the Bank of Montreal and Donald Smith. They proceeded to St. Paul and were taken by Jim Hill on a Sunday tour of inspection of the railroad. The first impression was good, plenty of settlers on the land, but beyond Litchfield the open prairie lay before them, and the visitors became discouraged. When at last a good crowd of people was seen gathered about a rude country church, and others were approaching across the trails —'What is all this?' said George Stephen —'It is a colony opened last year by Bishop Ireland. Already hundreds are coming from the Eastern States and from Europe; these people are going to Mass; this is what will occur all along the railroad.'— said his friends. From that episode Stephen was heart and soul in the enterprise."

In a letter some years later to Archbishop James Gibbons,

Bishop Ireland was able to take something of a proprietary tone about the Northern Pacific. "Bishop Grace and myself indulge in the hope that you will sometime take a recreation in Minnesota. I assure you, a visit to the Northwest, including a run on the Northern Pacific R R to the Yellowstone Valley in Montana is something quite attractive. Please think the matter over." (Exactly that trip was taken by the Baltimore prelate, when as a cardinal he visited St. Paul in 1887.)

An allusion to the difficulties of colonization is contained in a letter to Archbishop Gibbons on March 2, 1880. Bishop Ireland in making a place for a priest wrote, "He may come on to us as soon as he will be ready. Please, however, warn him that in coming to frontier missions in Minnesota, he is coming, for the time being at least, to no earthly paradise. Patience, and self-denial will be for him much needed virtues. The colonization movement so far seems to be a success. Bp. Spalding and myself secured before we left the East subscriptions to the stock in full and we have completed contracts for land in Nebraska and Minnesota."

At the site of Graceville Bishop Ireland had acquired the right to two hundred acres of land, and he made an agreement with a land-grant railroad for the control of 50,000 acres near Graceville with exclusive sale right. Much of it was disposed of to new settlers, mostly of Irish extraction. Before long, the Department of the Interior reversed an earlier decision, thereby throwing the railroad's title to the land into question. As a consequence, Bishop Ireland's claims were for many years a subject of litigation. Eventually the cases were decided almost entirely in his favor, on the theory that he had secured the land in good faith, but the whole procedure involved extensive real estate negotiations which consumed much of the prelate's attention and brought him much criticism.

A philanthropic attempt was made in 1880 to colonize a group of poverty-stricken families directly from Ireland. Father James Nugent, John Ireland's friend in Liverpool, who was an ardent social reformer, made arrangements for 309 victims of the famine in Ireland to emigrate to America and subsequently to Graceville.

The winter of 1880 was an unusually severe one which brought suffering throughout Minnesota, even to well-established settlers. For weeks at a time trains were unable to push through the deep drifts of snow and there were fuel shortages everywhere. The "Connemara" colony had come on a great wave of charitable enterprise and, although they had arrived too late in the season to raise their own gardens, fuel and potatoes and flour had been allotted to them.

Not only did these people from the west of Ireland lack the iron-clad vigor of the seasoned pioneers, but they early manifested a disposition to make the most of the paternalistic system under which they had been rescued and to let Bishop Ireland provide. The neighboring town of Morris had a Board of Trade activated by anti-Catholic sentiment which was bothered by all the Catholic bustling in Graceville. Delegations were sent over to visit the colonists and their reports on the iniquitous conduct of Bishop Ireland — who was said to be deliberately starving the colonists — were given space in the St. Paul and Minneapolis papers as a matter of course, but they also appeared at full length in Chicago and New York papers.

The bishop answered all the charges, but the rumblings went on until it is as easy today to find an old settler who will tell you that Bishop Ireland was a "hard man" as one who will say he was a great philanthropist, both sentiments deriving from the Connemara incident.

The Graceville *Transcript* began in March 1885 to tell anything that could be found out about the new school of the Sisters of St. Joseph in the village. The comings and goings of the sisters were painstakingly noted.

Several factors made this school somewhat different from other establishments. It began as a part Indian school, for which Bishop Ireland made the initial arrangements. He wrote to the Reverend J. A. Stephan, director of the Catholic Indian Bureau in Washington, by whom the matter was conducted through the Interior Department. Authorization was asked for the education of fifty Indian children from the Sisseton agency. The bishop pointed out that the school was situated near the shores of a beautiful lake in a most healthy district and the Sisters of St. Joseph were prepared to instruct the children in a common school curriculum, in housekeeping, dairying, sewing, and knitting.

One notation in the National Archives indicates that twenty-five Indian girls were allotted to the Graceville school and that the government paid one hundred and fifty dollars per capita for them annually. They were segregated from the white girls in a special building. When the Bureau of Catholic Indian Missions sponsored a display by Catholic schools for the Columbian Exposition at Chicago in 1893, the report sent to Washington from the "Convent of Our Lady," Graceville, stated that the school had been established in 1886 as a mission school by the Sisters of St. Joseph, with the aid of a benefactor, Katherine Drexel. This renowned member of the Philadelphia family later founded the Sisters of the Blessed Sacrament for the education of Negroes and Indians.

The convent reported four structures as follows: "1 Three story building, 50 by 60; 1 One half story building, 22 by 45; 1 One half story building, 20 by 22; 1 Two story building, 32 by 48." The value of the buildings was reported to be $12,000, the value of the land, $4500. Drawing was taught in addition to the common school branches. Needlework and general housework were listed as special branches of industry. Finally, the Sisters of St. Joseph stated that they were "actively engaged at present in preparing for the World's Fair."

The whole Graceville establishment was burned to the ground during the night of October 8, 1898. Two years before, the government had withdrawn its support of private schools for Indians and at that time the girls were sent back to the reservation. After the fire, the school was rebuilt near the church and named St. Mary's Academy. This boarding school was widely patronized by young ladies from the western part of the state and many elementary teachers were prepared there before graduation from normal school became a requirement. But never again did the townspeople see the three-seated wagon stop at the door of the convent and two sisters take their places in it for the long drive west to the reservation at Sisseton, South Dakota, where the Indian girls bound for the school had been met. No more did Mother Seraphine and Mother Jane, the Graceville superior, and later, Mother Cecelia Delaney, Mother Jane's successor, climb up a ladder and through a trap door for sleeping accommodations on these trips.

An Indian school for girls was opened at Avoca by the Sisters of the Holy Child in 1883 and continued by the Sisters of St. Joseph from 1890 until 1896, when the government withdrew support. Later on, in 1905, the school became St. Bernard's Hall, a school for little boys.

St. Mary's school at Waverly opened in 1886. Four sisters attempted to teach English to children of seven nationalities.

The school in Currie, which opened with 175 pupils in 1907, is remembered by the Sisters of St. Joseph as a sort of sylvan interlude, with their pastoral problems slightly complicated by their cow's propensity for running away. Neighboring settlers at times feared the injection of a dangerous foreignism by the aristocratic leaders of the colony. Chief of these was an Irish gentleman, John Sweetman, who desired to use his fortune to aid Irish emigration to the west. He conceded that his work failed in that respect, but the fact that the land in Murray County was sold to Catholic farmers from eastern cities satisfied him that at least he had had an important part in settling a Catholic colony in Minnesota.

In 1887, Bishop Ireland and John Sweetman had negotiated in Turin, Italy, with the founder of the Salesians, who has since become Saint John Bosco, for the establishment of an industrial school for eastern city waifs at Currie. However, the holy founder died the following year and Mr. Sweetman had been informed that since so many Salesians were needed in Patagonia none could be sent to Minnesota.

In 1882 Mother Seraphine Ireland had become provincial superior of the Sisters of St. Joseph in the province of St. Paul. The thirty-seven institutions opened during her years as superior, from 1882 to 1921, except for five hospitals and St. Agatha's Conservatory in St. Paul, all were schools in rural areas and nearly all were in Bishop Ireland's colonies. At one time or another the Sisters of St. Joseph taught in Kilkenny, Minneota, Marshall, Currie, Avoca, Iona, and Fulda. They also had schools at Anoka, Bird Island, Le Sueur, Morris, Le Center, St. Peter, Olivia, and White Bear. Schools which were closed because they were unsuccessful dropped out of mind completely. Failure did not exist for Mother Seraphine and what might have been done was not a proper subject of conversation.

Summing up in 1921, Sister Wilfrida Hogan, who was superior of the convent at Marshall for many years, wrote, "Since 1882, the watchword has been 'Progress.' Build, increase in number, spread out, and strive for the means of doing so. This we did, and we are still striving. It is now part of our life."

The usual pattern in the colonies was a grade school at first, with a high school added later. By 1890, many girls from all these parishes had taken the veil, for at that time the Sisters of St. Joseph had given the habit to a hundred and one girls born in Minnesota. Many more of those in the order had come to the state as small children and could remember no other home. The church and school had brought culture and hope to numerous families well-nigh isolated by the exigencies of pioneer conditions.

A characteristic example of the vistas of beauty and peace

opened up in otherwise drab lives is a letter of Father Joseph Guillot of Marshall, written from France to Sister Wilfrida at the convent in Marshall on June 22, 1904.

"As I came from Ars," he wrote, "where I spent a delicious day praying over the grave of the Holy Curé, whose beatification is to be celebrated next November, and where I forgot none of the friends far away, I had the pleasure of reading your most interesting letter. I am so glad that Memorial Sunday went off in a manner creditable to the Catholics of the parish.

"Anything like this goes a great way towards increasing the influence of Holy Church and attracting to her the American people. I am getting more and more awake to the fact that the Church must in season and out of season force herself to the attention of the public, and that one of the great duties of her priests and religious is to show her as she is: the greatest work of God on earth and the only channel of happiness and salvation. What a beautiful work and how captivating; but what a pity to feel oneself so unequal to the honor and task!

"I am as happy as the good Sisters themselves to hear of the building showing [off] in a fine new suit [of fresh paint] and I long to enjoy the sight."

When the frontier moved west and St. Paul priests — newly consecrated as bishops for the western dioceses — went with it, schools of the Sisters of St. Joseph were opened in Jamestown and Grand Forks, North Dakota, and in Watertown and Lemmon, South Dakota. Five hospitals were also established: St. Mary's in Minneapolis; St. John's in Winona; St. John's in Fargo; St. Michael's in Grand Forks; and Trinity Hospital in Jamestown.

Catholicism in North Dakota was merely an extension of the frontier of Minnesota. The pattern of progress repeated much of the earlier Minnesota story. The most popular priest in St. Paul, Father John Shanley, became the first bishop of North Dakota in 1889. His see city was at first

Jamestown, but later a change was made to Fargo because of better transportation facilities. One of his first acts was to buy the old Topliff mansion and bring the Sisters of St. Joseph whom he had known so well in St. Paul to teach at St. John's Academy in Jamestown.

He ruled by the charm and the force of his own personality and, as he had done in St. Paul, he wore himself out in a whirlwind of civic activities. When he died in 1909, it was generally agreed that he was the most popular man in the state. Catholics had won a measure of respect through his efforts but it was still possible to get a divorce and to drink illicit whiskey in spite of his vigorous campaigns. High praise was heaped upon him by one of his auditors who said, "I do like to hear Bishop Shanley talk. He sounds just like an old Methodist preacher."

As each new convent was in its way a replica of the motherhouse of St. Paul, so Mother Seraphine's visitations to the young missions in North Dakota were much like her earlier trips to Graceville, when it had been the farthest outpost from St. Joseph's Academy. The difference for us lies in the fact that still vigorous souls can remember her appearances in Jamestown and Fargo.

Her visits to the missions were always heralded in the newspapers and welcomed by the sisters. Her energy and gaiety were at once a spur and an inspiration to struggle against poverty and other obstacles to refinement and piety. While her word was law, the charm of her personality generally left her subjects liking the law.

The little bustle attending her arrival from a day's journey on a jolting train or in a buggy drawn by galloping horses was nearly always punctuated by the ringing of the bell for five o'clock prayer. Another might have felt the need of a nap, but not Mother Seraphine. Into the chapel, drafty or stifling according to season, she led the way to the hard benches and creaking pews. Hers was the most devout gaze at — or through — the altar's fading paper flowers and imitation lace.

Around the country in the various provinces there are yet mimics of the fine blast with which she blew her nose in the back of the chapel; of the loud, out of stop, "Holy Mary, Mother of God," with which she answered the Rosary. These facts are only part of the story.

They convey nothing of her gift for making meditation, not only a dynamic exercise, but a communal one. Let her be present in the last pew as the reader gave out the Gospel scene appointed for the day's contemplation and Mother Seraphine's struggle to imbibe the revelation was perceptible to everyone in the chapel. The sleepiest was awakened to emulate the pentecostal vigor with which she translated a parable from the shores of Galilee to the banks of the Red or the James. Sentimental hymn-singing had no part in the process — it was living, breathing Christianity.

Such personal realization might leave imitators breathless, but Mother Seraphine was refreshed by her tussle with the Scripture and she bounced down to the refectory with lighter step than the youngest. The odors of frying pancakes generally penetrated the chapel for an hour before supper in preparation for a repast considered filling and economical in those hearty, pre-vitamin days. Mother Seraphine's visit was an occasion for recreation at table, an exchange of news from St. Paul and the missions, of new buildings, of crowded schools, of the work of God progressing magnificently.

Bits about people, affectionate stories of foibles and sorrows, anecdotes concerning children were woven in and out. Most of the ridiculous family jokes which have become tradition originated with Mother Seraphine. There was, for example, her account of the visit of the Lutheran deaconess, who asked her what she did about the problem of keeping the sisters in nights.

In the evening, the parish priest and leading citizens called to pay their respects. The gracious hospitality and the touches of urbanity in these deferential exchanges emanated from Mother Seraphine, to be sure, but the sisters of the mission were expected to gather about and to participate with the high breeding of the people of God. Their sympathetic understanding of the neighborhood problems was taken for granted; sincerity and common sense, oiled with fervent prayer, were expected to supply any deficiencies in training.

Refinement and piety are often husks, but, given Mother Seraphine's enthusiasm and simplicity, they sometimes yielded culture and religion.

❧ VII ❧

Behind Convent Walls

AT THE same time the Sisters of St. Joseph were founding schools and hospitals throughout the state, they were not neglecting the heart of their activities, St. Paul.

Their first parish schools in the city served the Cathedral congregation. As the various nationalities branched off from the Cathedral parish, they opened schools almost simultaneously with their new churches, a procedure economically impossible in the country districts. Moreover, as Bishop Grace commented year after year in the *Catholic Directory,* Catholic parish schools were not necessary or even desirable in smaller places where in public schools both teachers and pupils were Catholics. The Cathedral, relieved of separate services for German, French, and English-speaking parishioners, found itself in less than two decades an Irish-American parish.

The first group to separate were the Germans, who built the Assumption Church in 1856. Since they had no building for a school, they were given one story of the brick building on the St. Joseph's Hospital grounds which was used for the English-speaking free school connected with the Cathedral parish, and Sister Radegunda Proff was sent from Carondelet to take charge of the German school. She took over on August 30, 1858. The official records for the school indicate that "Classes were held from 8 to 11 and 1 to 4. Tuition was 50 cents a month and the children paid a fuel fee for wood."

In 1860 a school building was erected at Ninth and Exchange streets at a cost of $400. This building was destroyed by fire on July 4, 1863, and it was replaced by a stone building, which is still standing although it has not been used as a school since 1888. There were "two masters for the boys and two sisters for the girls." When the Sisters of St. Joseph were replaced by the Notre Dame Sisters from Milwaukee in 1885, the enrollment was six hundred.

The reason given by Sister Ignatius Cox for leaving the Assumption school was that it was too difficult to supply from an English-speaking community teachers who could teach wholly in German. The parish histories put it another way. The people preferred to have their children taught by sisters who were members of a predominantly German community.

This nationalism extended beyond the school. With characteristic enterprise the Assumption parish maintained the church, an orphanage, social and charitable associations, and other activities on an exclusively German basis. In 1869 Bishop Grace wrote to Archbishop Martin Spalding of Baltimore to ask his advice about opposing, "without danger of scandal," the plan of the Germans in St. Paul to establish their own cemetery. He complained that the Germans were unwilling to take part in any work unless they had control of it and could manage it in their own way. A cemetery had already been established for Catholics and the bishop feared this move of the Germans would cause dissatisfaction among the American, Irish, and French Catholics. With or without scandal, the German burial ground did not materialize, but the living Germans held aloof from non-German activities as far as possible.

Sister Margaret Senselmeyer had charge of the English-speaking free school on the hospital grounds. In 1860 it was moved to the basement of the Cathedral and the name was changed to Cathedral school.

The second division of the Cathedral parish created the

French-speaking parish of St. Louis with its church near the old Capitol. The school there opened in 1873.

Change and growth in a diocesan institution were manifested in May 1869 when fifty-six orphans were transferred from St. Joseph's Hospital and the other establishments where they had been housed to the St. Paul Catholic Orphanage on Grove and Olive streets. Nine thousand dollars had been paid by the diocesan board of trustees for this property and in 1870 a large frame addition was made at a cost of three thousand dollars. The location was in Lower Town, within the new parish for the elite called St. Mary's. The orphanage averaged about eighty boys and girls until the boys were transferred to the new boys' home in Minneapolis in 1878. The girls moved to the present location at 933 Carroll Avenue, St. Paul, in 1883. Mother Seraphine was superior of the orphanage from 1877 to 1882.

Also in 1869 the Sisters of St. Joseph were asked to teach in a school for girls in St. Mary's parish. The school was opened on the corner of Ninth and Locust streets, with an enrollment of one hundred and fifty pupils. Between 1876 and 1894, the Christian Brothers taught the boys. After that the Sisters of St. Joseph had both boys and girls. In 1922 St. Mary's school moved into a new building at Eighth and Rosabel streets.

What was literally a practice-teaching school for the novices was opened at St. Joseph's Church, St. Paul, in September 1876. The long-time mistress of novices Sister Blanche Ryan was directress there and the teachers of the boys and girls of the parish were postulants or novices, for whom the short walk from St. Joseph's Academy was convenient.

There were eight houses, that is, convent homes, in the province when Mother Seraphine became provincial superior in 1882: St. Joseph's Academy, St. Joseph's Hospital, the girls' orphanage in St. Paul; St. Anthony Convent, Holy Angels' Academy, and the boys' orphanage, in Minneapolis;

St. Teresa's Convent, Hastings; and St. Michael's Convent, Stillwater. Of the ten parochial schools five were in St. Paul, Cathedral, Assumption (German), St. Louis (French), St. Mary's, St. Joseph's; two in Minneapolis, at St. Anthony and the Immaculate Conception; one in Stillwater, and two in Hastings.

In December of the following year the *St. Paul Dispatch* reported an "aggregate" of 1401 pupils in Catholic schools. Those credited to the Sisters of St. Joseph were the Cathedral school for girls, 207; St. Mary's parish school for girls, 115; German parochial schools, boys and girls, 351; French parochial, 140; orphan asylum, 53; St. Joseph's Academy, 52. A new foundation of the Visitation Sisters in St. Mary's parish, which drew from a wealthy and cultured clientele, had 25 students. The Protectorate of the Good Shepherd had 40 inmates.

St. Agatha's Conservatory of Music and Art in St. Paul was opened in 1884. Sister Wilfrida Hogan, at the end of Mother Seraphine's provincialship, remembered the early days of this foundation. "There was a house vacant on 10th Street right back of the hospital. No one cared to rent the house or to live in it, as it was the scene of a dreadful murder some years previous. Mr. Lick owned the house. I think he was serving a sentence in State's Prison at the time, but through an agency the Sisters obtained the use of the house and in it opened St. Agatha's Convent. It was conveniently located for the teachers of the Parochial schools and served its purpose until a better and [more] permanent one was provided. This was the present property on Exchange Street opposite the old State Capitol. It was called the Palmer house and it was purchased in the early part of 1886."

Mother Celestine was the superior of St. Agatha's from 1884 until her death in 1915. As Sister Wilfrida indicated, the conservatory was at first intended as a home for the sisters teaching in the parochial schools, but the financial return to be derived from teaching the arts soon determined its purpose. There were large classes for individual instruction in piano and painting and an ever increasing business in orders for whatever was the fashion in pictures and art needlework. The copying of classical and popular masterpieces was then very profitable and several sisters became experts. They made copies of fine pictures in collections in the Twin Cities and Chicago and Montreal. Later on three of them spent two years copying in European galleries. Many of the pictures were kept as permanent adornments of the convent walls, so that they were a cultural advantage to students and teachers.

St. Agatha's was followed by St. Patrick's parish school in 1885; St. Michael's parish school, West St. Paul, also in 1885; and St. John's parish school in 1892.

Many of the sisters who staffed the schools both in St. Paul and in the outlying towns, including three of the superiors, were from St. Louis. Sisters were moved back and forth from St. Louis to St. Paul, just as they are transferred from house to house within a province now. St. Paul was wholly dependent upon and closely allied to the mother province, St. Louis. It was only after the number of houses increased and the community grew larger that exchanges ceased and a greater sense of independence in local concerns became manifest.

After 1889 the number of sisters increased fairly rapidly. That year Father James McGolrick (later bishop of Duluth) went to Ireland and brought back thirty or thirty-five Irish girls for the community. In the next decade others from Ireland, Canada, and Prince Edward Island joined them. By the turn of the century there were 428 sisters in the province to staff the twenty-five institutions then under the charge of the Sisters of St. Joseph.

This seems a substantial growth in less than fifty years, but Sister Wilfrida commented in 1921, "There is no use getting a wrong estimate. The rapid growth in numbers and the number of houses opened within so short a time need not be considered as a great achievement, for it was premature and forced."

Right or wrong about the other missions, this stricture was hardly true of St. Joseph's Academy in St. Paul, for the story of which Sister Wilfrida herself is the best chronicler. Although the academy had its hard years, when widespread economic ills beset families that would otherwise have sent their daughters to the school, its foundations were substantial enough to weather all misfortunes.

While she was writing to another Sister of St. Joseph in St. Louis, who could fill in the gaps from her own experience, Sister Wilfrida attempted to portray the spirit of the St. Paul province as she knew it. The writer does succeed in removing a little of the family privacy which exists behind convent walls, but whether she is able to answer all questions about what goes on inside a convent is another matter.

Her narrative begins with her own school days and she builds up a revealing portrait of herself. The first comment likely to be made by anyone who knew her is that she was a "lady" in the sense presumably of gentility and precise taste in niceties. There could be no ruffled taffeta swish about her black serge ensemble, but some stateliness and manner still clung to her. She had the pluck to take in jobs of fine needlework and embroidery in order to eke out a living when she was sent as the first superior to Marshall, Minnesota, and there too she conducted a mandolin club for men and women in the evening. As an itinerant music teacher she traveled enough to be considered a gadabout, but with such dignified reserve that her trips caused no comment. The letters, written in 1921, when Sister Wilfrida was sixty-two, have a photographic detail we do not often encounter.

"My mother's ambition," Sister Wilfrida related, "was to give her daughters a good education. [That] the useful branches [must be] mastered went without saying, but this was not enough according to her ideas. Ambition led her on and she thought that no girl's education was complete without a little 'polish' in a Sisters' Boarding School. 'Polish' in her judgment meant music, painting, artificial fruit and flowers, birds in worsted work, and all kinds of needlework. To this might be added a study of Astronomy that in gazing on the stars at night we might be able to locate at least some of the constellations. This knowledge added to the practical things of life fitted any girl for the home and with a touch of 'The Usages of Good Society' was an open sesame to any modern court.

"In the early '70s plans were being made to send me away to school and often I would hear [my mother] remark, 'When Kate is a little older, I am going to send her to a Sisters' School.' At an early age I had a fair idea of what an education of this kind meant, for my sister who was some years older had attended two boarding schools, one at Shakopee, Minnesota, taught by the Benedictine Sisters, the other St. Joseph's Academy, St. Paul. I had visited both schools many times while she was in attendance, each visit giving me a new insight into boarding school life.

"While waiting for [my sister's] finishing years to be ended, I lost no time, but made preparations for the 'Day of my Inheritance' which was soon to come. I added to my wardrobe and provided myself with little articles of comfort that a girl would enjoy in boarding away from home. The decision as to what school I should be sent to was very quickly made, for [in] my sister's experienced opinion St. Joseph's Academy, St. Paul, Minnesota, was the 'best school' for me and it was decided that on the 'First Monday of September,' 1876, the Centennial Year of the Declaration of Independence, I would enter that worthy Institution.

"St. Joseph's Academy in 1876 was very unlike what it is now. The plot of ground purchased by Bishop Cretin in 1853 for a graveyard always retained its original shape and dimensions. Three years later — in 1856 — the city limits were extended and the bodies were removed to the present location [Lexington and Como], now called 'Calvary.' The plot secured in 1853 was transferred to the Sisters of St. Joseph for an Academy and the first building of the group was begun in 1861 and finished in July, 1863. It was through the portals of this building that I entered on that bright September morn, 1876."

There is an engraving of the original building as it was when it stood alone as Sister Wilfrida described it, before later additions were made. It still stands as the extreme end of the old main building, although other buildings are now attached to it on the north and east. "The structure is of yellow limestone four stories in height and quite majestic looking," Sister Wilfrida remembered. She thought the interior plan was similar to that of most convents of those days. There was an entrance hall with a staircase to a second floor where the chapel and schoolrooms were located. The first floor had parlors to the right and left of the entrance, a playroom for the students, and a library–music room. The dormitories and two classrooms were on the third floor. Storage and trunk rooms occupied the fourth floor.

To this building of 1863 an addition at the northwest corner was provided in 1871 exclusively for the sisters and "no student ever crossed its sanctified threshold. Its mysteries were never fathomed and years passed without any one of the girls even getting a peep into that secret cloister or knowing just what the nuns did when they were by themselves."

From the interior, Sister Wilfrida's description proceeded to the exterior arrangements. "These two buildings occupied part of the west half of the grounds; the other half to the east was devoted to orchard and garden. Vegetables of all kinds were grown and the plum and apple trees always bore a good crop which went far toward supplying the store rooms with preserved fruit in winter time.

"In front of the original building was a space covered with trees, shrubs, and flowerbeds. This space was [separated]

Water color sketch of the Chapel of St. Paul made by Robert O. Sweeny in 1852

Mother St. John Fournier of St. Paul

Mother St. John Fontbonne
of Lyons

Mother Celestine Pommerel
of Carondelet

Grey Nuns traveling through Minnesota

Bishop Joseph Cretin   Countess de la Rochejacquelin

The Ellens—Sister Seraphine Ireland, left, and Sister Celestine Howard

from the cornpatch by a picket fence which also extended across the front and along the opposite side from the cornpatch, thus enclosing a portion called the 'front yard.' It was quite ornamental. Two rows of tall trees led from the gate to the front entrance on either side of a gravelled walk; here and there were the flower beds of different shapes and forms. Some were round, others star-shaped or in a half-moon effect — the outline of each being marked by shells, rocks, or corners of brick set like little pyramids in rhythmic line. The gravel walk was also bordered by carefully selected rocks.

"At the rear of the building was the 'back yard' having the same area as that in front. A driveway occupied the center, running in a loop from the rear gate, and meeting its original line, thus forming an apex at the gate. At the right of this rear entrance were the barns, chicken house, and woodpile. The portion nearest the building had water pumps, clotheslines and the various accessories found in back yards. This was a most interesting spot, for we saw who drove in and who went out in the carriage. We watched the Sisters hang the clothes out on laundry days and there was always evidence of life in the back yard — a horse or cow wandered around and many a time the lordly rooster would lead his feathered flock up even to the steps of the back entrance."

Setting out for boarding school seventy-five years ago was an experience which Sister Wilfrida recalled in detail. "The first Monday of September had arrived. We set out early in the morning the day being favorable and all things in readiness. My mother in ordering the carriage ready said, 'Hitch up the black horses — they go faster. We will get there in good time and there will be no delay.' As I glanced through the window I saw the black horses in glistening harness drawn up to the gate, my trunk standing on end in the driver's seat of the carriage. Noticing the anxious look on my mother's face, my heart faltered. I was about to give way to my feelings when my mother informed me there was no time for tears, so I took a farewell look at my surroundings and very reluctantly followed the cortege out, feeling quite lonely.

"A brisk ride brought us to St. Paul in about an hour's time and as I was anxious to reach my destination and get the preliminaries over with we drove directly to the Academy. As we approached the stately old pile, with its round windows peering out of the gables on the roof, like the eyes of a monster, a feeling of awe came over me [such as] I never experienced on any former visit. Thoughts and visions came to my mind of medieval monasteries, the descriptions of which I had read in story books. I dreamed of foreign lands, for I was getting farther and farther away from home. My courage was abandoning me and only that my attention was arrested by our arriving at the door, I might have disappointed my mother's expectations."

What door bells were like in 1876, Sister Wilfrida explained. "We pulled a knob at the side of the door to announce our arrival. The mechanism of door bells in those days consisted of a knob on the outside of the jamb, connected by links of wire to a bell fastened near the ceiling in the rear of a hallway or adjoining room. Electric bells were not yet in use. A sweet-faced nun, whom I have known since to be Sister Scholastica [Duggan], answered our call. We asked for the directress and she showed us to the parlor on the right hand side. Sister Celestine Howard appeared in just a few minutes — she came through the door leading from her office into the parlor. She was gracefulness itself, as she stepped forward to greet us.

"With a low bow and genial smile she assured us that we were welcome. Business was transacted. I was to take, besides the general course of study, music, artificial fruit and flowers, and ornamental needlework. Regulations were gone over, but in a cursory way only, [Sister Celestine] thinking that [since I was] a sister of my sister I would show forth the same traits of character and be a close adherent of all the rules as she had been the previous year."

The dress regulations followed. "The conversation led to the subject of uniform. I had all the necessaries: 'For summer, black dress with white waist, hat or bonnet trimmed with white; for winter a black dress and cloak, hat or bonnet trimmed with crimson.'" Sister Wilfrida remembered that she had a summer hat, but for winter she specified that she did not have either a hat or a bonnet, but a black silk cap "which was newly fashionable then." On its side was "a crimson quill standing almost perpendicular, [with] a cluster of long white feathery strands like an aigret leading from a rosette at the base of the quill and floating across the top. To Sister Celestine's mind this white graceful plumage was superfluous. I listened to the pro and con of the argument, feeling somewhat uneasy lest the appearance of my head-gear be spoiled and my idol shattered, until I heard [Sister Celestine] say, 'Well, the crimson quill is quite conspicuous so we will leave it as it is.'

"My mother and sister departed for home and I was shown to the play room and given a place for my wraps. I next went to the study hall to be classified." Sister Wilfrida explained that classification is called registration now, but she gave no clue to the method of division into a so-called highest class, with graduating and subgraduating classes ranking still higher. There may have been some occult process having to do with age, size, or length of residence, to say nothing of depth of finish, which determined where the young lady would be placed, apparently quite often in a class all by herself.

"I was assigned a desk and given the necessary books after going through a short questionnaire. The classes were numbered by letter. The highest class was the 'A' and anyone finishing it might enter the graduating and sub-graduating

classes. I was put in the 'A' class. My teachers were Sister
Stanislaus [Vedder], Sister Stephanie for drawing, Sister
Scholastica for art and Sister Celestine for special class work.

"The front seats of the study hall were the important ones.
Jennie Maginnis (Sister Eugenia) who was to graduate that
year, sat directly in front of the teacher's desk. Near her
was Anna Doherty (Mrs. J. H. Donahue) on one side, and
Eva Trumbull on the other. These three girls were in the
graduating department and their books were far in advance
of ours. The 'A' class was the largest in the school. It was not
only big in number, but great in achievement; each girl
seemed to vie with the other as to who could play the biggest
pranks, or have the most fun. Some few whose names went
down in the history of the school were never forgotten. They
were remembered as being smart, efficient, fearless, daring.
And many a little anecdote was traditionally handed down
to those who replaced them in after years.

"On Wednesday afternoons we had instruction in Catechism given by Reverend John Shanley, who afterwards
became the Bishop of Fargo, North Dakota. Father Shanley
was newly ordained at the time, fresh from college and full
of humor. He made the driest of subjects interesting, always
supplementing the text by a story vividly told, in such a manner as to hold the attention of the most listless member. We
longed for Wednesday afternoon to come, for that hour was
all too short. . . .

"We arose early, said morning prayer and attended Mass
in the Chapel. That Chapel was the sanctuary of repose —
in it we found rest for our souls. How peaceful and calm was
its atmosphere! You felt it as soon as you entered. No sound
to disturb its silence — only the ticking of a clock or the quiet
rustle of someone telling her beads. It was always open and
never without some worshipper during the day or evening.
When overburdened by the trials of school life — and there
were many — we found solace there. To kneel at the altar
rail on Communion days and be so near the Tabernacle sent

a thrill through our souls. Even to look at the altars, half
hidden in the recesses of rich draperies of lace and damask,
was an inspiration to prayer and their symbolic meaning
was a reminder that we were in a holy place.

"No vaulted nave or Cathedral dome ever had the place
in memory that this simple room had in ours, with its
ordinary rows of pews, brown shutters, and bare pine floors.
Nor would any frieze or fresco be preferred to the plain
white walls and ceiling, devoid of any ornament but the
Stations of the Cross and one little relief in the center of the
ceiling for a hanging lamp. This was our Temple.

"We sang in the choir on Sundays and Feast days, also
on the First Friday of every month, when the Blessed Sacrament was exposed for adoration. On these Fridays an Act of
Reparation was read aloud either by Mother Agnes or Sister
Celestine. [Mother Agnes Veronica Williams was provincial
superior from 1876 to 1879; Mother Jane Frances Bochet
succeeded her and was the superior until 1882, when Mother
Seraphine took over.] No matter which one said it — as they
both read in such a prayerful tone and modulated voice —
it was beautiful to listen to and each word went deep into
our hearts.

" 'O worthy victim of the Most High, Thou dwellest under
the same roof with that chosen portion of Thy flock over
which Thou hast placed St. Joseph as patron and protector' —
this and other expressions echoed and re-echoed in our ears
for days afterwards. Blue barragan veils, two yards in length,
were worn in the chapel. They were of a bright cerulean
blue and made a strong contrast with the sombre black robe
of the nuns; the effect was pleasing.

"The regular routine of work went on day after day. Weeks
passed; the months seemed to grow shorter as the Christmas
holidays neared. There was little to break the monotony of
our every day life as no girl was allowed to go out even when
accompanied by her parents. The only time we saw the outside world was on Sunday afternoon when we took a walk

through the more secluded parts of the city. A venture was
never made beyond the brow of St. Anthony hill while on
those healthful expeditions. Only when 'Sister did not know
the way' and one of the girls had to lead — then we got into
the more thickly populated districts.

"On one occasion I remember being the cause of a breach
of decorum during a Sunday afternoon walk. It happened
like this. A young man who was spending a few months
at my home, to enjoy a rest and get a little country air, often
passed the weekend in St. Paul. My mother wishing to send
me a message asked him to call at the Academy to see me.
On his way out, he met the procession of girls. Knowing
that I was very likely among them, he thought that he might
fulfill his obligation by meeting me there on the street and
with a short interview deliver the message entrusted to him.

"He was riding a very spirited horse and what was my surprise when he dashed up alongside the rank, the horse pranc-
ing, taking sidewise movements forward like the chassé of
a dance. His eye searched me out and in a zigzag manner,
he approached. As he saluted, I stepped out of the rank
to receive the message which was delivered in as few words
as possible, for the horse was still dancing. In doing so, I
attracted much attention as was evident by the suppressed
sob, withdrawn breath — oh — I felt the weight of the occasion immediately and realized what I had done and what the
consequences might be.

"Returning to my place in the rank, I was met by the
curious looks of my companions, each eye bearing a question
mark. Anna Brownell voiced the feeling and called out,
'Miss Kate, who was the cavalier on that wonderful charger?'
I was too scared to answer, for I was thinking of Sister at
the rear end of the rank and of her decision regarding the
offense. . . ." Apparently this irregularity passed unnoticed,
for Sister Wilfrida said no more about it. The young man
was Lorenzo Markoe, son of the seminary professor.

"There was a Religious Reception on St. Teresa's Day,

October 15, 1876, at which all were present. The relatives
of the Sisters occupying the pews in the Chapel, we sat in a
line along the walls on benches. This afforded us a better
view and we were delighted to see the ceremony. When the
bridal train appeared, headed by the little girls out of the 'E'
class carrying the baskets containing the religious dress, we
were all on edge, for among the group of Postulants to be
received were Mary Werden, Lizzie Mackey, and Annie
Doherty, who were employed on the boarders' side and we
knew them better than the others.

"The singing was beautiful on that occasion. Sister Celes-
tia Prendergast presided at the organ and the rich plaintive
voice of Sister Victorine Casserly, who was my music teacher,
resounding through the Chapel, made one think of the
Heavenly Hosts pouring forth their praises before the
Throne. As the white robed group moved slowly up the
center aisle, Sister Victorine sang 'Go ye forth, O Sion's
daughter, See your King in bright array' — the enunciation
so fully expressing the meaning of the words that it could
never be forgotten.

"The Service began promptly. The Rt. Rev. Bishop Grace
officiated, assisted by several priests, among them our beloved Father Shanley, Father Ravoux and Father Bruton.
The organ pealing forth again, Sister Victorine's voice was
heard in 'O quam dilecta tabernacula,' How lovely are Thy
Tabernacles, O Lord of Hosts, for better is one day in Thy
courts above thousands. Who on listening to those sacred
words could ever doubt the 'hundredfold' in store for those
who have left all? Among those who received the religious
Habit on that day were, Sister Hyacinth Werden, Sister St.
Rose Mackey, Sister Irmina Doherty, Sister Thecla Ried and
Sister Eulalia Dress.

"On Thanksgiving Day, the girls were determined to cele-
brate in some way or other, not being allowed to visit their
homes or to go out anywhere. They planned on staging something in the study hall for the benefit of an audience. After

much deliberation, it was decided to produce 'Romeo and Juliet.' To present the whole drama with its numerous characters was more than could be prepared in such a short time, so they decided on the balcony scene. Anna Ward and Daisy Callinan were to take the roles.

"The only stage scenery that could be had was an improvised curtain hung on a clothes line drawn directly across the front of the room near the platform, where [the study hall was] divided in two parts. Juliet's costume was easily provided for; — but Romeo's? How could Romeo be made up? Anna painted her upper lip so that it resembled a mustache and put a little dab on the chin for a goatee. She had to look like a boy and therefore pinned her skirt so that it looked like tight pants. All were assembled in the study hall, the Provincial and Professed Sisters occupying the front seats. All the Novices were there and, lo and behold you, when the curtain opened, and Anna appeared in pants and mustache looking up at Juliet, the scene was too much. Mother Agnes left the hall and the entertainment was at an end."

Oral examinations were given twice a year, at the end of every session, Sister Wilfrida told. There would be a long line of examiners and a group of honorary onlookers sitting up before the victim. At the end of Sister Wilfrida's first session Bishop Ireland came and with him Fathers McGolrick and Shanley. There were priests from the neighboring parishes and sisters. When the "A" class was examined in geography, Sister Wilfrida related, "Bishop Ireland was the examiner. Questions were put hard and fast to my companions in class and then I was called on. I felt my knees get weak as I arose.

"'Where is Turkey?' was the question asked.

"I located two Turkies — one in Asia, the other in Europe.

"'Very good. . . . What are the inhabitants of Turkey called?' was my next quiz.

"By this time my tongue was getting thick and I felt it

going back to my throat. I tried to say 'Turks' but my tongue and heart were about to meet in the vicinity of my vocal cords, so I gurgled forth inarticulate sounds that struck his ear like 'Turkies.' He tossed his head back in the air and repeated, 'Tho inhabitants of Turkey are called 'Turkies,' then joined in the laugh that was enjoyed at my expense.

"How far these examinations went toward a passing mark I never learned, nor do I know what consideration was given on the balance sheet for the bright intellect which became speechless on those occasions and could not utter a word."

The next religious reception and profession the students were unable to attend, because of the large crowd. Sister Wilfrida wrote that three postulants the girls knew received the habit. Mary Manning and Mary Bohan taught music and Rose Waldron was a sort of hairdressing supervisor once a week and "she always gave us a drink of 'Sassafras,' when we were in need of a blood purifier. In the Spring we lined up in the 'Combing room' every morning before breakfast and drank a cup of 'Sassafras tea'." At the ceremonies Mary Manning received the name of Sister Adelaide, Mary Bohan, Sister Bridget, and Rose Waldron, Sister Martina.

"Immediately after Easter, the hammer was heard and the grounds became literally alive with workmen. The cornpatch of the autumn before looked like a stone quarry with all the rock that was hauled in for the erection of the building. [This addition was to be the central unit of St. Joseph's Academy, adjoining the building of 1863 on the east.] Our playground was taken from us, but we were allowed to walk in the front yard, which was a privilege. Many a one could give the dimensions of masonry better than solve a problem in Algebra or analyze a sentence in Kerl's Grammar.

"Just about this time, too, our attention was given to the preparations for the 'Exhibition' [graduation] at the end of June. Professor Manner had received his education in Germany and he belonged to the class of musicians that we usually associate with long hair and Limburger cheese. He was of medium height, light complected, and he spoke with a decided foreign accent. Among the various musical circles of the time, he was thought to be in the first rank as organist, teacher, and vocal instructor. This was often lost sight of by the girls and they thought of him only as he appeared when he encountered the seventy or more recreant students of his musical art. . . .

"Sister Celestine liked the open air, because it helped to give volume to our voices. The space being larger required more effort on the part of the speaker to make herself heard." However, the exercises at the end of Sister Wilfrida's first year were held in the study hall. On account of the building in progress, it was impossible to have an open air performance, such as Sister Wilfrida had attended the previous year when her sister had graduated. In the program of June 28, 1877, there were eighteen numbers. Gold medals and crowns were conferred. Jennie Maginnis, who was later to be Sister Eugenia, was the only graduate. There were two "Grand Square" pianos on the stage. All the pianos in the school at that time were square, Sister Wilfrida stated. An upright piano was a rare thing.

In September 1877, the Class "A" student was anxious to return, but, she wrote, "my mother thought otherwise. Fearing lest I should join the Sisterhood, she deemed it more prudent to keep me at home to continue my education under private tutorage than to have me return and become more infatuated with convent life. Two years elapsed before I saw St. Joseph's again." Then, since she had been "real good" for two years, her mother did not object when she asked to attend the annual exhibition for June 1879. The academy building was now one of "grand proportions, set in the central part of the grounds." Inside the new east entrance was an elevator and there were many changes in arrangement. Sister Celestine Howard, she found, had been transferred to the St. Louis province to be one of the general directresses of schools there.

In spite of the changes, Sister Wilfrida wrote, "The fire that smoldered in my heart was re-enkindled and there and then I decided that this was my destiny; to this work I would devote my life. After many conflicts within and without, the final arrangements were made for mo to ontor the Noviliate on September 21st, 1879, in order to be in time for the Reception on December 21st, 1879.

"On entering the Novitiate, I was greeted by many of the Sisters whom I had known at school, as they gathered around me with their words of welcome. I was happy to be in their midst. To my supreme delight the Novitiate occupied the room that was the Chapel when I attended school. My bed was assigned me, on the evening of my arrival; it was in the dormitory on the second floor of what was the 'Sisters' Building' in 1876. When the new school addition was completed, the whole house underwent a change. The arrangement was a very good one for it kept the apartments of the Sisters entirely separated from the boarders. There was a secular side to the institution, but there was always and ever the religious side, which was distinct and removed from the temporal things of this world."

Sister Wilfrida recalled exactly what went on in "the little corner" which Mother St. John Fournier had said a Sister of St. Joseph must keep to. "The first charge given me was that of the Novitiate and my Mistress' room adjoining it. The cold weather coming in early Autumn added to my labor. A large heater in the center of the room had to be fed with fuel — it was a wood burner — and needed big blocks of wood to keep it going. The only means of conveying those blocks of wood from the woodpile to the woodbox alongside of this great heater were my arms and feet. . . . Many a trip I took . . . up along the porch, through the hallway, and up the stairs to my woodbox. I grew strong and waxed fat on this physical exercise and I was more fortunate than some of my companions who had to carry their wood supply up two flights of stairs to the Sisters' dormitories. The boarders' apartments were heated by hot air furnaces installed with the new addition.

"In the Novitiate were two rows of desks along the walls on both sides with benches without backs, a table at the end near the Mistress' room, and a square piano just inside one of the entrance doors. I had to sweep this large room and dust the furniture, including the inside shutters on the ten windows. I had to learn my prayers, mend my clothes, and practice an hour a day on the piano. The remaining time I spent in the general work of the Community as on laundry day, to give a helping hand in turning the wringer, or taking the clothes out of the boiler, or working the washing machine. The Postulants also took turns in the kitchen, two weeks at a time and there were other works at which we took turns. We never forgot our turns for the one ranking before always reminded the next that it was her turn to do so-and-so.

"On the evening of December 10, Mother Jane, the Provincial, assembled the Postulants and mapped out for us the order of Retreat exercises and we followed the meditations and spiritual reading very carefully. Sister Marcelline Dowling made the [exercises of the] retreat with us. We had no eloquent conferences of any kind, our whole sermon being the living example set before us in dear, saintly Sister Marcelline, as she entered into that Retreat communing entirely with God. Rt. Rev. Bishop Grace received the Vows and gave the Habit; there were two Novices to make Vows and seven Postulants to receive the Habit. The books being signed and the officiating Prelates departing, we retired to the Novitiate to learn how to dress ourselves [in our new garb] and to practice the precepts set before us.

"There were full numbers in the Novitiate at this time as the Junior Professed remained in the Novitiate for five years after Profession. There was work enough for all. An increase in the number of boarders came with the increase of accommodations. Modern inventions to lighten labor were not known at St. Joseph's Academy in the early 1880's. The city water had not been extended to this part of the city yet, and even if the new building was fully equipped for hot and cold water, the water had to be pumped into the large tank on the fourth floor."

Here follows a description of the force pump, doubtless a replica of the one in use at St. Joseph's Hospital since 1854. The pumping, Sister Wilfrida said, "was done by a force pump in the furnace room. Four Sisters did the work, manipulating it in a way similar to that of a handcar, only the pump handle was one straight length of about 8 or 10 feet, the middlo of which was attached to the pump, the suction being effected by the action of the handle up and down. When one end went up, the other end went down, each stroke bringing water to the attic. It required united strength to force water from the cistern to the tank on the fourth floor. This occupation went along with the dishwashing, for the furnace room was handy to the boarders' refectory in the basement.

"The kitchen supply of water was brought from the well in the back yard. This pump had an iron handle, very cold to take hold of in winter time. It took two to pump water out of the well for the pump was stiff. We pumped the water into large tin boilers, carried it to the kitchen and deposited it in the reservoir on the back of the stove. I know this reservoir must have been a large one, for we often calculated that it held more than a barrel. Think of the amount of water used throughout the institution and all of it had to be pumped.

"The distribution of wood was also a problem, for each Sister in charge of a stove had to build her own fire every morning. She not only had to provide herself with wood but also with kindling to help start the fire. The woodshed was stored full of old boards, but they were not always cut in small pieces. This we often had to do and there was an axe left for our convenience."

In the novitiate there were regular recitation periods from

nine to eleven-thirty in the morning and from two-thirty to four in the afternoon. The curriculum included Christian doctrine, reading, rhetoric, grammar, mathematics, astronomy, natural philosophy (physics without laboratory work), elocution, music, writing, and drawing.

In identifying the teachers Sister Wilfrida made special mention of Sister Ignatius Cox. "She was the censor of the reading in the Chapel and Refectory. If I can read a paragraph straight through now, I owe it to Sr. Ignatius. Many a time she found it necessary, for the sake of the Community, to call my attention back from its wandering and make me repeat a sentence in a more intelligent way. One night in the Chapel, I was giving out the points of the morning's meditation and in reading the words, 'Examine yourselves and see,' I thoughtlessly read, 'Examine your sleeves and see.' It was outrageous, for the Novices had been examining their *sleeves* all day in repairing and replacing them. Another day I was reading in 'Christian Perfection' of a monk who had taken the wing of a pheasant. I read, 'He took the wing of a peasant.' Reading in the refectory was an ordeal. If we could have stood in some obscure corner it would have seemed easy, but we had to sit on a high rostrum in the most conspicuous place in the room, where the Professed members could see and hear us to a greater advantage.

"When Sister Celestine Howard returned from St. Louis in the Autumn of 1879, she supervised the work in the schools as the 'Highest Common Directress.' She devoted her whole time to the task and provided every means in her power for the improvement of the teachers. The Novices came in for a share of these advantages." Sister Wilfrida described the new classes and the teachers from outside the convent staff (including musicians and artists), and then she gave an entertaining account of a change in transportation for parochial school teachers. For many years they had walked to their schools, taking turns carrying the lunch in a large wicker basket, often with a hungry dog following them all the way. But, finally, Mother Jane bought a large wagon, like a Black Maria, for which John Delaney, the yardman, drove the horse and flourished the whip. In addition, he scolded latecomers and kept order.

"Time fled rapidly," the account continued, "and the close of the year 1881 approached. Our two years noviceship were nearly completed and it was nearing the time for our Vows. One of the seven died during the first year of her Novitiate. She was one of God's flowers culled in its opening bloom; the other six veterans were destined to weather the seasons of a lifetime, and offer a bloom at the end of almost half a century, perhaps longer, for five are still living and holding their own." The novice who died was Sister Cecelia Harrold, then 23 years old. The ages of the six others in the group at death were 55, 65, 72, 83, 84, 94. Sister Wilfrida died in 1944, aged 84; Sister Irenaeus Egan died in 1949, at the age of 94.

"The summer of 1882 arrived and with it a great many changes. . . . Mother Jane Frances' term as Provincial had expired and the newly appointed Provincial was Mother Seraphine Ireland, who had been Superioress at the Girls' Orphanage in lower town near St. Mary's Church. I had met her on a few occasions when I went to the Asylum for Benediction in the Chapel there. She was greatly beloved by both the Sisters and the orphans. No work was too hard or too menial for her to do. Being of a strong and robust constitution she usually bore the heaviest part of the burden and was first in laundry, kitchen, and at the scrubbing. She slept in the dormitory with the Sisters and led the common life in all things. I had this knowledge of her personality before she reached St. Joseph's Academy to be our Provincial.

"As soon as Spring [1883] opened, the hammer was again heard and an additional building was erected on the east side of the large central building. With this new wing came the heating plant. A laundry and boiler room [unit] was built at the rear of the grounds and a complete system was installed throughout the four buildings. About this time a new home was provided for the Girls' Orphanage . . . which is still in use on Carroll and Milton Streets. The next opening was that of St. Agatha's in the summer of 1884."

The boarding school at St. Joseph's Academy had more than a hundred students in September 1886. Sister Wilfrida said, "it grew with its surroundings. As the State grew and as the city grew, so did this school. It was and is the oldest institution of its kind in the State of Minnesota. The material was good, made up of smart, intelligent young girls, many of whom are now leaders in Catholic circles, reflecting credit on the Catholic Church in general. These were the palmy days at St. Joseph's when the surrounding country was enjoying wealth, prosperity, and a bountiful harvest, but a day came within the next decade when the farmer lost part of his crop and failure set in through various channels. The chinch bug came, the grasshopper did his work, and the seasons were not propitious to the reaping of this world's goods. The number of pupils enrolled grew smaller and for some years in the early 1890's St. Joseph's Academy suffered its reverses of fortune like many others during those trying times. . . . The returns from it did not meet expenses. Moreover the Novitiate was an expense as about one hundred or more subjects were brought from Ireland, the Community defraying all expenses in the majority of cases and many of them returned [to their homes]. . . .

"The year that Sister Hyacinth was made Directress of the Academy [1895] there were only thirty or thirty-five boarders. Ten years before this there were over one hundred. In 1895 or 1896, a 'Catholic Home Calendar' was issued and sold and the money went to pay the floating debts. During all these years there were always some drawbacks. The Sisters studied and prepared themselves by correspondence work and by attending Minnesota University. All this took money, and you must remember that the foreign-born subject was not prepared to take up the work. There was a drain on the income everywhere. . . . Considering all the foreign born subjects, they must at the present time [1921] outnumber the native born subjects. . . . The Canadian subjects were not educated and it took the Irish girls a long time to adapt themselves to the language and customs of the country. Both were causes of retarding the progress in the work of education."

The Sisters of St. Joseph were all aware of the difficulties enumerated by Sister Wilfrida. But, serious though their problems were, they did not allow themselves to be discouraged from yet another undertaking. As the sisters approached their golden jubilee in 1901 they were laying plans for the capstone to their educational endeavors in Minnesota — a Catholic college for women. In this, as in all their projects, they had the full support of their lifelong friend and adviser, John Ireland.

The Catherine Wheel

IN THE YEARS OF ARCHBISHOP IRELAND

✄ VIII ✄

"Consecrated Blizzard of the Northwest"

Since the discovery that minorities have some rightful place in American backgrounds, it is not unusual to hear an aged Minnesota historian ask, "I know about Bishop Ireland of course, but is there any other Catholic who should have a place in our Minnesota chronicle?" The query is its own answer on the status of early Minnesota Catholics and it suggests as well something of the closed lines of intercommunication between neighbors.

There may be a slightly pathetic emphasis on large crowds and eloquent sermons and model students in accounts inspired by Catholic efforts, but there is not yet a substitution of brick and mortar for spiritual achievements. John Ireland was gifted with qualities which made it virtually impossible for those outside the church to exclude him from public consideration. On the other hand, it was for his distinctions in Catholic ways that he was highly regarded within the fold. His public activities caused a sense of amused gratification to pulse through Catholics. At last there was somebody to speak for them in vigorous English, who remained nevertheless in heart and soul with them.

In 1886, Bishop Ireland had been a priest for twenty-five years. He was forty-eight years old and his character was set in the mold by which it was to be universally known during the next twenty-five years of his priesthood and after. Certain home-grown influences had shaped him. His dominant personality was marked by the individualism and prejudices of the frontier, by the nationalism and *parti pris* of a war chaplain; by the predatory tactics and the partisan politics born of free land. These were hard qualities, softened in a measure by his devotion to the "Irish church" into which he was born, by a somewhat broader education than his peers — in a French seminary, which, if narrowly professional, still opened the way to knowledge in other languages than his own — and by the cultural and cosmopolitan contacts provided in the responsibilities his superiors placed upon him. He was outspoken to the point of rashness, but that was a quality which Andrew Jackson had blessed in frontiersmen and it roused no odium in Minnesota. He was apt to overstate his case in pleading a cause. In a day when moral questions were treated with a touch of fanaticism by the most grave, his enthusiasm was considered laudable earnestness. There was never any argument about the fact that throughout his career he was a priest of blameless life. He had a genius for espousing causes which met the approval of effective public opinion. If at times he appears to have had a touch of the zeal which made an earlier apostle think the way to help the Lord was to cut off a man's ear, few in the nineteenth century separated wheat from chaff in such a thoroughgoing fashion.

A great deal has been made, in some quarters, of the fact that Ireland tore up much of his personal correspondence and advised some of his episcopal friends to do the same. What has been preserved from the fire reveals a frank and sometimes tempestuous personality, but never a mean and selfish one. Stray sentences — as whose do not — betray human disillusion and rancor, but the whole picture rounds out into an impressiveness which is arresting.

Writers struggled from 1878 to his death in 1918 to convey to their readers the secret of John Ireland's charm. The *New York Times*, the *New York Tribune*, the *Chicago Tribune*, the *North American Review*, the *Outlook*, the *Independent* —

these were the periodicals which strove in season and out to
describe the many-sided figure.

He was said to be tall or of medium height, but his frame
was always conceded to be large and muscular. His profile
was often said to resemble Dante's and in France they
thought he looked like General Washington. His eyes were
sometimes gray, sometimes blue. They were penetrating,
sharp, keen, but also kind, responsive, gentle. There were
soft lines around his mouth, some said. Generally note was
taken of his prominent chin and nose, which indicated his
determination. When he talked some thought it was his manner which held charm, for his matter, they said, was not
much. There was frequent allusion to his harsh, discordant
tonality, to his awkward gestures and unstudied mannerisms.
In France and Italy, as well as throughout the United States,
reporters had a way of starting back in Kilkenny and thread-
ing down through the simple biographical facts in an effort
to spell out the mystery of what made John Ireland great.

Amusingly enough, Minnesota writers were not intrigued
by the descriptive phrase applied to Ireland by Archbishop
Ryan of Philadelphia, "consecrated blizzard of the Northwest," which occasionally turned out as "consecrated cy-
clone" and testy Catholic editors made into "Church blizzard." It was as if the Minnesotans knew their weather and
found no fitting parallel therein for their favorite son. The
pages written into Minnesota histories by those who knew
him tremble with superlatives as they shrink from writing
of one whom they considered to be in himself an age, an
era, an epoch. On the Catholic side, the eulogists compared
him to Mont Blanc and felt the figure was still inadaquate
to convey the splendor of one who brought the church to
the age and the age to the church. Distant generations alone,
they felt, could compass the magnificence of this colossus.

His own generation recognized his worth sufficiently to
award him rapid promotion within the church. In 1884, at the
age of forty-six, Bishop Ireland had succeeded to full author-

ity when Bishop Grace resigned the administration of the diocese of St. Paul. At that time there were 130,000 Catholics in the diocese. The following year St. Thomas Seminary was opened upon the present campus of St. Thomas College. By that time any institution in which Bishop Ireland had a hand was looked on as a real estate venture through which the city would profit by increased assets and population. His standing in the city and state were so secure that every civic group endeavored to hear a word of commendation. The optimism about the future of Minnesota which was to color most of his later pronouncements enhanced the value of his opinions on what was "good for the country." There is ample evidence that the bishop even then was anxious to put himself right with American public opinion.

Then in 1888 John Ireland was advanced to the position of archbishop. And as the first archbishop of St. Paul he became a figure of national and international importance. Just as Donald Attwater, the English Catholic author and editor, could say on his first trip to the United States in 1939, "I made a bee line from the boat to Mott Street," meaning that the *Catholic Worker*'s House of Hospitality at 115 Mott Street, New York, naturally would have the highest interest for a European Catholic, so while Archbishop Ireland was alive European Catholics headed for St. Paul.

Minnesota was well known, especially in France and Italy. One can understand the manner in which Archbishop Ireland wrote to a friend in Rome to ask him to please inform the postal authorities that St. Paul, Minnesota, was a much more important place than São Paulo, Brazil, and much nearer to Rome. A letter from Cardinal Rampolla to Archbishop Ireland had gone first to Brazil before reaching St. Paul.

To Protestant Minnesota and to American people in general, Archbishop Ireland was even more of a phenomenon than to his colleagues in the church. For he was a living demonstration of the possibility that a devoted, practicing Catholic could be a patriotic American citizen. As early as 1863, he had written to O. A. Brownson to order the *Catholic Review* for Bishop Grace and each of the priests of the Cathedral parish, adding a characteristic and forthright paragraph on the intellectual quality of Mr. Brownson's writings. "I consider it a shame for any man, who pretends to have some theological or literary qualifications not to be a constant reader of the *Review* and I do blush that there should be in our country so many *soi-disant* Catholic writers, or rather I should say scribblers who are bent on opposing you. True I can explain this opposition; they are ignorant; they have just tasted, *summis labiis*, a few branches of science, and thinking they know all, because they never knew what is to be known, they boldly set down as an error whatever is not intelligible to them."

Mr. Brownson, a convert, in spite of his crotchetiness, represented the kind of appeal to intellectual non-Catholics which is provided today by the *Commonweal*. When John Ireland was away as a war chaplain, Father Caillet carried on the correspondence with the *Review* and sent messages to the Henry Brownson family, whom he had known in St. Paul.

There is no doubt that the groundwork for Archbishop Ireland's later expressions was laid by discussions in the Cathedral rectory in St. Paul. There, for example, they could understand him when he said, "In Protestantism, where there is no firmly constituted ministerial organization, the layman is more keenly alive to his responsibility, and lay action is more common and more earnest. . . . There is, on the part of Catholic laymen, too much dependence upon priests."

Certain cautious and retiring bishops were scandalized when the newspapers suggested that Archbishop Ireland was a new sort of Catholic, not in particularly good repute at Rome. This conviction was deepened by the fact that certain other suspiciously watchful bishops tried hard to render him less welcome at the Vatican, a campaign which was heedlessly carried on in the secular press, together with the spirited rejoinders of the Minnesota prelate. The display of selfish individualism, petty jealousies, and personal ambition on the part of the too human bishops on either side of the controversy presents a picture more striking than edifying. The net effect on the last quarter of the nineteenth century seems to have been the revelation to America that Catholics did not all think in an identical way and that they were not all told from Rome to which political party they must adhere. By this occult process, the lamentably uninformed American public also acquired a fairly good knowledge of what Catholic belief and practice meant. Within the limitations of his own time and character, that was the work of Archbishop Ireland — to reveal the church to America and America to the church.

Perhaps Dr. Folwell's estimate of John Ireland, recorded in *History of Minnesota*, may be taken as a good example of the over-all public picture of the archbishop in Minnesota. "He was distinguished in ecclesiastical circles on both sides of the Atlantic and his heart and hand were always in every good cause of his city, state, and nation. American through and through, he incurred no little censure because of his desire to see and his efforts to establish a distinct American Catholicity in this country. His commanding yet gracious presence and his powerful and brilliant oratory dignified many an important civic celebration. As an apostle of temperance he wrought a revolution among his own people and others sufficient to make an epoch in Minnesota history. No Catholic prelate in America has done more to bridge the chasm between the old church and the descendents of those who in times gone by broke from its fold."

John Ireland's campaign against alcohol antedated by many years his elevation to archbishop. While he was still the pastor at the Cathedral his sermons and addresses on the

evils of drink drew wide attention. He dated the establishment of the first total abstinence society to a plea scrawled
on a scrap of paper by one who was himself an example of
the evil effects of drink. Taking the pledge was an important
part of the crusading activities. In common with other cru-
saders of the time, Ireland depended upon a doubtful physi-
ology for the lurid consequences which might attend any
consumption of alcohol. The degrading moral results of
chronic alcoholism were attributed to even moderate drinking. Engaging in the liquor business was a serious transgres-
sion of the moral law. Nevertheless, despite this inflexibility,
his earnestness and sincerity were a powerful spur to self-
control and Ireland had early come to be looked upon as a
force for law observance and uprightness in the community.

The moral opinion of the temperance advocates was puri-
tanical and narrow, however. Most of the European immigrants came from countries where the drinking of alcoholic
beverages was taken as a matter of course. They took very
unkindly to teaching which insisted that any consumption of
alcohol led to alcoholism. Even Father Mathew, the great
temperance apostle of Ireland, was censured in Catholic
circles for coming close to declaring even the most moderate
use of alcohol a moral wrong. Germans were not abstainers,
but they were apt to be moderate drinkers, insistent on re-
taining their right to drink along with their language and
customs, whatever Ireland had to say.

Among the Catholics, Ireland worked upon the hard-
drinking Irishmen with marked success. Part of his enthusiasm for founding colonies in Minnesota might be laid to his
fear that the temptations of drink would be too strong for
the Irish if they remained in the large eastern cities. This
is borne out by accounts of the colonization rallies in New
York in 1879, which commented that Ireland's "immigration"
talks were veritable temperance lectures. The Irish did little
fussing about the physiological basis for the cherry-red
stomachs infected by rum which were stock-in-trade of a

good temperance harangue, or about the theological confusion between use and abuse of alcohol. Many of them had already experienced the physical and moral effects of abuse — there was no need to be technical or anonymous. It was a great deal that there was someone to point the way to salvation. John Ireland's cleverness kept him from making any really questionable statements, except perhaps in his insistence that engaging in the liquor business was an unequivocal evil. But he had the blessing of Pope Leo XIII on his work and in the early years the ardent sanction of his local superior, Bishop Grace.

In politics the Irish were less easily swayed. John Ireland was an adherent of the party of Abraham Lincoln and the Republican leaders represented statesmanship to him even after they had chosen social and economic ideals allied to wealth and power. When they failed repeatedly in their promises to him, he did not discern the inevitable lapses of partisan politics from religious standards. For the most part, the Irish, the most vocal Catholics, belonged to the Democratic party and their conviction that Ireland was a great man seems to have had no appreciable effect on their voting column. While the *Irish Standard*, started in Minneapolis in 1886, was not the prelate's official paper, its language was filial and enthusiastic, except for occasional expressions such as references to the Republicans as "the party of pirates to which His Grace belongs" and "this is the langauge of diplomacy His Grace uses."

Fashions of thinking about public questions have changed with the passing of the conditions which created the problems, so that upon hearing that Archbishop Ireland could remark publicly, "I am not afraid of the man with an extra dollar in his pocket," the contemporary reader is apt to dismiss him as a slave of Wall Street. Archbishop Ireland belonged to his time — he did not see two world wars and a great concentration of wealth and power. In any case, as Mr. Dooley once said, "The trusts are heejus monsthers built up by the inlightened entherprise iv the men that done so much to advance progress in our beloved country. On wan hand I wud stomp thim undther fut; on th' other hand, not so fast."

The archbishop's political blast against bimetallism and Bryanism in 1896 appalls the modern reader with its accusation that the opponents of hard money were secessionists, anarchists, socialists, and what have you. But in 1889, to the assembled hierarchy of the church in Baltimore Cathedral, he had dared to say: "Socialism — it is, in its first outburst, the shriek of despair from the hungering souls upon which presses the heavy hand of greed and injustice, reasons for many of its demands are found in Catholic theology, which teaches that the human race does not exist for the benefit of the few, and that private property becomes common property, when death from starvation is at the door."

Archbishop Ireland's social and political pronouncements were generally criticized at the time for their modern and liberal tendencies, but there were a few critics like the *Irish Standard* and *Kennedy's Own* of Minneapolis which brought out the fact that he opposed strikes because they were bad for business, he believed that capital's right to profit preceded labor's rights to bargain in its own behalf, he thought that the claims of manifest destiny were reason enough for war whatever the demands of humanity. Nevertheless, he taught the social gospel of his lifetime friend Pope Leo XIII and the great French liberal Count de Mun.

The key to the conflict is the fact that the doctrine of the Mystical Body with its ramifications in the liturgy and social charity had not yet been elaborated in the way that Pius X was to clarify its implications for all men. It is significant that Archbishop Ireland classified Pius X as a worker for holiness and admired him less than his beloved statesman-pope, Leo XIII.

Peace with victory was the only palatable condition of affairs to him and he told veterans after the Spanish-American War that it was not such a bad thing to have had the war in their time, because it helped to keep alive the country's patriotic ideals. Tammany Hall and all its adherents were "bad for the country."

There is a common characteristic for many of his friends, like James J. Hill, Cushman K. Davis, Stephen B. Elkins, Chauncey M. Depew, and others. As characterized by the *Dictionary of American Biography* they include a railroad-builder, a senator, an industrialist, a wit, and a broker, but the common description is that each was also a plutocrat. Archbishop Ireland himself had a fortune of $1,500,000 in 1893, invested largely in land holdings in the Midway district of St. Paul. In 1894 his friends in New York loaned him $500,000. This was intended to clear the diocese of debt and the loan was secured by mortgages on his land. In 1896, he failed financially and gave up his land holdings to settle with his creditors. There was said to be no loss to any individual Catholic, but only to his personal fortune, which he had been amassing in order to build a Cathedral and a school.

Monsignor John Ryan in his autobiography summed up the archbishop's economic position when he commented that Ireland was not "an economic reformer, as was Ignatius Donnelly. In fact, he regarded the 'Sage of Nininger' whom he knew very well and who for more than forty years was almost his neighbor in Minnesota, as something of a demagogue. All this is true and more. The Archbishop's associations were the pillars of the contemporary economic order, men like James J. Hill, president of the Great Northern Railway, and William McKinley, President of the United States, rather than with such critics of the order as Ignatius Donnelly and William J. Bryan. Nevertheless, he was at heart, liberal and progressive in his attitude toward economic institutions, and their proper functions. He differed with the reformers not so much with regard to desirable objectives as in his evaluation of economic facts and tendencies."

John Ireland often made wrong decisions in economic and political matters in the light of what he probably would think if he were living today, but he had a clear eye for Gospel truth and the liberty which belongs to a child of God. He was not fearful of giving offense to either his political friends or foes. The further one delves in the private correspondence of the presidents from Benjamin Harrison on through President Wilson, the more one is convinced that — entirely apart from his well-known Republicanism — these men respected Archbishop Ireland's person and influence in a marked manner.

Part of his appeal for both politicians and churchmen was his knack for speaking with hard common sense about contemporary problems. At a meeting on "pauperism" in St. Paul in 1885, for example, Ireland said, "In all large cities there is a tendency to what may be termed unjustifiable poverty. . . . One method of curing pauperism is to investigate cases and thus prevent imposition upon one society or another. . . . I believe a great deal can be done by making employment a basis of relief. Make every tramp and able-bodied pauper earn the charity that is bestowed upon him. If a man isn't willing to go and earn his meals at a city wood-yard or some other such institution, in one sense it is better for humanity that he should starve."

At the same time he had a genuine respect for religious charity. In a talk on "Charity in the Catholic Church" given at the meeting of the National Conference of Charities and Corrections in 1886, he made a simple explanation of the scriptural basis for Catholic charity and a clear description of the supernatural motives which must activate true charity. He gave an understandable picture of the organization of Catholic charity in religious orders. Over and over he presented variants of the idea that "the identification of Christ with the destitute and the suffering has sunk most deeply into Catholic tradition," or "the personification of Christ in suffering humanity invests all forms of misery with a divine halo." But nothing about woodyards.

A series of full-scale controversies centered around John

Ireland after he became archbishop. The matters assumed
a national and an international character because the hierarchy of the United States and Europe took sides which were
sharply colored by their personal animosities and admira-
tions. It has always been deplored that the details of the
rivalries and quarrels as well as the theoretical discussion
of the points at issue received such noisy attention from the
press on both sides of the Atlantic. The willingness to be
heard in his own defense by the man jocularly dubbed "the
consecrated blizzard of the Northwest" may at times have
departed from the reticent dignity characteristic of the hierarchy of the time, but it did nevertheless dispel the clouds
of ignorance which shrouded everything concerning the
Church of Rome in the minds of Americans. A by-product
was a better education in their own beliefs for nineteenth-
century Catholics.

Some of the matters which stirred the country were the
condemnation of other secret societies than the Masons, the
question of the single-tax theories of Henry George, the
Knights of Labor, the Catholic University, the World Parliament of Religions at the Columbian Exposition of 1893,
the Apostolic Delegation, Cahenslyism, Americanism, the
Faribault-Stillwater compromise school plan, and the campaign for Archbishop Ireland's elevation to the cardinalate.

John Ireland had early taken a vigorous stand against
Cahenslyism, the movement of the Catholic German immigrants in the United States for exclusively German religious
institutions. The German religious leaders in this country
and abroad feared that the immigrants would lose their
faith unless they retained their native language and customs.
So concerned had one organization of benevolent men in
Germany, the German Catholic Emigrant Aid Society, become that it commissioned Peter Paul Cahensly to present
two memorials to the pope requesting German bishops and
priests for the German immigrants in the United States. This,
they felt, would ensure German sermons in churches and

Left, Mother St. John Ireland, Mother Celestine Howard, and Mother Seraphine Ireland in 1885; right, Sister Wilfrida Hogan

Sister Antonia McHugh

Archbishop John Ireland

Mother Seraphine Ireland in 1925

Reception and Profession Day, 1951, at St. Joseph's novitiate in St. Pa

St. Joseph's Provincial House, St. Paul

the exclusive use of the German language in parochial schools.

There had been immediate and almost unanimous opposition to this action on the part of American bishops. John Ireland had been in Rome in 1887 on other business and he and Bishop Keane of Richmond presented to the Holy See the American bishops' opinions.

Ireland had made his position very clear in numerous speeches and sermons. He said that America was not a Congo to be partitioned off at the will of foreigners, however well intentioned. He maintained that all foreigners must gradually learn English and mingle freely with Americans. He felt that children who were taught their religion in a foreign tongue would be unable to answer questions concerning their belief by other Americans and would soon come to regard all religion as something foreign and old-fashioned.

There was lay opposition to the Cahensly plan as well. Wisconsin passed the Bennett law forbidding the exclusive use of German in schools. Senator Cushman K. Davis of Minnesota declared on the floor of the United States Senate that the apportionment of Catholic bishops in the United States by nationality quotas was a great peril.

The conviction of the American bishops prevailed and the pope eventually denied Herr Cahensly's petitions. The German immigrants in the United States, however, continued to form their own little communities, with their own churches and schools. For many years after the official rejection by the church of Cahenslyism Ireland was forced to combat excessive nationalism among the Germans and other immigrant groups. He continued to urge throughout his life Americanization of all immigrant groups.

The German or Cahensly problem and other trenchant issues were well known to the priests and sisters of Minnesota. They were on the firing line with their leader for a Catholicism which was integrated with American democracy. A certain aggressiveness colored their spirituality and, while it was seldom deviant from church teaching, tended to make them hustlers for secular standards in school and for great achievements in church buildings. Cardinals and princes and political leaders sought St. Paul because of its archbishop. All these guests were welcomed by the clergy and they were brought to St. Joseph's Academy to meet the sisters and the students. These were cosmopolitan experiences which added to the church in Minnesota a measure of self-reliance which cannot otherwise be explained.

One of the issues that concerned the Sisters of St. Joseph directly was the Faribault-Stillwater compromise school plan, which involved a form of state support for parochial schools. The part that the sisters took in Archbishop Ireland's experiment in 1891 in a state-supported parish school in Stillwater is told in a revealing fashion in the *Minneapolis Journal* for January 9, 1892. The account of a visit of inspection to Stillwater by a reporter is enlivened with a sketch by the cartoonist "Bart" of a Sister of St. Joseph.

In Faribault, where Dominican Sisters were the teachers, the same plan was being tried as in the schools of Stillwater. The Faribault story was told in the *Journal* for January 12

Bart's cartoons of Stillwater-Faribault teachers

with an appropriate sketch, but the reporter, having visited Stillwater first, seemed a trifle critical of the Dominican habit, in the manner of a connoisseur.

The reporter began his story on Stillwater with a bit of dialoguo.

"'Can you direct me to the public school near this corner?' the reporter inquired of a bright little girl whom he met in front of St. Michael's Catholic Church in Stillwater.

"'Oh, you mean the Catholic public school. That is right back of the church, in the tall building. I thought you meant just the public school.'"

From this dialogue the reporter explained that the school was supported in the same way as the other public schools of the city, although it was attended by the same scholars as before the transfer, from all parts of the town without regard to school districts.

"They are instructed," he wrote, "by sisters of the church, who wear the prescribed dress of the sisterhood. The long black veil flows down from the head over the shoulders and back. Under it the head is encased in the close-fitting white hood, and the shoulders and bust are covered by the white cape. The full black gown, with flowing sleeves and simple gathering at the waist, complete the familiar picture. From the neck is suspended the crucifix and from the waist the rosary. These teachers are engaged by the schoolboard and paid from the public fund."

There was less opposition in Stillwater than might have been supposed, considering that everyone considered this an experiment in what was an especial hobby of Archbishop Ireland and in what they feared was an episcopal goal in the Catholic church — the support of all the parochial schools by the state. It was pointed out that Stillwater was a city of thirteen or fourteen thousand people of whom possibly two thousand were Irish Catholics. Seventeen hundred children were enrolled in the public schools and 202 in the parochial. Aside from the Protestant objection to the action of the school board, the German Catholics and Lutherans of the town, both of whom had parochial schools, were demanding an explanation for the refusal of the state to support their schools as well.

Sister Hyacinth had been transferred to Stillwater to fill the position of principal in the Hill school, as the parochial school was renamed. The five sisters were examined in the usual manner, "were found well qualified to teach," and were granted certificates and engaged on the same terms as the other teachers. The textbooks were changed in the schools and religious pictures were removed from the rooms.

The reporter described what he found to be the "marked inferiority of the parochial school building." It was a tall four-room brick structure, located about fifty feet in the rear of the church. The schoolrooms were eighteen feet high, with windows on three sides, "many of them with neither blinds nor curtains. The blackboards, formed by painting the plaster, were four feet from the floor and were of poor quality. By means of steps the children were able to reach the board." The rooms were warmed by stoves, without provision for ventilation. Two of these rooms were "seated with desks of an exceedingly ancient pattern, as awkward and uncomfortable as the slab bench of our forefathers." By means of pictures, flags, and other decorations, the teachers had made the rooms as neat and attractive as possible. One class had been temporarily located in the convent in a room altogether too small for school purposes, with a low ceiling and limited lighting space.

According to the reporter for the *Journal,* the superintendent considered the sisters qualified to instruct, but he thought there was a "subtle influence which a teacher exerted, even unconsciously, and susceptible children would be influenced by them." The sisters, he said, asserted that they were "always for the church first" and then what they could do for the schools they would do to the best of their ability. The superintendent admitted, however, that the church work of the sisters in no wise interfered with school-work. Again the reporter pointed out that the building had the "Catholic church building stamps upon it" in its "high ceilings, panelled walls, and long, narrow halls and stair-ways. One thing was very conspicuous in all the rooms and that was the absence of every vestige of Catholic emblem, excepting in the wearing apparel of the teachers them-selves."

Superintendent Wilson had referred the reporter to Sister Hyacinth for an interview, but she greeted him with the statement that she would not be interviewed. It was with difficulty that she was induced to state the facts in regard to worship in the schools. There were no religious exercises during school hours and after that the building reverted back to the church and it was none of the public's business what was done at that time. She was quite bitter at the public for the comment that the experiment had called out. She pro-fessed to be indignant that such prejudiced reports had been printed and still insisted that she would not answer ques-tions or be interviewed — that she believed it was not re-quired. She and all the other teachers were very willing that the rooms be visited.

After a short stay, during which it was apparent that Sister Hyacinth had perfect control of her pupils and was a good instructor, the interviewer inquired again as to what work the sisters did in the church out of school hours — were not the teacher's relations to the church the same as before she became a public school teacher? "The sister was very indig-nant at this," the account read, "and thought it perfectly impertinent of the public in this free land to inquire into the home life and religious worship of such as herself. How-ever, she stated that her connections in the convent at home were the same as ever. All that had been reported about the sisters supporting the parish church she said was ridiculous."

In one of the rooms "the young sister became quite excited and enquired quite emphatically if her visitor were a reporter . . . She said that a good deal that was not true had been published about her particular room and it would have to stop or someone would get into trouble."

In the next room the reporter was "met by a smiling sister, who looked quite accustomed to her profession of charity. She seated the reporter in the farthest corner of the room where retreat was impossible, and turned the tables on him completely, by calling out some two dozen small urchins with drawings of squares and circles in various combinations, on slates, and had them file by for his inspection. When she sent them back to their seats for more material the reporter took a hasty retreat, utterly routed."

Upon leaving the school, the reporter had sought out the Reverend L. H. Morey, a Presbyterian minister, who considered the dress of the sisters "particularly obnoxious."

Within a few days, Archbishop Ireland left for Rome to present a memorial upon the school question and the German or Cahensly dispute. He was upheld by Pope Leo XIII in the compromise plan insofar as circumstances made such a departure from the parochial school system necessary, but even before he had presented his plea to the pope, the Protestant ministers of Minnesota had succeeded in alarming the public sufficiently to withdraw public support for the two schools, at Stillwater and Faribault.

An active enemy had been the *North*, a paper for Scandinavians published in Minneapolis. In cartoons and long articles the machinations of Archbishop Ireland were excoriated, with numerous references to "John of St. Paul," "the carpenter's son of St. Paul," and "John Irelandism." It is a curious fact that the archbishop seems never to have replied to any of these attacks. He simply refused to notice their obvious connection with the anti-Catholic bigotry of the American Protective Association, which he maintained would disappear if no attention was paid to it. Denunciations of the church in the Sunday sermons of the Protestant ministers, on the other hand, as they appeared in the papers on Monday, he answered in the following day's papers. The treatments tend to seem dryly apologetic today, but more than one distinguished Catholic attributed his conversion to the course of instruction he received in reading Archbishop Ireland's argumonto in the newspapers. He often preached on Sunday evening at the Cathedral and the church was crowded to the doors, whether he appeared once or for a series of instructions.

Sister Wilfrida Hogan was sent to Stillwater in 1894 and she found that "the echo of the famous Faribault-Stillwater Plan was still in the air, and the importance in attracting so much world-wide attention was felt by everyone. The good resulting from it was that the school stood the test and that the teachers made good their ability to handle the situation. . . . The Catholic school in Stillwater gained a prestige in the fight that it never had before, and it has been a success since."

In another place Sister Wilfrida commented that the attic at St. Joseph's Academy was full of papers regarding the Stillwater plan, but, she added, "it caused such a fight all over the whole world at the time that perhaps the controversy may as well rest in peace."

The experiment was tried again in still another town, Waverly, a year later. From 1893 to 1904 St. Mary's school there was a consolidated parish and public school, in which the sisters worked under the supervision of a state superintendent and received a salary of forty dollars a month from the public school administration. As early as June 23, 1894, the *Loyal American,* an American Protective Association paper published in Minneapolis for Scandinavians, was referring to the Waverly school as "John Irelandism." It was simply the Faribault plan at work in Waverly, the editor commented, as the fact that Sister Eugenia and Sister Alphonsine Welp were receiving public school salaries proved. In 1904 public support was withdrawn, but the Catholic school continued to operate.

For almost every aspect of John Ireland, prelate, patriot, publicist, there is a divided opinion — not perhaps so marked in Minnesota as in that wider area on both sides of the Atlantic where the echo of his periods has not quite died out. But there is certainly one statement that can be made about him without fear of contradiction. It is that he was a friend of the Sisters of St. Joseph. To the sisters he was father and friend in an individual and personal way, but he also represented to them the church and the state. It is a tribute not so much to his impressive jurisdiction as to the charm of his personality that there is to this day almost no perception of the fact that for full forty years he headed a veritable family dynasty which governed the Sisters of St. Joseph in St. Paul. Although there is an occasional retrospective criticism of the members of the family who were even closer to the sisters than the eminent archbishop, he stands for them on a pedestal apart, fascinatingly human, but incapable of error.

Naturally, Mother Seraphine and Mother St. John and Mother Celestine were looked on as Archbishop Ireland's sisters, but they were persons of purpose and ability in their own right. They were not born superiors any more than he was born an archbishop. All came up the hard, intangible, invisible way to appreciation by those who professed the same thought and design. The Oriental ideal that the leader be the person most indistinguishable in his group was intrinsically theirs, for they strove to uplift the whole community with themselves, but in the Occidental fashion, they stood above their fellowship, elevated by general recognition of their spiritual talents.

Mother Seraphine had advanced from directorships at St. Joseph's Academy, St. Teresa's Academy in Hastings, St. Anthony school, and the St. Paul Girls' Orphanage to the provincial superiorship. Mother St. John had been directress of Immaculate Conception school and superior of Holy Angels' Academy and convent. Mother Celestine, after directorships at Immaculate Conception school and St. Joseph's Academy, had become general directress of schools in St. Louis province, supervisor of elementary schools in St. Paul, and finally superior of St. Agatha's Conservatory of Music and Art.

No one is now living who can remember an earlier picture than that of the various convents headed by one of these sisterly generals with Mother Seraphine as the beloved chief. But it was in the very early days that exclusive possession of John Ireland as a brother was forgotten in the general ownership implied by such observations from all the sisters as, "What does Father John think about this?" and "Father Ireland suggests we ought to do that." He was the friendly counselor and trusted friend of the sisters individually and collectively.

His long narrations about things and people in Europe and eastern United States were preventives of narrow provincialism and concentration on the mentality of their separated brethren. He looked on the sisters as an integral part of his Americanizing process. For although they were not all native sisters they were at least English-speaking, and by the time he became influential, they were able to forward his plans to make Catholic schools adhere to the same standards in secular branches and American citizenship as prevailed for the public schools. He wanted all the teachers to take the regular examinations for certification. In the Baltimore Plenary Council of 1884 he had worked hard to have this become a principle of church discipline. In these proposals he was greatly aided by his like-minded sister, Mother Seraphine, especially after she began her long career as provincial superior in 1882.

Externally, Mother Seraphine combined charm and rigor. Internally, even those who felt that she was harsh and too quick to believe aspersions agreed that all her vitality was centered in devotion to God and the community. These characteristics she shared with her brother, and on a smaller

— or perhaps feminine — scale she developed the same reck-
lessness in undertaking large projects with small collateral in
hand. She worried a great deal about how bills were to be
met, but she never developed good business sense or hard-
headedness. Rather, she depended on the strength of her
midnight vigils and her unceasing prayers, as well as the
managing powers of her devoted sisters.

Mother Celestine remained her dependable friend, with
greater shrewdness, more caution, and less frankness than
her chief. She it was who accepted the burden of fitting
country girls to teach in the schools, who prodded Mother
Seraphine to rigid disciplinary measures, and who acted as
a check on her cousin's too visionary plans. Mother Celestine
would try to hold back her plunging cousin, but when decisions to expand were made despite her warnings, she
strained every nerve to get the money together. In this she
utilized St. Agatha's Conservatory, where the sisters did a
brisk business copying classical and popular paintings and
teaching the arts then in fashion.

The need to make money tended to slow up the process of
original work at St. Agatha's and teachers at other schools
had students producing creative work before the sisters had
turned from china painting and the other stilted crafts. The
artists were sufficiently aware of this cultural lag and perhaps
the musicians were also, although it is doubtful whether
anyone realized at that time that the trend also represented
a spiritual lag. The greatest good they could imagine was
meeting the present needs of the community.

At one time they had accumulated enough at St. Agatha's
to brick an old building. It had been a long struggle. Just
when the pile of money needed was complete, Mother
Celestine said to the sisters, "How can we spend it for bricks
when Mother Seraphine needs it?" No one objected to hand-
ing over the money. A sister who spent a lifetime at St.
Agatha's said that there was more of a family spirit then than
now. The poverty struggle was real as evidenced by the

poor food and the debts. Habits were worn out before they were paid for, but everyone prayed hard and they felt they were struggling for God. The sisters loved Mother Seraphine and Mother Celestine in spite of their harshness.

The two orphanages were sporadic sources of income for the sisters, when donations were unusually generous. Mother Josephine Gleason was the superior of the girls' orphanage in St. Paul from 1884 until 1916 and Mother Xavier had charge of the boys' orphanage in Minneapolis from 1885 until 1906. Gifts of the charitable were the support of the orphans. Two sisters from each institution went out through the state at harvest time begging, and another sister from either house went around the city on a wagon periodically, soliciting food from the market, hotels, and bakeries. The Orphans' Fair in St. Paul and their Fourth of July picnic in Minneapolis were patronized by the different parishes. In time as much as $10,000 per year was realized at these functions. Archbishop Ireland lent his personal assistance with prizes and money and often with an address.

As time went on, St. Joseph's Hospital became a source of revenue on which Mother Seraphine could depend, but this was not true in the beginning. Not until 1895 was the hospital incorporated, when it was deemed necessary to borrow money to expand. The first money borrowed by the community was $40,000 for that purpose, and Mother Seraphine was said to have worried over it inordinately. She wondered how they would ever get it paid back. Archbishop Ireland was not so timorous. When several of his friends in Europe asked him to invest their idle money for them, he loaned it to the sisters and sent the interest to the investors. St. Mary's Hospital in Minneapolis, which had been bought from the Sisters of Mercy in 1887 for $80,000, was in this way entrusted with $20,000 from an Italian countess.

In the long run one of Archbishop Ireland's greatest services to the Sisters of St. Joseph was his insistence on professional qualifications for educational and charitable work.

He had no patience with the literal-mindedness which would have tied the sisters to the seventeenth-century social conditions prevailing when their institute was founded. He felt that the genius of the church lay in its adaptability to the needs of every age. Again and again he exhorted the sisters to make their institutions comparable to the best secular schools and hospitals by use of the most recent discoveries and techniques. This point of view is noteworthy, for the position of women was still sheltered and of little consequence in the public opinion of the early twentieth century. While the Sisters of St. Joseph cannot be said to have achieved the high ideals Archbishop Ireland placed before them or to have gone higher still in perfecting a program for the social needs of the present era, there is no doubt that an early and unusual grasp of professional demands is part of their heritage from Archbishop Ireland.

Under his urging the sisters destined to teach were given more and better training, a greater emphasis was placed in parochial schools on the academic standards insisted upon by the accrediting agencies, and administrators and teachers utilized more efficient classification systems, new curriculums, up-to-date material.

Very much the same changes came to hospitals as to schools, when certification was insisted upon. In 1893, Mother Bernardine Maher, superior of St. Joseph's Hospital from 1884 to 1920, engaged a teacher of nursing from Johns Hopkins to train the sisters and any other young women who wished to become nurses. Before that the only training the sisters had was what they acquired in service from the doctors. It was of a superior character, because St. Joseph's was a center for the St. Paul College of Medicine, and the medical men were of a high caliber. Nevertheless, the trend demanded professional qualifications and Mother Bernardine saw to it that the sisters met all the requirements of the new course.

In 1896, ten sisters and six lay women were graduated

from St. Joseph's Hospital Training School. Within a few years, the number of young women desiring training increased to such an extent that the sisters were no longer able to do much bedside nursing. Instead, their time was taken up with supervision and they lost a measure of personal relationship with the patients. Hospitals soon changed their character also. They were no longer places to which only the poor and the outcast came. The advance in surgical technique and the history-making surgery of Dr. Arnold Schwyzer at St. Joseph's brought people to the hospital from all over the state. In no time the hospital was so crowded that the insistent rich were more apt to get the beds when there were any.

Five Sisters of St. Joseph served as nurses in the Spanish-American War for eight months in Cuba. Mother Seraphine and Reverend Mother Agatha from St. Louis spent some time with them before Christmas 1899. Later on St. Joseph's expressed a willingness to care for naval veterans at sixty-five cents per day, the lowest rate offered in any hospital in the country.

As superior of St. Joseph's Hospital, Mother Bernardine, although not of the Ireland family, was close in their counsel. There were others too, for Mother Seraphine, Mother St. John, and Mother Celestine were companionable people who made warm friends in women of comparable stature and intensity. Besides Mother Bernardine, their friends included such admirable women as Mother Madeline at St. John's Hospital in Fargo and Mother Josephine at the St. Paul Girls' Orphanage — women of high cultural and administrative merit in their time.

John Ireland shared with his sisters the ability to make and keep warm friends among persons of talent and conviction who drew admiration for their own programs as much as for their support of the illustrious archbishop. As they were consecrated bishops, these men were referred to scornfully in some quarters as "the young Irelanders," but more objective observers acknowledged their individual superiority.

Outside the religious community of sisters and priests the Irelands also had a wide circle of friends and admirers. However, they were not always the favored, not even in the early days before the storms of controversy raged around the archbishop.

When Mary Mehegan, for example, went to the Cathedral to be married to James J. Hill, it was discovered that Father Ireland had forgotten to deliver the message that the bride wished Father Caillet to officiate at the wedding. Father Ireland offered to take Father Caillet's place in the ceremony. However, the future Mrs. Hill declared that she would like to have Father Oster officiate if Father Caillet was not available. Although Mrs. Hill and her family were bound by close ties to Archbishop Ireland, it is a little-known fact that their gift of $500,000 to the St. Paul Seminary was not a personal token to the archbishop, but a recognition by James J. Hill of the esteem of his wife for her pastor, Father Caillet. To neither of the churchmen were these matters of any moment whatever — the munificent gift made God's work possible. That was all that mattered.

One of John Ireland's continuing campaigns in his relationship with the Sisters of St. Joseph was his effort to do away with the office of lay sister. Lay sisters had been received by the Sisters of St. Joseph during their early years in St. Paul and some were still being accepted through the 1880s. The first translation of the French Rule in 1847 refers to them as the "servants of the Sisters," an expression omitted in all later English versions. They wore a distinguishing dress with a black cape and a headdress different from that of the "choir" sisters. They participated in the religious exercises only in part, ranked below the other sisters at table, and were engaged exclusively in the domestic work of the convent.

This classification was a custom which Archbishop Ireland

could not abide. It was European to his mind and utterly opposed to American practice and principle. "It's a wonder they don't burn the house down," he would say in his irritation. He continually advised against conferring the lay habit and after Mother Seraphine's accession, it was seldom given. The few who had received that habit earlier continued to wear it, until the archbishop's insistence was finally carried to Rome and the provision was changed for the whole congregation. This occurred in 1908 when he accompanied Mother Seraphine, Mother Celestine, and the two highest superiors from St. Louis on their visit to the Holy Father.

A sister who has lived in St. Paul for many years has said that she believes the archbishop's power made the St. Louis motherhouse keep hands off the St. Paul province. "The archbishop had great foresight," she said, "and he was in a position always to give our community the lead. Priests used to say, 'You can't have any other sisters than the Sisters of St. Joseph,' or 'watch the blackbirds take a back seat when the archbishop dies.' Mother Seraphine and the archbishop were very close. She never told any of his confidences, but everyone knew she was powerful with him. Priests who were in trouble with the archbishop would go to her to intercede for them. She wanted the archbishop to think the community was perfect — she never told him anything that would change his mind."

Technically, the archbishop of the diocese is not the superior of the Sisters of St. Joseph, for the congregation has managed its affairs autonomously since 1860, according to its approved constitution. The sisters stood in relation to Archbishop Ireland in the position of any lay Catholic for the external affairs of his jurisdiction, but there was a large twilight zone within which the sisters preferred to follow the archbishop's suggestions and guidance.

That the Sisters of St. Joseph were the archbishop's *pupillum oculi* is firmly believed by the sisters and priests who remember him. Numerous stories are told to prove it. The pastor from Bird Island, for example, once brought in blue-prints for a new school, and the archbishop said, "I really don't know school building requirements. Take all these up to Mother Celestine and be guided by her judgment."

"I have already shown them to Mother Marianna and she has approved them," said the pastor.

"And who is Mother Marianna?"

"The superior of the Sisters of Notre Dame at Mankato, whom I intend to have in my school."

"Not at all. You will do much better to have the Sisters of St. Joseph. Take your plans to Mother Celestine." And so it was.

In all his dealings as a man of affairs, a fairly hard picture of the archbishop remains. He was a typical American of his times — a war veteran, a hustler, and a western booster. But there is a more tender and intimate side which remains the familiar picture in Minnesota. Perhaps it is the true likeness. This picture is traced in the many stories from confirmation days, of which the following is familiar.

The class at St. Michael's Church in West St. Paul was up for examination. A little eight-year-old girl was asked, "Where does the soul go after death?"

"Heaven," she answered, "or Pup-pup-Purgatory." And stopped still.

The archbishop waited. Then he smiled broadly as he turned to the pastor. "There is another place," he said, "but I guess you people here on the West Side don't know much about it."

This was the pleasant person every Sister of St. Joseph knew, one who appreciated all her efforts far beyond their deserts. He had put it into words for them at the celebration of the golden jubilee of the coming of the sisters to St. Paul. In spite of his personal relation to this particular group of sisters, the archbishop never lost sight of their meaning as an agency in the work of the church, or of his position as a prelate of that church. "Much as I know of the Sisterhood

and of its works, angels only know them as they are. . . .
The Catholic Church understands woman's soul, and draws
all her energies into its service, as no other religious society,
no other institution of any sort, has ever been able to do.
This, on the part of the Church, is supreme wisdom. . . .
To its sisterhoods, the Church commits a very large part of
its work; and so effectively do they perform their task that
they take rank among the Church's choicest and most valuable agencies."

On the warp and woof of the archbishop's fancy the
picture of the Sisterhood of St. Joseph in St. Paul traced
itself while he spoke that morning, as it was wont in the long
ago to strike his boyish gaze. Those far-off days flitted before
him. The awe and trembling timidity were back, with which
he would approach the little cottage and struggle into
speech in the presence of its inmates. "Never since," he
declared, "in all my wanderings revealing most stately and
renowned convent sanctuaries, was I in feeling — and, verily
shall I believe, in reality — confronted with visions of life
so supernatural, as when, then, I would rest my eyes on St.
Paul's early Sisters."

With a fine sense of drama the archbishop had opened his
oration with the story of their arrival. "It was the third day
of November, 1851, in the early morning dawn. A steamer
from St. Louis was making fast its cordage to the levee of the
village of St. Paul, and soon from its deck stepped ashore
four sisters of the community of St. Joseph."

Then the names and events of the first day in St. Paul,
the names and characteristics of the sisters who came in the
next few years. "Yes, I see the Sisters in their poor shanty-
home, in their rustic schoolroom, in their tiny chapel; I see
them, amid the green grasses of summer, amid the deep
snows of winter, stepping demurely across the vacant field,
spread out between Bench Street and the romantic three-
story Cathedral on Wabasha Street: I see them gliding into
their seats near the Virgin's altar; I hear their sweet voices,

as docile to the bishop's commanding intonation, those voices spelled out in holy music thrilling canticles, and compelled by their magic power the whole congregation to mingle with them in harmony."

However true the strictures on Archbishop Ireland's failure to emphasize spiritual and supernatural values in public questions, however blind he may have seemed to the inroads of secularism and materialism, there is no doubting the quality of the golden jubilee challenge to the Sisters of St. Joseph. "To work, then, devoted Sisters! To your hearts and hands we entrust the children of the Church, especially the daughters of the Church, that, while you endue their minds with all the graces of human knowledge, you build them up into firm and devoted Christians. Teach them truths of earth; but teach them also truths of Heaven. . . . As they will be, so will be the Church itself, whose life and destiny are so closely interwoven with the life and destiny of its members. . . .

"The Church is the dispenser of charity. . . . Again to work, devoted Sisters, for God and for the Church! Open your hearts to every ill, physical and moral, with which poor humanity is smitten. Feed the hungry, visit the sick, comfort the afflicted. . . . The work of the Sisterhoods is the work of God; God alone could uplift human nature to such planes of holiness and self-immolation. But it is, also, the work of human nature, co-operating with divine grace, and rising with it to sublime heights of sanctity and sacrifice. . . .

"If between the future and the past there is to be a difference, it will be that in the future the opportunities of our sisterhoods will be more abundant, that greater demands will be made upon their energies, and that they must be richer in the virtues that inspire to high efforts and draw down copiously the graces of divine love. . . . With the love of Christ abiding in you, dare to rise ever higher than the world around you. . . . In your institutions, let there be no routine, no deadening conservatism. . . .

"I am a firm believer in the higher education of women: I covet for the daughters of the people, for so many of them, at least, as circumstances and position permit to aspire so high, the opportunities of receiving under the protecting hand of religion tho fullest intellectual equipment of which woman is capable. In this regard I offer my congratulations to the Sisters of St. Joseph for their promise soon to endow the Northwest with a college for the higher education of young women; and I take pleasure in pointing to this college as the chief contribution of their community to religion during the half century to come."

The involved proceedings connected with the founding of the Catholic University, with the archbishop's alleged politico-ecclesiastical ambition for the cardinal's hat, and with all the other famous controversies, must be passed over here with the most casual mention, for it is all too obvious that "the consecrated blizzard of the Northwest" blew more bitingly elsewhere than at home. "Leave me to my prairies," he often said.

❧ IX ❧

A Fountain Springing

JOHN IRELAND'S praise in his golden jubilee speech of the plan of the Sisters of St. Joseph to establish a college for women was welcome encouragement to the sisters. But the archbishop's share in the creation of St. Catherine's College was not merely verbal.

There had been talk about founding a college from 1887 on. Mother Seraphine knew the time was right for starting a college, but aside from that conception, the project was quite nebulous in the minds of the sisters. There was none of this vagueness in the archbishop's mind, however. In 1892 the foundations for a college building were laid at "Academy Heights." This tract was a part of the holdings of the archbishop in the Midway district. But during the depression of 1893 the plans had to be abandoned and the land was sold to meet pressing obligations.

Then in 1900 Archbishop Ireland gave all the rights of a special edition of *The Church and Modern Society*, a collection of his sermons and addresses, to the sisters for their college. The sisters were grateful and eventually the sales of the book, throughout the state and as far afield as the Pacific Northwest, brought in sixty thousand dollars. But they long remembered the weary days of peddling the books, the humiliation in begging for help. It was Mother Seraphine's enthusiasm that kept them going. Nothing mattered to her but the advancement of the community.

In 1902 Archbishop Ireland was instrumental in obtaining substantial material aid for the college. Hugh Derham, a rich farmer at Rosemount, had gone to the archbishop to ask what worthy cause should be helped from his bounty. Ireland told him of the plans for a college and Mr. Derham gave twenty thousand dollars for its erection and another five thousand for a scholarship. In later years, when the sisters were discouraged in their efforts to get money, Mother Seraphine would recall the early struggles and the gift of Mr. Derham. "It may not seem very large to you," she would say, "but it gave us the courage to go on. He well deserved to have Derham Hall named for him."

The cornerstone for Derham Hall was laid in 1903. With it the dreams of Archbishop Ireland and Mother Seraphine took on substance. But it was two years before the building was completed and almost a decade before the college proper emerged from the preparatory school.

It was the first postulant to enter the Sisters of St. Joseph in St. Paul from a North Dakota home address who was actually to realize the Irelands' dreams for St. Catherine's. This was Sister Antonia McHugh. Mother Seraphine gasped at some of the developments under Sister Antonia, not in disapproval, but as a sort of reminder to the community that all of them were not acts of God and the letter of the law was still in force. From the point of view of the archbishop and Mother Seraphine, it can be said that for the last twenty-five years of their lives, Sister Antonia brought the most twinkles of satisfaction into their fading eyes and the deepest *exegi monumentum* joy into their hearts. It is doubtful whether even the rising pile of the great new Cathedral of St. Paul gave them the peace they found in contemplating the College of St. Catherine.

The comparisons and contrasts among the individualities of the distinguished brother and sister and their independent disciple are multiple. Finally, the only fair way to regard each is as an exceptional personality, battling with practical exigencies born of the moment. Each met the day with the equipment in gifts and training peculiar to the person. If there is no exact counterpart for any of the three on the present horizon, neither do we have a replica of the milieu in which they displayed their powers.

A frontier environment comparable to that which the Ireland children had known twenty years earlier in St. Paul was the atmosphere in which Sister Antonia passed her girlhood. Her father, Patrick McHugh, was born in Ontario, and he spent six years of his early life steamboating on the Great Lakes. After living two years in Buffalo, where he took a business course, he moved to Omaha. There, in 1872, he was married to Rosa Welsh. In Omaha, also, on May 17, 1873, was born his oldest daughter, Anna, who was to be Sister Antonia.

When little Anna was three years old the family left Omaha in a covered wagon for Deadwood, Dakota Territory, a pioneer town built between gulches in the hills. There Mr. McHugh erected the first hotel in the mining village and named it I-X-L. The nearby Home Stake Mine, surrounded by the spruce-covered Black Hills, had its own gold rush, just less showy than the earlier California trek. Grace McDonald, the first teacher in Deadwood, lived at the hotel and spent her evenings teaching little Anna McHugh to read. When the child was six, she and her mother spent a year in Chicago because of Mrs. McHugh's illness. City and school were strange experiences to the little girl, who had seen apples in Dakota, but never a banana. "Two bits" was the only name she knew for any medium of exchange, but the new paper dollar her father put into every letter for her began her funding experience. At St. Patrick's school, where the Sisters of Mercy were her teachers, she saw a statue of the Virgin Mary for the first time.

In 1882, when Anna was nine, the family made a trip to Omaha in a stagecoach freighted with gold bullion and passengers fearful of attacks by Indians or road robbers. At

Omaha, the McHughs took a train for Sidney, Nebraska, to visit relatives, a visit often recalled later for its association with Willa Cather, whom they met there. After returning to Omaha, the family continued their journey to Grafton, in the northern part of Dakota Territory. There Anna's father took up land in Walsh County, making final proof on it in 1884, and Mrs. McHugh's pastry was one of the attractions for which the claim house gained a reputation. As soon as the pre-emption claim was proved up, Mr. McHugh filed on a homestead in Cavalier County, in the present townsite of Langdon. The claim had only a sod shanty for a year or so, but in 1885, a fine residence was erected which remained the family home.

After two years in the Grafton ungraded school, Anna, at twelve, was taken to St. Joseph's Academy in St. Paul in order to have careful instruction for her first communion. She was enrolled in the fifth grade, with Sister Alphonsine Welp as her teacher, Sister St. Rose Mackey being the directress of the school. She enjoyed boarding school and music lessons and returned to Langdon for her summer vacation, where her father, a delegate to the territorial legislature since 1884, was engaged in numerous political and business ventures, involving wheat, horses, and county seats.

In the fall of 1886, it was decided that Anna was to go to school in Winnipeg, to the Academy of the Holy Name Sisters, because it was only fifty miles away and the family could drive there or send her on the Great Northern train. For the next five years she remained in the French convent boarding school, completing three years of high school and taking music and drawing lessons as extras. She knew French well and she was accomplished in needlework. Her teachers remembered her talent, outspokenness, and fine manners.

After she had attended this academy for some time she applied for admission to the novitiate of the Sisters of the Holy Name. Her father, however, objected strenuously to her entering the convent and decided that she should "see the world" in order to get out of her head that foolish notion to "take the veil." He took her with him to the North Dakota Constitutional Convention in Bismarck, which he attended as a delegate. She remained with him all the summer of 1889 and went on with the delegates for a tour of Yellowstone Park at the end of the sessions, chaperoned by the wife and daughter of Delegate Leach from Cassleton. Park visitors then rode in four-seated stages drawn by six horses and the three weeks which the delegates spent there provided an opportunity for Anna to develop the bent for geography which characterized her later teaching. Moreover, a young professor of geology from the University of Indiana was in the party and his knowledge of curious rock formations furnished invaluable aid to the others.

Finding that his daughter's mind was no easier to change than his own, Mr. McHugh told her that if she was determined to enter a convent, he would prefer some place where two languages were not in use as in Winnipeg. Why did she not go back to the convent where that lovely Sister St. Rose was? They spoke English there. She agreed to his proposal and in 1891 she entered the novitiate at St. Joseph's Academy in St. Paul.

Thus it was that on August 15, 1891, when she was eighteen, Anna McHugh received the habit of the Sisters of St. Joseph and the name Sister Antonia. Thereafter, at every reception ceremony for many years, her clear high soprano sang, "Go Ye Forth, O Sion's Daughters," as the candidates, dressed in bridal gowns and veils, entered the chapel. Many sisters can still remember the bell-like tones in which the words enveloped them on their own day:

> "Not on Thabor's heights so holy,
> Where we taste such sweets today,
> But on Calvary's mountain lowly . . ."

During her novitiate, Sister Antonia helped Sister Dominica with the first and second grades at St. Joseph's school, next door to the church where she had made her first communion in 1885. As soon as she was professed in 1893, she taught the third and fourth grades at St. Joseph's Academy and she progressed with her class from year to year until they and she had reached high school. Sister St. Rose was still the directress at the academy when Sister Antonia began to teach there, and it was to her that the young teacher complained on her first day that she had taught everything she knew and that she had nothing for the next day. That must have been the last time she experienced that difficulty, for, as far back as anyone can remember, she fairly spouted material and never had finished when the class hour was over.

A summer school for the sisters with teachers from outside was organized at St. Joseph's Academy in 1891 and night classes and Saturday courses were regular thereafter. Sister Antonia and other teachers went to the state university during the summers. She took biology and botany at Minnesota and various subjects from teachers who came from the St. Paul Seminary, such as Shakespeare, Emerson, Browning, and Tennyson from Father William Sheran, and ethics from Father Joseph Campbell.

Archbishop Ireland had early talked of the necessity of training sisters to become professors in the new women's college that was being planned. One group within the community, however, thought that the sisters would be tempted to pride if they held academic degrees. They considered that it was sufficient preparation to pursue the courses, without being presented for graduation honors. Sister Hyacinth Werden, who had been principal in the Stillwater compromise school, and who was to spend two years making an exhaustive survey of the organization and practical working of the St. Anna Stift, the Catholic Sisters' College of Munster in Westphalia, adhered to this view. To Sister Antonia's mind this was worse than nonsense — she was sure that those who had this notion were too fearful of failure to make the effort to achieve standards.

Archbishop Ireland's well-known ideas about the desirability of state certification for every religious teacher settled the audible opinions. It is said that he selected the first group to be sent to the University of Chicago for training. They were Sister Antonia, Sister Mary Joseph Kelly, Sister Margaret Kerby, and Sister Clara Graham, who sought degrees respectively in history, science, Latin, and English literature.

Sister Antonia would have preferred to go to Harvard or to some other school in the East, but she felt later on that the teachers she met in Chicago more than made up for the disappointment, since several of them became active protagonists in furthering her projects for expanding and developing St. Catherine's, once the college got under way. The sisters went to Chicago every summer for twelve weeks and took as many courses as they were allowed to register for. During the year at home in the convent they worked at correspondence courses from the University of Chicago in order to progress more rapidly. When Derham Hall finally got under way, they remained in Chicago throughout the year. Sister Antonia received a bachelor of philosophy degree at the end of the fall quarter in 1908; a bachelor of education in June of the following year. In 1909 she received her master of arts degree, writing a thesis on "Franklin's Mission to France."

A fairly complete collection of her notebooks, term papers, and examinations makes it possible to reconstruct her program at Chicago. This material has unusual interest for the striking resemblance it bears to the content of the courses Sister Antonia taught at the college. Here, for instance, in her own hand are her records of the lectures of Richard G. Moulton in the literary criticism of the Bible, which were known to hundreds of students of "Bible" or what the catalogue called "Hebrew History." There was a series on

history in general and the Greek classics in particular. No
one ever got through one of Sister Antonia's classes without
acquiring some ideas about the geographic backgrounds of
history — her notes indicate that she must have taken everything offered in geography.

The sisters lived at the Home for the Friendless on Chicago's South Side while they were attending the university.
This was a cradle-to-grave charitable institution in charge of
the Sisters of St. Joseph from the St. Louis province. Thus,
there were orphans who could be taught in Sister Antonia's
supervised practice work. When the restrictions against
practice teaching in public schools by those wearing religious
garb bore down on the Sisters of St. Joseph in Minnesota in
the 1920s, she recalled the kindness of the Chicago examiners of practice teaching in going the long distance to
35th Street to observe her technique. Her Winnipeg training
stood her in good stead when she took an examination in
French one summer and was given credit for four years of
work.

Dr. George E. Vincent, who was later president of the
University of Minnesota and head of the Rockefeller Founda-
tion, was dean of the faculties at Chicago while Sister
Antonia was a student there and she knew him well. Dr.
James Angell, who was later to be on the Rockefeller
Board and the Carnegie Foundation, was Sister Antonia's
teacher of psychology in Chicago for two years. Dr. Trevor
Arnett, who later went to Ann Arbor, was the treasurer at
Chicago. Dr. William Rainey Harper, Chicago's president,
was an admirer of Archbishop Ireland. There was a lasting
mutual esteem between Sister Antonia and all these educators upon whom she counted in the pursuit of her educational plans.

What the archbishop and Mother Seraphine thought of
this sister or that appears to have been a matter of as much
moment as at an earlier day it had been to know what the
Vatican thought of Archbishop Ireland. In later days, Sister

Antonia would say quite frankly, "The archbishop liked me. I would talk to him. He knew I wasn't afraid of him."

In the spring of 1909, just after Mother Seraphine's return from Europe, Sister Antonia wrote from Chicago to a former student who was then a sister in Graceville, "Let me tell you our great pleasure — Mother Seraphine and Mother Bernardine walked in to see us on Saturday. Oh! I was so glad I almost clapped my hands with glee. We had them all to ourselves for two whole days. They left this morning and in spite of all, the happiness is now but a memory. Mother told us most interesting things about her travels."

Sister Marie Teresa Mackey, one of the three artists who were then copying in European galleries, wrote to her sister, Sister St. Rose, about Mother Seraphine's visit in Europe saying that she would like to write to Mother Seraphine, but she did not know whether she was the same at home as in Italy, where Sister Marie Teresa "never saw anything like how kind she was." And she went on, "She has gotten it into her head somehow that I tell the Archbishop things. I think I would have to be a little more sure of my footing, before I would say anything to him. He has given me many a chance to say things if I wished."

The "things" related to the artists' desire to take more lessons and do less copying and apparently they must have been said at some point, for later on, Sister Marie Teresa wrote, "Mother told you no doubt that we were to stay two years and take lessons. But I can assure you if Mother Celestine has her way we will do neither. What her object is in trying to prevent our having lessons, I do not know. I hope the Archbishop will keep up the song; if he does not it will certainly fall through." Mother Celestine was still evidently more interested in profit-making artistic enterprises for the sisters from St. Agatha's than in giving them training for creative work.

Going outside the convent for higher education was a distinct departure from custom. Yet each of the sisters thus developed a stronger individuality and an assurance about the proper way to conduct activities in her field. Sister Antonia was regarded as aggressive and domineering, but she differed from her companions in degree rather than in kind. Nono of them contemplated any departure from either the letter or the spirit of their religious profession. They felt that they were merely carrying out the prescriptions of the Third Plenary Council of Baltimore which insisted that Catholic schools should be at least as good as public schools of similar grade. These pronouncements and the ideas of Pope Leo XIII on the subject they had heard many times from Archbishop Ireland. While superiors made no effort to prohibit these changes, neither did they present a clearly implemented program and the result was that each sister developed according to circumstances and her own initiative.

Derham Hall was not completed until January 1905. From September 1904 until January 1905 two schools were housed at St. Joseph's Academy. Sister Eugenia was in charge of the day school, Sister Hyacinth of the boarding school. (St. Joseph's Academy now became a day school only; the new academy to prepare students for the college was a boarding school.) As soon as Derham Hall was completed, Sister Hyacinth and seventy students moved into the new building, and St. Catherine's was officially opened. At this period, however, St. Catherine's was really a small high school with an additional handful of young ladies of uncertain age who were grouped together as "specials." The college was still some years in the future.

Archbishop Ireland, as always, was looking to the future. He selected St. Catherine of Alexandria, celebrated in Christian antiquity, as the patron saint of the college. He spoke often of the ancient cult which had fired artists and writers so that the wheel upon which Catherine was tortured and the palm which betokened her martyrdom had been known for centuries as symbols of learning and holiness. In later years the name *St. Catherine's* would be reserved for the college, and the high school would take the name of the first building, Derham Hall, but at this time *St. Catherine's* was applied to the high school as the nucleus for the college to come.

Sister Wilfrida Hogan lived at St. Catherine's in 1907 and she has said that although the first general retreat was not held there until 1915, the opening meant a great deal to the sisters. "We always loved St. Catherine's. We loved it before it was. There is something fascinating in nature's own bowers before man civilizes them with square and compass. We long for the primeval forest because the landscape gardener has given us too many mathematical lines. Who can improve on 'God's Temples,' with their infinite variety of color and form? They are far beyond the touch of human hand. During my stay at St. Catherine's in 1907 for about eight months, I lived all my free time in the woods — a morning walk up and down the 'Old Government Road' which runs diagonally through the grounds, a noon rest under the trees on 'Rose Hill,' and in the afternoon I penetrated into the depths of my favorite grove, 'where silence made music of dream and shade'."

In this early period St. Catherine's was indeed extremely remote and cloistered. The tract upon which Derham Hall was perched was separated from streetcars by miles of unrelieved mud. Scattered farmhouses were all but invisible in the distance. Deep oak woods and dense thickets of hazel bushes would have prevented any exposure to passing traffic, had there been any.

Added to this nearly total separation from society was the rigid code of boarding school regulations. There was not an unsupervised breath drawn in the course of the day. A few minutes after breakfast a bell summoned everyone to the study hall. Five minutes later bedroom doors were locked by a prefect and no student could return to her room until it was opened for her at night. Thursday was the free day instead of Saturday, because if one had to go to the dentist or to some other permissible destination, with a chaperone of course, there was less danger on Thursday of meeting an adolescent of either sex on the street. Permission to go out with your well-certified brother — say to Thanksgiving dinner in a hotel — was rarely given, for "How would people know he is your brother?" The large roster of masculine cousins who attended the neighboring St. Thomas College was regarded with horror and nothing so unseemly ever occurred as permitting a St. Catherine's student to go out with one of them.

There was harmless fiction in the library that might be withdrawn on Sunday afternoon and returned Sunday evening. The books were shelved in sectional bookcases — always locked except at the moment of withdrawal — in a room which under later crowded conditions was considered commodious enough for only two offices. Ladylike walks were encouraged as far as "the stone," a rough glacial specimen placed discreetly back from Cleveland Avenue, where occasionally a sleepy horse was driven past. As Sister Wilfrida remembered, the woods were remarkably lovely and relatively free of access, with an amazing variety of wild flowers. These were better known than might have been expected, because of the necessity of making herbariums for botany class with twenty-five identified flora.

There might have been an inclination to vegetate in this enclosure, but Sister Antonia blew all that kind of complacency out the window. She was just one of the teachers, not an official, for the first ten years after Derham Hall opened, but no girl ever took her lightly. "Energize yourself" she would pronounce and they moved. There is an endless calendar of her oft-repeated dicta. Gathered up, they sound like Benjamin Franklin's smug maxims, but her audience was not discriminating — dared not be. Consider the fate of a young lady who cited a reference as "the green Russia book."

Or the many who heard that their recitations were "perfectly true, perfectly general, and per-fect-ly mean-ing-less." Then there were those who were "as clear as mud" and those who "acted like ostriches." Long recitations were often "windy."

Things outside of class deserved attention too. "I don't see how people live who can't read. It's terrible to have a stagnant mind. . . . Things for sale are in windows. . . . Only horses were meant to hang their heads. . . . Self-pity is a destructive force. . . . Fill your minds with great things and there will be no room for trivialities. . . . She who would be a woman must avoid mediocrity."

Room 12 was Sister Antonia's history classroom and the place whence apples and advice were dealt out with an impartial hand to the starved and the maladjusted. This was a pre-mental-hygiene era, but "12" was the locale of a clinic where the girls found out what was the matter with them — generally without wanting to know. There were also in that room pleasant half-hours of talk for the taking — about books and stars and music and pictures. There was breadth of view and inspiration inside that door, enough to last for years and years. It was always the hub of the universe to the students, even though not officially so designated. The seriousness of the client's condition could be gauged by the fact that the door of Room 12 was open or closed. This fact might be ascertained from the top of the stairs with the aid of the glass on the fire extinguisher opposite, and the victim's friends would know whether the matter under consideration was a subject for prayer or penance.

The room itself radiated personality. In the center there was a great polished space marked off by the circle of classroom chairs through which no one ever walked. More interesting were the huge and thriving ferns on tall stands, ivy carried home from Mount Vernon, *passe-partout* pictures of the Dying Gaul, the Reading from Homer, Achilles, the Mona Lisa (this was a colored print in the center front), below it Van Dyke's "Footpath to Peace" in water colors.

That Mona Lisa — students often saw the same nonspecific smile on the placid face in the plain brown rocker below it. There was a tall case filled with filing boxes for thousands of mounted pictures which were a never-failing source of wonder — they were almost as explicit as the history teacher. Maps small and large sharpened up the poor student for the brisk examinations on the wide world's face.

Sister Antonia did not go to Europe until 1922 and again only in 1932, but she had conducted her students back and forth through every cathedral and castle and up and down every mountain and river long before. They wondered what Europe had to teach her, for they felt that the old Greeks and Romans would rise from their tombs to greet her as a friend. The intricacies of symphonic music fascinated her and she talked so often about the individual instruments and their combination and about various effects they achieved that students absorbed some appreciation in spite of themselves.

Perhaps of sheer necessity, the boarding-school regulations became almost imperceptibly less severe as each year passed. Two bona fide college girls left after three weeks in the fall of 1909. They "just couldn't stand" the restrictions and the "old maids" who were called "college girls." That departure may have had something to do with liberalizing policies.

In 1911, the first sister to have earned a bachelor's degree before she entered the community came to teach at St. Catherine's. She was Sister Ste Hélène Guthrie, Sister Antonia's favorite student at St. Joseph's Academy, where she had come from Blooming Prairie as a boarder for the sixth grade through high school. She attended the University of Minnesota for four years and then taught two years in public high schools — the time required to secure a life certificate — before entering the novitiate. Sister Ste Hélène had a winning personality and a gift for teaching English thoroughly and well. She had the students' confidence as well as their devotion and she represented an entirely new point of view.

Sister Antonia and she remained intimate friends and for twenty-five years they controlled the whole policy of the college. When Sister Antonia's ideas were extravagantly visionary, Sister Ste Hélène sat down and worked out the details. When Sister Ste Hélène was thought to be too young and frivolous to have any ideas, Sister Antonia listened to her and put the plan through as her own.

In the beginning the recruitment of students was of paramount importance. Before one criticizes too severely the charm method, the needs of the moment must be remembered. Sister Antonia's relations with the students were a great deal like the catalogue's description of the food — good, wholesome, and abundant. She was vocal about sentimentality and emotionalism. Yet her favorite student from 1910 to 1912, just before she became dean, stands in her class record book all the way through as "Ruthie." She treated her like that too. Sister Ste Hélène had favorites, but she escaped some censure because there were so many of them.

There were other influences on the students, of course, good, bad, and indifferent. They told in the lives of the students, but there was never any doubt about Sister Antonia's being the dominant force.

In the summer of 1911 Sister Antonia got permission to go to Omaha to canvass for students. There she met a high school senior, a non-Catholic girl home from Oberlin, who became interested in St. Catherine's. The girl wrote to the University of Minnesota to inquire about the college. The registrar wrote back that he "had never heard of it." Sister Antonia dashed over to see Dr. Vincent, who by that time had become president of the university, to say, "Your Mr. Pierce has made all this trouble for us." Mr. Pierce was "called on the carpet," as Sister Antonia told it. It seems that he had never thought of St. Catherine's as anything but a high school, but thereafter he remembered that it was a college.

Mr. Pierce may be excused for not having given St. Catherine's its proper status, for despite Sister Antonia's protestations, the college was still largely a product of her fertile imagination. True, two students entered their junior year in college work in 1911, and that is the year assigned in official listings as the opening of the college. The two young women graduated in 1913, the first alumnae. But Sister Antonia could hardly count them, because as she was wont to say she had "started the college without leave or license from anyone." She just opened it.

In 1914 Archbishop Ireland insisted that she be made dean of the college, and thus she became the first distinct college official in the history of the school. This, of course, was an entirely extralegal prerogative the archbishop exercised, but Mother Seraphine followed his advice on this, as on other matters.

Whatever the legal niceties of the situation, Sister Antonia when she became dean did her best to make St. Catherine's a college in substance as well as in name. Six graduates from St. Mary's Academy in Graceville and a few more from Derham Hall high school were the nucleus. This group was augmented by sending some of the sisters into college classes, especially from the novitiate which had been moved from St. Joseph's Academy into a separate building on Randolph Street in 1913. Some students who had no funds were given complete educations free. Some came because they got what they wanted. Sister Ste Florine was an attraction in the French department, although in high school her flourishes in etiquette of the extreme French type were wearing. She had been instrumental, for example, in adoption of the rule that students retire from classes by pirouetting out the door backward, at the same time bowing gracefully to the teacher.

The general lack of recognition of St. Catherine's as a college still hampered Sister Antonia's plans, however. The Oberlin student had transferred to St. Catherine's, had finished high school in 1912, and had returned for one year of college. But, although there were students from states bordering on Minnesota at St. Catherine's, she was for some years the only one from a state as far away as Nebraska. It was even very difficult to hold the Derham Hall graduates or to interest the girls from St. Joseph's Academy or St. Margaret's Academy in Minneapolis. They went to the university.

As early as 1913 Sister Antonia had begun insisting that it was necessary to have recognition in the North Central Association of Colleges and Secondary Schools. The association's legislation was so worded that it was difficult for Catholic institutions to conform. With a little help from the archbishop, she persuaded the superiors to let her try for accreditation. After the first meeting that she attended, she and the heads of other Catholic colleges got together to plan what could be done. The first great obstacle was the required endowment. It was Sister Antonia who proposed that they impress upon the association the fact that the lives of the sisters, who gave their services without remuneration in Catholic colleges, represented an equivalent to the necessary endowment. She was chosen spokesman for the group and with the aid of an old friend and teacher from Chicago University, Professor Charles H. Judd, her point carried. St. Catherine's became a member of the North Central Association in 1916 and the way was thus opened for all Catholic colleges to become members.

Derham Hall had housed the whole high school and college until the first building exclusively for the college was built in 1914. This was the present Whitby Hall, known for a few years as "the other building" and then as "College Hall." It was to hold the music and science departments, in addition to an auditorium and a residence for students and it was built and paid for by the sisters at a cost of about $300,000. Since the superior, Mother Frances Clare, fell on the ice and broke her leg while the building was going up, the supervision devolved upon Sister Antonia. She kept on teaching medieval and modern history but more and more her lectures became a species of broadcasting. She had a clerk take the roll and correct papers but she was often called away to the telephone or a conference in the middle of the period and the substitute was ineffectual.

With factory-like speed sisters were hurried through college and shipped away for graduate work. College and high school graduates began to enter the novitiate. The instant they were released from the religious training required by Canon Law, Sister Antonia insisted on taking them over. Teachers' meetings and the dean's assembly talks to students followed the same notes and were nearly indistinguishable. There was one on student government which began vigorously, "No such thing!"

The older trained members of the faculty were not easily swept into the whirlpool, but the young sisters grasped the intellectual challenge and pleasure which foot-loose travel and study, the necessary concomitants of Sister Antonia's ideas in education, brought them. Not a few scars must be attributed to the reckless distribution of opportunities. The future problems were not apparent to Sister Antonia who regretted aloud that she was thirty-six before she earned her master's degree and forty before she saw New York. She made a rule that her faculty must have doctor's degrees before they were thirty-five and she insisted that seeing New York should be included in the graduate course.

Not a great deal of thought was given to the integration of this rapid education with the obligations of a religious teacher. Archbishop Ireland is supposed to have said at some time, "There is no such thing as Catholic spelling or Catholic geography." When that remark was elevated to a principle and repeated to a young sister who timidly voiced doubts about her course of study, it settled the matter. If she remained unconvinced, she was apt to have a new address by fall. "Such nonsense! Don't be a baby!" routed all scruples before they had a chance to develop.

An admirable account of Sister Antonia's assemblies, written by an alumna fifteen years ago, records that "character

training or the building of a life was almost the unique subject of her Assembly talks, which were for many years one
of the good reasons for coming to St. Catherine's. Wednesday after Wednesday she lashed us into a fairly homoge-
neous student group. She drove at practice, at homely virtues — honesty, cleanliness, industry, dependableness, a nice
consideration for others. Who could ever forget her urging
us to 'chisel' our characters, to accomplish hard things, to be
women of good sense? She taught us that the ideal of sound
and strong Catholic womanhood is big, simple, noble, and
practicable. We knew that the Dean's words, however hard,
were loaded with life and experience, that her spirit had
somehow paid for the wisdom that she was imparting with
pungent energy and splendid courage. . . .

"We felt in her, first of all, an omniscience that was little
short of terrifying. She knew everything about us, every
thought, every idle dream, every latent possibility. She
knew with absolute certainty our every vagary in word and
deed, and for these latter there was sure to be a dreadful
and swift reckoning. It was plain that she would tolerate no
indirectness, superficiality, bad manners, slovenly thinking,
sham or nonsense in any shape or form. We loved this discipline: we had confidence in its source: we felt its chasten-
ing power. . . . For the initiated, there was another manner. She was alert, uncompromising, omniscient still, but
gentle, of queenly amenity, of tireless helpfulness, of keen
vision, showing the most cordial interest in the present and
future of each one of us. She loved us with an affection that
had in it a certain hardness that we liked better than even
the gentleness that was just as surely there. To the same
extent that she terrorized us in the class room and in the
assembly, Sister Antonia won and fascinated us in her ever
memorable individual conferences. . . . She respected us
too much to accept from us a standard lower than the
highest. . . . She has loved us each individually and strong-

ly, who has chastised us a plenty and not without calling us the while an 'unspanked generation'."

Archbishop Ireland made weekly visits to the college whenever he was in St. Paul. By the time Derham Hall was built, he had passed into what was known as his "tranquil old age" and his absences from the city were fewer than in his stormier years. Word flashed around when he came of an evening and the sisters ran to the Derham Hall parlor to greet him. He knew every one of them and always asked each about her particular field. He had been educating priests for St. Thomas College and the St. Paul Seminary for so long that he felt at home with teachers.

No sister was embarrassed to join in the conversation. He always had new things to talk about, for he accepted many invitations to banquets and meetings, and many distinguished people came to visit him to the very end of his life. He held out against women's suffrage for a long time. Indeed, the only time he spoke in favor of it seems to have been in London at the request of Lady Aberdeen. There even his courage may have quailed when speakers were hissed who opposed the ballot for women. His heart was in colleges for women, however, and he had objected strenuously to the move to condemn Trinity College when it was opened near the Catholic University in Washington, D.C.

It was rather in the field of promotion, obviously, than in current educational theory and practice that Archbishop Ireland was skilled, but his influence on individuals and groups was great. If he came to St. Catherine's in the daytime he visited classes and talked to the students. He attended every recital and program and made flattering comments about each. He walked all over the woods talking Minnesota history. All his diplomatic and political experiences he related in an entertaining fashion and he listened to everything the sisters had to tell him. He never came without bringing books and magazines. On more formal oc-

casions he presented rare volumes or precious objects for the
archives. Publicly and privately he encouraged Sister Antonia, and he kept his eyes open to see that she was not
being hampered in her plans.

As early as 1918 Sister Antonia began to ask the General
Education Board of the Rockefeller Foundation for funds.
Normally, the family sense of ownership tends to obscure
the leadership of any one person in a religious group. But
when Sister Antonia went outside the family pocketbook
for funds, the buildings seemed to be hers. To secure an
appropriation, it was necessary to match the amount given
by the foundation in New York with a sum twice as large.
The new archbishop, the Most Reverend Austin Dowling,
who had succeeded John Ireland after the latter's death in
1918, agreed to assign $200,000 of his Archbishop Ireland
Educational Fund to St. Catherine's. The fact that it took
three or four years to complete the drive was a severe check,
which greatly decreased the value of the benefaction in
Sister Antonia's eyes. Dr. Vincent, who had left the University of Minnesota in 1917 to become head of the Rockefeller
Foundation, took a special interest in seeing the matter
through the final channels.

Sister Wilfrida expressed what was perhaps a fairly general opinion among the sisters not stationed at St. Catherine's
when she wrote in January 1921, "Sisters St. Rose and
Antonia were in N.Y. on business — the Endowment Fund.
An expert accountant examined all the books lately — all
these things require method, wise, wily method. The Educational Fund amounted to nearly six million, so C. S. C.
will get its two hundred thousand and no doubt the business
in New York was to get the one hundred thousand from
J. D. R. — It takes all people to make a world, and it takes
all kinds of people to do the different *phases* of work in a
Community."

In June of 1921 Sister Wilfrida went to the commencement at St. Catherine's and thereafter she wrote, "The

Archbishop spoke beautifully at the Exercises. He is very much interested in the work done at St. Catherine's. I noticed a new 'ring' in his voice that day, so different from the first time he visited the College. He is now really as enthusiastic over St. Catherine's as was his predecessor, which means much for us. . . . The map of the grounds for 'A greater St. Catherine's' may be interesting to you. It plans for twenty-five years in the future. We will have received our reward by that time, either in this life or the life to come. . . . This plan of the grounds is according to the new Archbishop's ideals. I remember that last year one sketch of the grounds was drawn up, but did not meet his approval. So they changed it and now this is the final plan. . . . I always wanted something definite and to have them stick to it. They are forever changing — I do not think he will allow much of that. He has some very fine ideas."

The Carnegie Corporation under Dr. Angell gave $25,000 for books in 1926 at the rate of $5000 a year for five years and in 1931, another $15,000. The General Education Board made a second grant of $100,000 for the new science building, Mendel Hall. Since that amount had to be matched with $200,000, Sister Antonia organized the College Board of Trustees for investment and funding operations. The largest endowment — $300,000 from the General Education Board — was used partly for the erection of the Health Center. This building, which contains the swimming pool and the gymnasium as well as teaching and correctional units and facilities for health and nursing education, is now called Fontbonne Hall.

Earlier Sister Antonia had taken great interest in building the chapel. Mary Ellen Chase, who has incorporated things she heard and overheard at St. Catherine's in three of her books — by direct, indirect, and oblique reference — says of the chapel, "When I first knew St. Catherine's in 1921, it consisted of three pleasant buildings on a hill which sloped to the high bluffs above the Mississippi. Sister Antonia

was then planning and praying into being a chapel which
from its porch should command a wide sweep of the western
horizon. This chapel was to be called the Chapel of Our
Lady of Victory, a name which, I thought with no hint of
blasphemy, contained a double significance."

The contractor for the chapel later wrote his memories of
Sister Antonia's supervisory activities. Two events stood
out in his mind — they were the time she persuaded the men
to work on Thanksgiving by giving them their dinner and
the day she sent cigars to the men who worked on Saturday
afternoon. For the first occasion the contractor's comment
was, "The men got a wonderful dinner, and everybody was
happy." For the Saturday, he wrote, "Sister Antonia was
so pleased about this work being done that she gave a box
of cigars to each of these men because they were willing to
forget an afternoon off and work to please Sister Antonia.
She even called me up at home to thank me because I had
gotten the work done."

This was the production angle, of course, and who could
be so perspicacious as to mention the social encyclicals or
the rights of labor? Rather read on in the contractor's testimonial, "I was much pleased with doing this chapel for
many reasons. First it was a place to worship God. It was a
beautiful chapel and I believe I had satisfied Sister Antonia's
wish which I was told could not be done. Sister Antonia was
a woman who knew what she wanted and she was pleased
when she got a real job. It is now over twenty years since we
left this job, and seeing the shape the building is in to-day I
believe anyone will admit that Sister Antonia's dream came
through."

There were other problems than building which absorbed
Sister Antonia and perhaps tended to give a bit of plausi-
bility to the Lady Abbess picture Mary Ellen Chase and
others drew of her. One such problem was the organization
of training for teachers in the parochial grade schools. The
regular curriculum leading to the bachelor's degree was

conceded to be adequate training for teaching only at the high school level. After the establishment of the novitiate in the new building on Randolph Street, adjoining the college campus, it had been expected that St. Catherine's could be used as a training center for the young parochial school teachers living there. And during the early years St. Catherine's faculty members with elementary-level qualifications did teach professional courses in the novitiate. Sister Antonia, for example, taught geography.

This kind of training did not satisfy Sister Antonia. She was as eager as John Ireland to have Catholic elementary schools recognized as the equal of public schools. That meant providing the sisters who taught in them with as much training as public school teachers. Although parochial school teachers were not required by law to have state certificates, Sister Antonia believed that the sisters should have them anyhow. The certificates would indicate to the public that the staffs of parochial schools were as well qualified as those of public schools. In addition, if the teachers had certificates, parochial school pupils would have no difficulty entering public high schools.

The initial step toward getting certificates for all the sisters teaching in elementary schools who did not have them was to bring them to St. Catherine's in the summer to take examinations in the elementary branches under the immediate supervision of the state superintendent of education. At that time examination was an acceptable method of securing first-grade and second-grade certificates. This was not a generally satisfactory plan, although it continued for five or six years. Some of the sisters had taken advanced standing examinations and had far more college credits than required for graduation from a normal school, but their credits in education were not acceptable at the elementary level. And St. Catherine's faculty simply was not prepared to offer an adequate number of the type of courses the elementary-level teachers needed. The community recog-

nized that, although differential calculus and quantitative
analysis could be offered economically to the sisters, they did
not compare with methods in reading and arithmetic. Chau-
cer and Tacitus were also available and likewise unsuitable.

Sister Antonia saw that the only thing to do was to send
the sisters to a normal school. Accordingly, in the summer of
1921, a group of one hundred were settled in a building
rented from Concordia College near Moorhead Teachers'
College. They were welcome at the normal college because
they worked hard and generally earned good grades, but
they were unable to graduate because one requirement was
a two-hour course in supervised teaching. Since the model
school was a public institution and the sisters were in
religious garb, they could not teach there. In addition, they
were denied the privilege of teaching under observation in a
parochial school. Opinions of the state attorney general for
1904, 1915, 1922, and 1923, held to the principle of the
state constitution that no religious garb could be worn in
the public schools. Practice teaching was deemed to be
the same as any other, and the same negative ruling applied even when the county attorney at Alexandria wrote
the attorney general that he couldn't see that the nun's garb
wasn't a neater dress than the flapper's.

Since North Dakota had no antigarb law covering practice
teaching in the 1920s, a number of the sisters transferred
to Valley City Teachers' College in North Dakota for graduation. In any case, practice teaching was not an absolute
requirement in North Dakota, since another course might
be substituted. The sisters who were teaching in Grand
Forks and Jamestown were given an opportunity to attend
the normal school throughout the year until they were
properly certified; lay teachers were hired by the Sisters of
St. Joseph to replace them while they were going to school.

Because of the expense involved in sending the sisters to
Valley City, however, the only general remedy was for most
of them to continue at Moorhead for several summers until

they had adequate methods courses and then to complete work for their bachelor's degree at St. Catherine's. The sisters who could not be spared from their teaching to take courses at the college during the academic year attended the regular summer school at St. Catherine's, hoping to achieve degrees with majors in education before death overtook them. Since the State Department of Education recognized degrees from St. Catherine's, the sisters were thus able to obtain certificates, even though they had not been able to graduate from a teachers' college.

Sister Antonia moved ahead as rapidly as possible to educate members of St. Catherine's faculty to give a two-year nursery school and kindergarten-training course at the college. Although the normal schools were jealous of their rights and objected to the expansion of St. Catherine's curriculum to include elementary education, the State Department of Education and the North Central Association recognized this department in 1931. Part of the sisters' difficulties were thus solved, since practice teaching by the sisters enrolled in this department could be done under college supervision in the parochial schools. Certificates were likewise granted to teachers completing this course.

Each year more sisters entered the community with previous normal school training, and the problem of giving them adequate training was lessened. In the meantime, Sister Antonia somewhat reluctantly relinquished part of the burden of preparing sisters for teaching to the Diocesan Teachers' College, established in the old James J. Hill home in St. Paul. Here there were normal classes in the summer and on Saturdays at first and after a few years on a full-time basis, with accreditation from the University of Minnesota. In 1951 the Diocesan Teachers' College was incorporated into the education department of St. Catherine's.

In 1938, after the matter was settled without protest to the state, the Department of Education reversed itself, by declaring that since the compulsory attendance law presupposed qualified teachers, parochial school teachers must be permitted to satisfy the requirements of normal schools. The decision was brought about, not by the Sisters of St. Joseph, but by the Benedictine Sisters of Duluth, a teachers' college city. The new arrangement allowed practice teaching to be done in a private or parochial school and to be supervised by a public school teacher. Credits from an accredited Catholic college are now also accepted by a public college in Minnesota as teacher preparation, due care being exercised at all times not to brush the public with the garb.

These activities brought Sister Antonia into frequent contact with the hundreds of sisters who taught in the parochial schools. The majority of the St. Catherine College students prepared for high school teaching and when shortages occurred in the sisters' academies, they were employed there. Therefore, Sister Antonia was also known as the last word on high school teaching; and she did everything in her power to raise the standards of teaching in Catholic high schools, insisting on proper preparation of the teachers in order to ensure accreditation by the North Central Association.

Sister Antonia stood for all liberalizing and progressive policies and she liked being appealed to for unusual opportunities and the relaxations of religious restrictions. Although religious superiorship would seem to have been essential to Sister Antonia's program, she never held any office higher than that of local superior at St. Catherine's from 1931–1937. She was elected by popular vote a delegate to the St. Louis General Chapter of her community in 1936 and she is credited with securing permission for sisters from Ireland to visit their homes and with implementing the change to celluloid from linen guimpes, which were a laundry problem. At home she provided moving pictures and other recreational features for all the sisters.

Upon Sister Antonia's being named president of the college in 1929, Sister Ste Hélène became the dean and the two remained in these positions until 1937.

Archbishop Dowling never had the great personal interest in St. Catherine's that Archbishop Ireland had had, but he supported the college program and he encouraged the students in every way possible. And he had a very real appreciation of the contribution of the Sisters of St. Joseph to the college.

Once, when he brought the papal delegate Archbishop Pietro Fumasoni-Biondi to St. Catherine's, he said to him, "You have visited eighty or more dioceses in the country and by this time you are used to the modesty with which we describe ourselves. . . . We know that you have visited many excellent colleges. . . . The interesting thing here is that this college has grown to be what it is solely through the services and devotion of the Sisters of St. Joseph. You have met twice in two days Mother Seraphine, the foundation stone of St. Catherine's, and if one should inspect her heart I believe the college name would be found engraved upon it. St. Catherine's was her ambition, although when she first dreamed of it, the dream seemed impossible of fulfillment. Yet these buildings have grown up, where years ago was but a wilderness and empty fields. All of this has been done without any very great gift to the college, except what came from the diocese, in the entire history of the institution. Therefore I ask you to think of St. Catherine's as a symbol of the devotion and zeal of these consecrated women."

In his commencement addresses, the archbishop considered current problems. He urged that Catholic women must be an active and intelligent force, not only in the home, but in public. "The world," he said, "looking on from the outside, is not in sympathy with Catholic education. It considers Catholic institutions as mere places for teaching religion. Have they forgotten that the science of God is knowledge? Is man as a moral and social being bettered because of his mathematics, his natural science? Is it not rather because there has been holiness in his heart and because of his realization of the great and all-wise Power?"

He told the graduates of 1930 that we think of the Catholic church as eminently successful, because we have a physical equipment which is full of promise. But so far, he said, we have made very little impression on the country. To do that we need to know the world's mind, to think its thoughts, and to know what is in the hearts of the people. "Ours is a world of conflicts," he said; "a phenomenon like the world war was possible because civilization then was built around wealth. We say that such a thing must not happen again. The minds of men must be changed for the business of life in this world and I think that you and others like you . . . have bright possibilities for doing much in the world."

Dr. Melvin E. Haggerty, dean of the College of Education at Minnesota, in a monograph published in 1937, evaluated the St. Catherine College faculty for the North Central Association. "The faculty here described," he wrote, "is that of a four-year college for women with the usual liberal arts curriculum and with special curricula in library work, in nursery-school and kindergarten training, in music, and in physical education. The faculty is composed of fifty-one persons engaged in teaching and in the administration of the educational program. The enrollment is about 450 in the regular academic year, giving an approximate faculty-student ratio of 1 to 9."

Interestingly enough, Dr. Haggerty emphasized the youth of the faculty. "The median staff member is young, as compared with corresponding groups in other institutions. The fact that this faculty is, on the average, four years younger than liberal arts faculties in general and that the full professors are six years younger than those of corresponding rank in similar colleges has important bearings upon the prophetic future of the college. The resultant energy and alertness should be given consideration in judging the present competence of the faculty as a factor in the growth of the institution. During the past five years fourteen individuals, about 25 per cent of the total group, have engaged in graduate study and travel in this and foreign countries. The institution has itself arranged and paid for such study and travel for ten individuals that were already members of the staff. Others have been newly added to the staff after such preparation."

Sister Antonia was cited as an individual case. "The president of the college was until 1922 a professor of history. She holds the Bachelor's and Master's degrees from the University of Chicago, has studied at Harvard University, has travelled extensively in Europe, belongs to three national learned societies, and has within the past five years attended the meetings of eight such organizations. Full time is now given to administrative duties. . . . The president of the institution appears to be in active charge of the educational program. Under her direction the entire plant, consisting of seven modern college buildings, has been built up, and the college enrollment has grown from nothing to about 450. Considerably more than half the faculty have during the past three years conferred with her concerning educational matters, and apparently she makes most of the decisions concerning instructional needs and the monetary support of research.

"Aside from her responsibilities in monetary matters, the dean of the college [Sister Ste Hélène] is active in directing the educational activities of virtually all members of the staff. . . . [She] is a professor of English, holds the Bachelor's and Master's degrees from the University of Minnesota, has studied at the University of Chicago, has spent a full year in study at Oxford, and has travelled throughout most of the United States and extensively in Europe, with excursions into Asia and Africa. Experience covers teaching in public and private high schools and in college. This person holds membership in two learned societies and has attended meetings of six such societies within the five-year period."

These accomplishments, be it stated, were relatively meager as compared with the study and travel experiences of sister after sister on the faculty, who, as Dr. Haggerty pointed out, tended to be about thirty-five years of age. But that was not the half of it. The college buildings and grounds were developing a manner and an air, under the minute direction of Sister Antonia. There was the gate, for example, and the wrought-iron fence enclosing the huge campus. Lincoln's rail splitting was no match for its toll. There is still in the thinning woods a shrill echo of staccato tones that gave orders for smooth green slopes, a graceful mall, trim maples, sweeping willows, a marble statue of Christ highlighted by the sun, the lagoon placidly mirroring the saints' figures on the chapel's façade. The grass almost had to be planted blade by blade to keep the hillside from washing down into the Mississippi.

Once the grass was stationary, Sister Antonia moved into flowers — miles of them. Walks were bordered — not just with peonies, but with seasonal flowers from tulips to asters. A reporter who interviewed Sister Antonia during the year before she died wrote a self-conscious account of how starved she had been for beauty as a child on the Dakota prairies and how, because lilies had represented the most unattainable flowers to her then, she would now plant every species of them.

Whatever the truth of that, there were tulips first — in staggering quantity — then peonies, petunias, dahlias, snapdragons, asters. Small gardens here and there featured more exotic and delicate blossoms. Inside it was the same. Arundel prints, Piranesis by the dozen, steel engravings, etchings, and then antiques, paisley curtains, rugs, first editions, autographs.

Naturally, eating with elegance had a slightly different

twist from Sister Ste Florine's lessons in table etiquette. There was more attention to what to do with the silver and what about the service plate. The food had some new qualities added to the old catalogue description — good, wholesome, and abundant.

Pipe organs with varying numbers of manuals appeared. A three-manual Reuter with carillon attachments estheticized chapel attendance. Marcel Dupré and Pietro Yon played concerts in the chapel. Sister Antonia gloried in the organ's mellow tones and she liked to have it played all through Mass, by itself if hymns were not being sung. During May, she had the round-like Lourdes procession hymn sung in its entirety every morning at Mass. There was Benediction in the evening after supper, a hymn, and night prayers for the girls in the soft glow of amber lights.

The library is a perpetual miracle to anyone who trailed along on one of the recklessly prodigal buying tours, shuddering at the quick succession of "I'll take this," and "Send me a dozen of these," or "Please order it for me." The "basic sciences" and "modern languages" came in for their share of largess. Mental tests and direct-method Latin swept in. There was never the same sense of security about a faculty member who was just too old to have been run through a battery of tests. If you knew a person's I.Q., you knew what you had.

The standard of living rose. When the college opened, Eric, a man with a wooden leg, drove Dolly and the carriage with the fringe around the top for the priest every morning. That was the sole transportation facility for some years. Later, a more imposing sense of the fitness of things added a large Pierce Arrow car.

There is a corporateness about a religious order which defies every extravagance of individualism. The body is quiet, denies or affirms nothing, feels secure. No sister can "go it alone." None does. Any achievement is accomplished solely through the combined spiritual and intellectual effort of the group, working under the prescribed discipline they have promised to observe daily throughout life. The long, unspectacular battle which the faculty at St. Catherine's and the thousand-odd Sisters of St. Joseph throughout the province have fought with themselves to preserve the letter and the spirit of their rule makes Sister Antonia's accomplishments the heritage of each.

She mastered difficulties in the same spirit as the pioneers in the old log chapel on Bench Street, and her contribution flows in the same stream, despite their obvious differences. If her acquisition of an honorary doctorate from the University of Minnesota, of the papal medal Pro Ecclesia et Pontifice from the Holy Father, of a chapter of the conservative Phi Beta Kappa Society for the college, would have been unattainable and possibly undesirable ends to the earlier sisters, so the primitive inefficiency would have disturbed her. She was charitable as a whole convent at times, lavishly giving away educations — some of them to young women who might not otherwise have had an opportunity to develop a religious vocation — but there was still some shortening in her view of universal brotherhood. The invincible power of the individual was the cornerstone of her structure. Individual liberty was the cry of the age — in religion as in business. Mother Seraphine kept a better balance, because she clung more passionately to the exercises of the common life and thought. But success to her too had a tinge of individualism. For example, she never spoke of missions which had failed — they simply did not exist. And when she was old, she boasted shamelessly of the brick and mortar accomplishments of the community.

Neither Mother Seraphine nor Sister Antonia was influenced by the burgeoning of social Catholicism toward the end of their days, especially after World War I. Least of all did Sister Antonia realize that her ideal of equaling Vassar or Wellesley was not enough for her college, that a newspaper description of the college as a "big time school" was not very high praise, because it failed to take into account the central purpose of any Catholic college, to make better Christians as well as to impart intellectual training. Sister Antonia, like many others of her generation, did not think of class and race prejudice as failures in charity. A multitude of affairs had taken her away from free and uninterrupted contemplation of the more simple truths.

The president of the College of St. Teresa in Winona, who was a lay woman with a doctor's degree from Cornell, made it rather difficult for Sister Antonia to remember that our Father's house has many mansions. But St. John's University at Collegeville, Minnesota, perhaps came in for the least favor; the principal thorn was its complete indifference to the emoluments of accreditation by the North Central Association. This was sheer suicide, she predicted, but somehow St. John's held on as successfully as the other colleges in the same fields and in addition its officers worked out with President Hutchins and Mortimer Adler of the University of Chicago a program integrating philosophy and theology which vitalized their own purposes.

The Liturgical Movement centered at St. John's, which aimed to diffuse social charity and understanding through increased lay participation in the official worship of the church, was something with which Sister Antonia would have nothing to do. "Why, I have been in all the churches in Rome," she would say, "and I never heard a Missa Recitata. What is good enough for the pope is good enough for me." The Psalms were beautiful poetry and she taught them vigorously, but the thought of connecting the Psalms with the Divine Office for socially activated prayer was too irritating to be considered. To her mind this whole commotion was doubtless of German origin, reminiscent of Cahenslyism. She accorded little consideration to the Gregorian chant, whatever Pius X had to say. Polyphony was prettier and better suited to women's voices.

But no amount of misconception could hold back the flood

of social charity in any case. A young student at St. Catherine's was writing even during Sister Antonia's presidency
of "how an effective faith in the Mystical Body of Christ
could solve the present problems of society; of how social
Catholicism, generally practiced, could overcome such evils
as war, class hatred, unequal distribution of wealth, inter-
racial prejudice, the totalitarian state. . . . Increasingly as
we found ourselves in the divine life, we also discovered the
Negroes — as other Christs, as more than brothers. . . .

"Late in the afternoon," she wrote of a Liturgical Day, of
a few St. Catherine's students, "we finished our discussions
and gathered in a semicircle to say Compline together. Our
room was a west room and the college is situated on high
land, overlooking miles of gorgeous country. The great thing
as we prayed was that in the infinite bounty of God our
prayer was most pleasing to Him, for it was the prayer of
Christ and of the Mystical Body which we were offering. It
was but a small thing that the Psalms were magnificent
poetry, and that we were looking into the winter sunset."

❧ X ❧

Women Who Know the Poor

ARCHBISHOP JOHN IRELAND lived only long enough to see the College of St. Catherine through its first half-dozen years. But with his extraordinary vision he probably would not have been surprised at the rapid development of the college in the next decades or at its present position among women's colleges in the country. Nineteen young women had received bachelor's degrees from his hands before his death in the fall of 1918 and the college had passed its most important test by gaining membership in the North Central Association in 1916. The program for exchange of students from foreign countries was already under way in spite of the European war. Lay faculty members of distinction had been hired to take the places of young sisters who were studying in various universities and a good college program had been launched.

Both size and quality of enrollment at St. Catherine's have increased rapidly since 1918. Students from all parts of the United States have been attracted by the reputation of the English, Romance language, and science departments. In addition each year an increasing number of day students from the Twin Cities choose St. Catherine's for its high scholastic standards and its emphasis on spiritual training.

Recognitions from educators for physical equipment, for excellence of library, and for well-trained faculty have come swiftly. Friendly relations with officials at the University of Minnesota have been accepted as a matter of course, summarized with a citation to Sister Antonia for "creating at the very doors of this University one of the really important colleges for women in America, with a substantial and beautiful plant that attracts each year nearly a thousand young women."

Sister Antonia was dean of the college from 1914 to 1929, president from 1929 until 1937. For six years before 1937 she was also mother superior of the sisters at the college. From 1937 until her death in October 1944 she lived in retirement at St. Catherine's, virtually an invalid. Sister Eucharista Galvin succeeded as superior and president until 1943; Sister Antonius Kennelly held the offices from 1943 to 1949; Sister Antonine O'Brien is at present holder of both the religious and executive positions.

Varied backgrounds have tended to keep these administrators alert to the Catholic ideals, scholarship standards, health program, and professional training which Sister Antonia vigorously advocated for twenty years. Sister Eucharista holds a doctor of philosophy degree from the University of Chicago with a major in American history, Sister Antonius spent four years in graduate study at the University of Munich to earn her doctorate in chemistry, while Sister Antonine prepared for an Oxford master of arts with two years of study in England.

The archbishop's death in September 1918 left Mother Seraphine the last living member of the quartet that had led in Catholic affairs in Minnesota for so long. Mother St. John, well known in Minneapolis as an able school directress, had died in December 1897; Mother Celestine, coordinator of the parochial school system and superior of St. Agatha's Conservatory of Music and Art, in June 1915.

In 1921 Mother Seraphine too retired from active leadership. General church law had made some changes in all religious communities in 1918; long-term superiors might complete the term they then held, but thereafter six years was the limit of time allowed in any religious office. Mother

St. Rose Mackey, who had been the provincial assistant since 1910, succeeded Mother Seraphine, and the last of the Irelands retired from official position in the religious community. (A niece of Mother Celestine, Sister Annetta Wheeler, however, continues the family line as a Sister of St. Joseph.) Mother Seraphine had been the eighth provincial superior. Six have held that office since her long term of thirty-nine years, with Mother Aquin Enright assuming the position in August 1951. Mother Seraphine remained a provincial councilor until 1927, although she did not live at the administrative headquarters established in the novitiate on Randolph Street in 1921 and in the new Provincial House adjoining it in 1927. After 1927 she lived in simple retirement at St. Joseph's Academy.

In the years left to Mother Seraphine before her death in 1930 she was able to watch with pardonable pride the growth of the established enterprises of the sisters and the founding of new ones. Not all survived, but by the time of her death, the sisters had charge of ten academies, thirty parochial schools, and two orphanages, as well as St. Catherine's College and five nursing schools, which had been opened in St. Paul in 1893, Minneapolis in 1900, Fargo in 1904, Grand Forks in 1908, and Jamestown in 1917. From 162 sisters in the province at the time of Mother Seraphine's accession as provincial superior, the community had grown by 1930 to 913, hundreds of whom had been received while she was superior.

Mother Seraphine never forgot the day the papers announced in 1902 that the new building for which the Sisters of St. Joseph had filed plans with the city building department of St. Paul was only the first of a series of buildings for a new college. But she outlived the promise and saw the fulfillment. The Derham Hall opening in 1904 had her as an enthusiastic guest, as did the opening of Whitby in 1914, Caecilian in 1921, the Chapel of Our Lady of Victory in 1924, Mendel Hall in 1927. Only the Health Center — now

Fontbonne Hall—in 1932 was erected too late for her to see it.

Few people preserve the vigor of their powers and their optimistic outlook longer than did Mother Seraphine. The sisters visited her frequently and she went about to the convents happily until the final few months of her life. Churchmen who had been friends of the archbishop continued to call upon her, as much for the vitality of her own presence as to renew their memories of his. She read a great deal and enjoyed discussing her reading with others. Her interest in community matters remained keen, although the worries of her more responsible years she relinquished to others. The tense vigils she had kept in the chapel in earlier times became sweet conversations with her Lord and many a sister saw her bowing and throwing kisses toward the altar as she left the chapel when she thought she was unobserved.

During her last illness an instance of her utter devotion to the community's interests was provided in one of her wandering hours. One night she said to her nurse, "Why this is the archbishop's house."

"Yes, Mother," the nurse answered, humoring her.

"Does he mean to give me the whole place?"

"Yes, I think so," said the nurse.

"Go out at once and get a lawyer. I want to deed it over to the community before it is too late."

The Irelands had a large share in building for the Catholic church on the good ground of Minnesota. Few who were privileged to know any of them will forget their dominant personalities, their bounding energy and enthusiasm, their complete devotion to the causes of the church. Their accomplishments were a spur to the later leaders of the religious community.

During the depression years of the thirties, the war years and the postwar years of the forties, the Sisters of St. Joseph continued to widen their services. A large plant for a boarding and day school at 6600 Nicollet in Minneapolis was opened in 1931 and named for the pioneer school Holy Angels. In the same year such a large addition was made to St. Joseph's Academy in St. Paul that it was virtually a new institution. Ten new parish schools were staffed during these decades and all the hospitals added substantial buildings to their earlier equipment. St. Mary's Hospital in Minneapolis had started out in 1887 in the converted Murphy mansion. It had been a show place of the city but even with the supervision of the famous architect L. S. Buffington its reconstruction did not make it an entirely satisfactory hospital. Modern buildings and residence halls for nurses had been built in 1890, 1918, and 1929. St. Margaret's Academy began in 1907 in two palatial residences also designed by Buffington for the McNair and Wilson families, which likewise required and received numerous additions.

By 1951, the centennial year of the sisters' arrival in St. Paul, there were 2430 pupils in their ten high schools and 17,224 attending their grade schools; 938 students were enrolled in the college; 1050 patients were being cared for daily in the five hospitals; there were 125 orphans in the two orphanages and 72 mothers and infants in the infant home. Students of nursing education totaled 178, exclusive of those in the college program.

In North Dakota about one hundred sisters staffed four schools and three hospitals, located in Jamestown, Grand Forks, and Fargo. A new three-million-dollar hospital located near the campus of the University of North Dakota in Grand Forks was to be completed in 1951. St. John's Academy in Jamestown, a combination grade and high school for boys and girls, had an enrollment of 367, while in Grand Forks a total of 1100 students were taught in the two parish grade schools and the Academy of St. James. In Jamestown the generous support of the pastor there for forty-six years, Monsignor Edward Geraghty, and a large legacy from a Jewish gentleman of the town, Morris Beck, made possible the erection in 1951 of two new buildings for school purposes. St. John's Hospital in Fargo, the largest of the three hospitals in North Dakota, has the oldest and largest nursing school in the state.

It is fitting that the first of the sisters' foundations should have remained one of the most important to the lay community and to the sisters themselves. Always the leading high school in the province, St. Joseph's Academy became a veritable preparatory school for the St. Paul Normal School, a nondenominational institution, after 1896 when the academy was accredited to the University of Minnesota. An appreciable number of those holding responsible positions in St. Paul public schools indicates this fact.

When the academy was opened in its present location in 1863, it was considered too far from the city for day pupils and served primarily as a country school for boarders. As the city grew out in that direction the patronage exceeded the limits of available space and addition after addition had to be erected. After the founding of St. Catherine's in 1904–5, the school took no more boarding students and after 1909 the grades were dropped. More room was given to the school after the novitiate moved to Randolph Street in 1912, but new students filled it promptly. The new buildings added in 1931 were a chapel and library wing on Western Avenue and a four-story wing on Virginia Avenue, providing an auditorium, gymnasium, administrative offices, and classrooms.

For some years before these additions were built, it had been necessary to refuse admission to many students because of lack of facilities. After the additional space became available, nearly a thousand students could be accommodated annually. Splendid young women, many of them daughters of St. Joseph's graduates, have continued to seek the century-old academy for their high school course. They come from all parts of the city and the suburban towns. A high percentage go on to college at St. Catherine's or at the University of Minnesota and the four thousand members of the alumnae association make a substantial contribution to the intellectual and cultural life of St. Paul.

However earnestly Hollywood strives to picture convent life, the results are ludicrously unreal. This marked lack of success is a more glaring failure because it falls within the field of Hollywood specialization — the telling of love stories. Screen researchers have gone too far afield to discover that the whole answer to convent secrets is contained in the one word *love*.

Fortunately, an artist who did not depend upon Renaissance costumery for his effects has left a clear and timeless picture of every convent. Saint Luke in two verses of the Acts of the Apostles has painted the picture and written the history of all religious orders.

"Their possessions and goods they sold, and divided them to all, according as everyone had need. And continuing daily with one accord in the temple, and breaking bread from house to house, they took their meat with gladness and simplicity of heart; praising God and having favor with all the people. And the Lord increased daily together such as should be saved."

Therein are all the essentials of convent life — the voluntary poverty, the mutual charity, the prayer together, the common life, the humility and peace. Saint Luke was, of course, describing the early Christians, a minority group segregated and limited to its own society by the pagan majority. What the majority feared was the thing they sneered at. "Look at these Christians," they said, "see how they love one another." They had sensed the secret which was expressed by St. John, the beloved disciple, in a familiar phrase, "Little children, love one another." The fears of some later Christians were not then a source of concern. The early Christians did not worry about the suppression which might follow if the world discovered their standards nor did they hesitate to reveal their difficult ideals lest they be held accountable for an open practice of the love they believed as truth.

There was of course a good deal of misunderstanding of convent life. That there was little standard of comparison for daily life behind convent walls in the Minnesota experience was illustrated early by a letter which W. P. Murray wrote to his six-year-old daughter from Caracas, where he spent the year 1868 in connection with some business affairs of the legation of the United States. Even after the turn of the century Mr. Murray seemed to be the only authentic voice to tell the public what nice people Catholics were to do business with. He was invited to recount early Catholic history at the celebration of the golden jubilee of the diocese and on several occasions the papers printed his glowing recollections of his Catholic friends.

It is therefore somewhat disconcerting to read Mr. Murray's description of the ceremony of the taking of the veil at the Convent *Carmelitos* in Caracas. His interest derived from the fact that he "had never seen anything of the kind" and he "thought it might be worth looking at." So he went to the church of Santo Pablo where what he called the "ceremony of transferring the living into the dead" was to be performed, going early that he might be sure of a good place. Without knowing a word of Spanish he fabricated a romantic tale of disappointed love concerning the young lady in the ceremony and he told this tale with flourishes. The mystery story ending had touches of "iron wall swung again upon its hinges" and "another was added to the sisterhood."

Almost as fanciful was the sentiment of the editor of the *Northwestern Chronicle*, the weekly of the St. Paul diocese, after witnessing the reception at St. Joseph's Academy on December 8, 1866. Tears filled the eyes of several as they pensively thought of the heroic sacrifice. Expressions like "the bloom of youth," "life in its brightest garb," "world strewn only with roses," "renouncing forever," may have been a shade less stereotyped than they have now become, but they represented no better approach to the meaning of the ceremony than Mr. Murray's.

Neither Mr. Murray's fanciful imagination nor the *North-western Chronicle*'s desire to speak sentimentally of tears and strains of sweet music could quite obscure, even in the early days in Minnesota, the real truths of convent life. At least as early as September 8, 1866, Bishop Grace was explaining the origin of convents in a sermon on the "Evangelical Counsels," when he took as his text the words the Saviour spoke to the young man who said he had from his youth observed the commandments: "If thou wilt be perfect, go, sell that thou hast, give to the poor, and come, follow Me." The bishop showed that in the religion of Christ, besides the precepts which are for all, there are counsels of perfection which we are not obliged to follow, but which unite us more closely with God.

Again and again, through a hundred years of religious professions, St. Paul's bishops and archbishops have reiterated the same sentiments. "Be not ashamed, Sisters," they have said, "of the lowly and the poor. Think it not a disgrace, but a privilege to be associated with them. The church rejoices in the number of her poor. They are her richest treasure, her brightest ornaments, by the virtues they practice. Christ gave it as one of the evidences of His divine mission that the poor had the Gospel preached to them. It is among these that are cultivated the virtues of humility, of meekness, of patience, and of charity, which, though unseen and despised by the children of this world are the meet subjects of the contemplation of God and His angels. In short, to be a true Sister of St. Joseph, you must love the poor."

Great buildings and large numbers are not indubitable signs that the Lord has prospered a work, nor is long life alone a proof of predilection. The test which the church makes of the lives of those she would raise to her altars as saints is a close scrutiny of their practice of charity. The only virtue which a saint must be shown to have possessed is heroic charity — social, universal, personal, and real. Charity is what the church asks Catholics to observe in her saints and to imitate, not their peculiar mannerisms or their human failings.

Archbishop Ireland knew two priests who have since been canonized. One was Saint John Bosco who exercised heroic charity toward delinquent boys in Turin, Italy. He was a poor peasant who had a difficult time to get together the means and the ability for his education as a priest. Yet, with no letter of recommendation he persuaded the Turin reformatory officials to let all the inmates out with him on Sunday. He took them to the country, offered Mass outdoors for them, prayed with them, played games with them, and returned them all to the prison without the assistance of guards. Don Bosco's own home became a hostel for waifs and strays, who frequently annoyed his aged mother by pulling the washing from the line and strewing it about in the mud. The man who is now a saint remained indulgent to the culprits unless ethical principles were involved.

The other saint was a curé in rural France, not far from the town in which Archbishop Ireland made his seminary studies. He was the curé of Ars, John Mary Vianney, canonized for his wonderful pastoral zeal and his unflagging devotion to prayer and penance. He had been such a backward student in the seminary that his directors questioned the wisdom of ordaining him, lest he be so defective in theology that he could never hear confessions. Yet it was in the peculiar pastoral office of guidance through the confessional that the curé of Ars displayed his heroic charity. He subsisted on a most illogical and unbalanced diet and annoyed those who tried to keep his house up to standard by giving everything edible and wearable to the first needy person he met.

There is no way of determining just what the curé of Ars or Don Bosco would have done on a visit to the Belgian colony at Ghent, Minnesota, with its mixture of Hollanders, Icelanders, French, Germans, and Irish. Their admirer, Archbishop Ireland, on one such occasion asked a confirmation class, "Do we see here this morning the unity of the church?" To which a child's answer was, "Oui, parce qu'il y a ici toutes les nations." The recurrence of that idea in Archbishop Ireland's public utterances especially about Negroes, for whom he would have broken down all barriers, hurries us on to the conclusion that his was a universal charity. But he tolerated the denial of American citizenship to Orientals and the notion that they could never be assimilated. This despite his enthusiasm for the one hundred Chinese converts at St. Vincent's Church, St. Paul.

One or a hundred defects in judgment on passing affairs do not alone determine the worth of a figure in history. Archbishop Ireland often quoted Pope Leo XIII's encyclical on the writing of history in which the Holy Father said that the church had nothing to lose from telling the truth about her past and went on to say, "If the Gospels were written today, the stories of Judas and Peter would doubtless be omitted." This principle is the fine heritage Archbishop Ireland left to Minnesota, for he spoke and acted with such frankness that even his limitations show up like warnings which hardly diminish his stature. One thing he made crystal clear — that Catholics in their schools and hospitals have a central aim which is not in conflict with the differing purpose of others. The methods he used to show this were not always perfect for every age and people, but they suited Minnesota in his time.

The community of the Sisters of St. Joseph presents a more complex picture. The strange word which the founder used to describe the little design he conceived was *annihilation*. It rasps on modern ears. That which was to be reduced to nothing was selfishness. Each member of the little institute and all the members collectively were to spend themselves in unselfish love. The details of the plan were mid-seventeenth century, but the "little design" was as revolutionary as the New Testament and as out of harmony with its time. The Holy Rule contains a manifesto in the special art of social love in this passage:

"That the sisters may preserve and increase the zeal necessary for doing and suffering with patience all that is difficult and revolting in the service of their neighbor, they shall frequently reflect that it is Jesus Christ Himself whom they serve, and that all those whom they assist are members of His Mystical Body; that it is He Himself who receives their services, and who, on the day of judgment will say to them: 'Come, ye blessed of my Father, possess you the kingdom prepared for you from the foundation of the world. For I was hungry, and you gave me to eat; I was thirsty, and you gave me to drink; I was a stranger, and you took me in; naked, and you covered me; sick, and you visited me; I was in prison, and you came to me.' Who is there, that, meditating on these truths, will not be animated with zeal?"

The temper of the seventeenth century is apparent in the omission from the Holy Rule of the Sisters of St. Joseph of the great social prayer of the whole Mystical Body and the substitution of more individualistic prayers and devotions. It was not so general a matter of knowledge in the seventeenth century as it had been in the sixth and as it was to become in the twentieth, that the person who would lead a life dedicated to society must be interpenetrated with a high regard for social worship. There was more to this than the length of the prayers, for all unconsciously even piety had gradually come to emphasize personal rather than social aspirations, so that souls who were blessed by their heavenly Father with their own daily bread did not worry too much about the quantity or quality of their neighbor's blessings. "Give us" too often meant "give me" or "me and my friends."

Three hundred years ago the pious founder of the Sisters

of St. Joseph could not bring himself to refer to the congregation he had established by any title but the "little design."
This reticence derived not so much from a modest desire to
refrain from boasting about something he had built as from
a shrewd perception that quite probably the institute would
be suppressed if there was talk about it. For uncloistered
orders had not yet received the approval of bishops.

The strange new sisters were more like lay people than
nuns, because their prayers were just the common ones that
any good Catholic said. They were not bound to say the
Latin offices and their required prayers were short. The
prayers could be said while the sisters worked if necessary,
and if a duty of charity interfered with the customary hour
of prayers, they might be said later in private. They dressed
with less classical uniformity than the long-established
orders. The habit was not carefully thought out, as it would
have been if a saint had sat down to plan its symbolism. It
was just a dress of "common stuff," or of "black woollen
stuff," or like "the dress of humble widows," or simply "not
singular."

The first prescription was that the skirt be "not too long"
in order to avoid being in the extreme of fashion with the
prevailing long skirts. At great intervals there was a modi-
fication toward "long" skirts which finally settled at "two
inches from the ground." The headdress was at first indistinguishable from that of the ordinary Frenchwoman. It was
a white linen bonnet covered with a black *taffetas* hood. A
white kerchief was worn about the shoulders and knotted at
the neck. After the French Revolution, Mother St. John
Fontbonne added a short veil which was like that worn by
widows in her time. For the same reason, the kerchief was
replaced by a white linen guimpe. In times of persecution,
the sisters were not squeamish about donning secular dress
temporarily. On occasion in certain parts of France after the
Revolution and in the hostile sections of the United States,
especially in Louisiana and Pennsylvania, they disguised

themselves in lay apparel, but there is nothing in the archives to indicate that the sisters in Minnesota ever wore any other dress than the habit.

The radical departure of the Sisters of St. Joseph was that they combined the life of prayer and personal sanctification with the life of charity in the spiritual and corporal works of mercy. All religious women since New Testament days had been praising God and praying for blessings upon all mankind in the Mass and Divine Office — the extension of the Mass throughout the hours of the day and night. In addition, but without the inspiration of the Divine Office, the new community of the Sisters of St. Joseph would seek the poor and help them wherever they found them. They knew that they had to be holy first in order to perform the works of zeal, but the personal practice of social charity was an integral part of their way of life.

The Rule is explicit about the work of the congregation. A few quaint phrases from early editions have been omitted, but the idea of the consecrated work remains unchanged. The first English translation of 1847, for example, retains directions for the making of soup for the poor and the care of girl tramps, which do not appear in later revisions. But no portion of the Rule as it is known to thousands throughout the world today fails to emphasize the duty of social charity in a dynamic fashion.

The New Testament presents a picture which may tend to fade as time goes on. Large and long-established organizations show an inclination to move slowly and to compromise, except where stimulus comes from zealous visionaries within or without. Numerous examples may be seen in labor unions, cooperatives, the Red Cross, medical and legal societies. Sisters are neither saints nor radical Catholics, although now and then examples of each occur within religious orders. All that the sisters do is limited to their own business of practicing the Gospel precepts and the result, by and large, is a better than average practice — an example, indeed

— of the Christian virtues. Whether they have an exaggerated notion of the need for imposing buildings and elegant equipment is a serious question both in and out of the cloister. Whether concern over balancing the budget has obscured the counsel and promise, "Seek ye first the kingdom of God and His justice and all these things shall be added to you," is a subject much discussed by lay Catholic Action groups.

Convent life is a radical departure from the glamour and the self-indulgence of a comfortable, gadgetized world, yet in its own area it is simply a normal, conservative existence. Some years ago, a retreat priest came in briskly for the five o'clock conference at one of the large summer retreats at St. Catherine's. "Since our last conference," he said, " I have been visiting the prison at Stillwater. I went about the wide corridors and through the cell-blocks and kitchens and the factories. The order and cleanliness were impressive. Silence was the rule — the men did not look up to stare as visitors passed, but went on with their work in an exemplary fashion. As I went through the institution I was impressed by its resemblance to a convent. But how different it was! For there the fellowship is made up of men who are forced to remain together because they hate society, while you have come into this unity because you love society."

The striking analogy finds a counterpart in the history of the Sisters of St. Joseph in the period of the French Revolution, when their community was at first suppressed and then refounded with the original Rule. At that time, the great cry in France was for liberty, equality, and fraternity. Taken by themselves the words have the sound of cornerstones for universal brotherhood, except that history has proved they can be used for a universal brotherhood of hate. In that tense period of pride and vengeance, the sisters demonstrated the power of even a small cell of love against a hurricane of hatred. Perhaps they also showed that the meaning of *annihilation* in Father Medaille's use of the word

is facility in adaptation to the needs of any age and circumstances — to bring love to those who stand in want of it. In
Minnesota, the very achievement of those things they have
struggled for so painfully carries with it a challenge fundamental to their purposes. It is to be hoped that at their coming of age mature reflection upon their history will draw
them and their friends closer to the common ideal.

There are two hundred and seventy-five times as many
Sisters of St. Joseph in Minnesota as there were in 1851 and
their institutional property has increased in valuation from
nothing to ten millions. From the standpoint of population
and business the sisters have done so well that they are
taken for granted by everybody in Minnesota. Unlimited
credit is extended to them everywhere, while Protestants and
unbelievers vie with each other in proffering good will. In
spite of the many complaints by Catholics concerning the
rising costs of high school tuition and hospital services, all
the waiting lists grow longer and longer. Parents and pastors
of parochial school children have only one complaint — there
ought to be more sisters.

That is a point at which Protestants stop short. How to
go about making a sister is a mystery they do not care to
comprehend, although they do not object to having their
curiosity about convent life satisfied if the subject can be
handled indirectly and without turning into an opinion poll
at the end. For the way of life has a subtle appeal to the
imagination and provokes the question as to what would
happen if every woman became a nun. What goes on inside
convents is almost as little known to lay Catholics, but their
question, if any, is what would happen if no woman became
a nun. In the foreseeable future, neither contingency appears
likely to come to pass in Minnesota.

A century of state history seems to give assurance that an
appreciable number of Catholic women will continue to
replace the aging sisters in convents. In Minnesota the
Catholic population comprises roughly a fifth of the total,

equaling approximately the combined population of Minneapolis and St. Paul. Minneapolis would represent the twenty-seven counties comprising the diocese of St. Paul and the whole population of St. Paul would be relatively that of the other dioceses: St. Cloud, Crookston, Duluth, and Winona. According to the latest general statistics, one and one-half per cent of Minnesota's Catholic population resides within convent walls. That is, of every two hundred Catholics, three are sisters; of every thousand Catholics, fifteen are sisters. While there are almost a thousand times as many sisters in the state as in 1851, the Sisters of St. Joseph now represent less than a third of the total number and their parochial school pupils are roughly a third of the whole group within the archdiocese.

Despite the fact that there is a considerable amount of homogeneity about the girls who become Sisters of St. Joseph, the easily determinable likenesses do not tell the whole story. Most of them are natives of Minnesota or North Dakota, from ordinary Catholic families, of no particular social or economic status, with no pronounced ideas about how to cure the ills of society. Some are from farms or small towns, some from the Twin Cities. The majority have attended Catholic grade or high schools, but a few come from Protestant homes and public schools. The typical girl has finished high school and is eighteen years old. She is energetic and enthusiastic, healthy, full of fun, devoted to her family, and possessed of a love for God which seldom displays itself in unusual outward piety. So indistinguishable is she from the other girls in her high school class that if she had married and become an ardent Christian mother, no one would have been surprised. As a matter of fact, it is conceded that the identical traits characterize the unselfish mother and the self-sacrificing sister. But it is still a mystery how, with exposure to the same proportion of movies and television and convent school and comic books, some girls choose marriage and some take the veil.

The guaranteed security and the assurance of inspiration and refreshment that go with nuns' veiling make it less of a risk than that involved in the kind worn by brides. Yet it is doubtful if this occurs to anyone who contemplates being a sister. To be sure, she may not have become a very old nun before her idealism shows a few starts of irritation at the oft-repeated platitudes of her neighbor at table. It is invariably the appeal of God to her individual soul that makes a Minnesota girl give up her family and possessions in order to serve the Master more entirely. Although it is a consciously supernatural act, it is, nevertheless, universally understandable. Many novelists have woven their plots about the psalm which expresses the urgent impulse of religious vocation, "Whither could I go before Thy spirit . . . if I should take to wing at dawn, and settle at the farthest sea, even there Thy hand would seize me and Thy right hand take hold of me." Because the earliest Christians formed a special kind of group, many persons in every age have desired to imitate them as far as changing conditions permit. Sensitiveness to the simplicity of the original organization grows duller with inevitable changes in standard of living. One of the oldest of little convent jokes is a humorous reference to the fact that Saint Louis of France, a king, practiced poverty although he dined from plates of gold.

The Most Reverend Austin Dowling, after he succeeded Archbishop Ireland, frequently adverted to their early environment in order to recall to the sisters their original aspirations. "When you recall the Church in St. Paul fifty years ago," he said on the occasion of the golden jubilee of five sisters in 1928, "you can scarcely believe your memories: that it was so small, that the prospect seemed so dark. . . . In the days of the Apostles, the Church travelled in the hearts of men like St. Paul and had not a building. . . . If the Church in our diocese is today more beautiful than it was in its humility . . . it is because there have been humble, devoted lives, a constant group of faithful servants of Christ who went around in silence, in devotion, to do the works that Christ bade us do in His name. We all join in recognizing that it is the work of Christ through His servants, through these humble Sisters who did their duty, some in exalted positions, others standing by a range in a kitchen, or perhaps engaged from day to day in other corporal labors. They came here as strangers, and all commingled in Christ. It makes no difference; there is no glory to one more than another. It is Christ who has done it — their hands have served Him. . . .

"It is one thing as a young girl in the glory of youth, with the piety that comes in childhood and adolescence, to utter these words of obligation that have held you fast through all these years. . . . Today you know what religious life is; how you are tried by yourself and by others; how, because it is an imitation of Christ, there are burdens to bear; how one carries a cross as Christ did. . . . When you made your vows, you did not know yourselves. But from year to year . . . you have revealed yourselves to yourselves. You pray, you give your hearts to God's service; you look abroad and try to find the effect of what you do and desire and pray for, and you find it not. . . . You have had a picture of life as it is — different from what you dreamed it would be in the day of your exaltation . . . and yet, for all that the years have revealed to you, you would not recall one moment of them."

Of Mother Seraphine, the archbishop said on this occasion, "Her spirit is as keen and her devotion as lively and her heart as much in the diocese as when she came here as a young girl."

Mother Seraphine died on June 20, 1930. Archbishop Dowling said that as the most distinguished Catholic in the parish, her funeral must be in the Cathedral. At the funeral services, as he sketched the changes that had come to Minnesota in the course of her lifetime, he told of the high hopes of the pioneers that St. Paul and not Chicago was to be the great city of the West. No one could imagine in 1852 that railroads would ever be built beyond it. The Civil War brought one transcontinental railroad and the unemployment following the war caused more roads to be built with government aid. Then St. Paul and Minneapolis subsided, with their opportunities lessened. Minnesota became a corridor state, through which many passed, but not many remained. Mother Seraphine had lived through all these times, for she had even known the first Cathedral of St. Paul which had given the city its name. "It is she and those like her," the archbishop declared, "that make a city glorious, women who know its poor, women who alleviate their sorrows and who teach their children, women with great hearts and splendid imaginations to meet Christlike the needs of the multitude."

Seeming to forget the splendor of the occasion, the archbishop went on to speak of Mother Seraphine's relations to her sisters. "Many a time she criticized them," he said, "many a time she seemed harsh, but that was only to meet the ideal she had in her heart for them, for she loved them tenderly. When she ceased to be 'Mother' the inherent motherhood in her character remained and she still mothered them all as her own. Had she not a right? Had she not trudged the streets of St. Paul for the poor? Had she not in her old age dared to build her College of St. Catherine? And it was to her a daring thing to do, for, like her brother, the Archbishop, she never forgot the poverty of her childhood. So she too thought of St. Paul as poor, and she wondered — as if the buildings came by magic — that building after building was added to this, the crowning achievement of her life.

"Now, though I speak of her as if she worked alone, yet I must and do include all of her sisters. She was a fine chief with splendid imagination and daring to do what she conceived. I think of her today and of her many associates — dear old nuns — who on the way have dropped into the peace of everlasting rest. They upheld her arms and they passed, without notice, into the grave, but she was with them for years. She shared their troubles and labored with them. Generation after generation of sisters came and she filled them with the same courage. Therefore, it would seem treason that this dear old saint should pass away without some authentic voice of the diocese being raised up to thank God because she lived."

The older sisters were sure that Mother Seraphine "knew the poor." Some of them had gone with her long ago about the streets begging for the orphans or they had gone out selling calendars to pay the bills for their own food. That was as it should be, for they were "the poor Sisters of St. Joseph" who had been told by their pious founder long ago that they were to labor to establish an obscure institute, just a "little design." They understood that times had changed and that an air of magnificence seemed to be necessary to prove to the world of today that they were capable of rendering any service. But they were content that God had blessed their hard work and given success to the sisters under the strange conditions. They were tired and happy in the blessed rest they had looked forward to for so long.

Some of the younger sisters wondered if they themselves really were "women who knew the poor." They had not experienced, but had merely heard of grinding, searing poverty. Few of their pupils were from very poor homes. It was so easy, even in studying the encyclicals, to fall into the way of thinking that the rich were always benevolent to the poor. Their own lives were simple, but they were also without cares for any of the necessities that harassed even well-to-do people outside the convent. They often laughed when their friends came to visit or when they went to their own homes for a week in the summer at the concern lest the sisters feel they were missing something that was going on in the world. They tried to explain that they were so busy with their work and their prayers that they had no time for pangs of regret, but people couldn't believe that.

With all the sisters conveying a little information and a

crumb of inspiration at the recreations, the convent conversation was generally interesting enough, and although intended only to be refreshing, it supplied sufficient current news to keep busy people who could not take time to read all the up-to-the-minute things from missing important occurrences. As a matter of fact, they often said they were better informed than their friends who pitied them so much. The sisters could never understand why they themselves were in such a hurry to return from their home visits. With shame they often confessed that any house seemed cramped and restricted after they had lived in large airy rooms for so long and their center of interest seemed to have changed so that they felt lost without the convent routine. The sheer physical comfort of the methodical life they could hardly do without.

This was a matter of each sister's own personal practice of poverty and she had plenty of reminders to keep herself detached from even the simple things of life. But there was also the problem of the whole group being "women who know the poor." The young sisters could not remember that St. Joseph's Hospital had been literally a public poorhouse when it opened. That had lasted for some years, but as soon as the city was able to erect its own institutions for the care of the indigent, public aid and patients were no longer sent to St. Joseph's. The church was no longer considered a proper agency for general care of the poor.

Methods of caring for the sick had undergone such changes that the gentle home nursing and the solicitous invalid care which the sisters had provided in the early days were no longer satisfactory. For forty years, the sisters had been the only nurses and they had done all the cooking and scrubbing and cleaning. They read to the patients and wheeled them on the verandas. They pumped all the water to the various floors or carried it up the stairs. The patients were for the most part poor, so poor that they could not have been given proper care at home. Or they were strangers who were taken suddenly ill away from home. Many men who had led hard lives on the frontier were brought back to a sense of virtue as well as health during their sojourn at the hospital. Protestants frequently came to a new sense of tolerance for the church through observing the kindness of the sisters. No one thought of a hospital as a business in those days.

Now it was increasingly difficult to be sure when business interests ended and social charity began. Mother Bernardine Maher had done capably what was necessary in her time. She had insisted on meeting the best standards of nurses' training and on serving the public with the finest scientific methods and equipment then available. Now another sort of educational coordinator was necessary with a vision capable of recognizing when the hospitals were meeting essential standards and when they were compromising New Testament ideals in social charity. The problem of balance between too much and too little emphasis on efficiency in health services should be faced honestly by the standard of St. Paul's instruction to the Romans:

"Wherefore you must needs be subject, not only because of the wrath, but also for conscience' sake. For this is also why you pay tribute, for they are the ministers of God, serving unto this very end. Render to all men whatever is their due; tribute to whom tribute is due; taxes to whom taxes are due; fear to whom fear is due; honor to whom honor is due. Owe no man anything except to love one another; for he who loves his neighbor has fulfilled the Law."

The first summer after Archbishop John Gregory Murray came to fill the metropolitan see of St. Paul, the summer of 1934, he gave a weekly conference to the sisters attending summer school at St. Catherine's under the general title, "The Sister of St. Joseph as a Religious Teacher." With that theme he traced the history and meaning of convent life and the story of the Sisters of St. Joseph since their foundation three hundred years before. There could be no mistaking the meaning of his final appeal:

"If we think we are not heroic enough to adjust ourselves to conditions that seem to us personally to be just as humiliating, just as disappointing and just as distressing as were the conditions under which our Savior lived His public life, then let each of us ask: Have I come to religion for myself alone or have I come for God? Am I willing to find God wherever He may be pleased to reveal Himself, whether in the dullard in the class room or in the hospital or in the orphan asylum where there are conditions that seem to demand a superabundance of charity apparently at the price of my love of solitude and peace? . . . If I am determined to live a life that justifies me in the claim to be a Sister of St. Joseph, then, indeed, I may not only hear the greeting that was given to the good thief but I may rejoice in the multitude of those who receive the same greeting through my apostolic life."

Father Medaille sealed the little design with the words, "He that neglecteth his own way shall die." The Minnesota years of the Sisters of St. Joseph carry the same challenge tempered with the benediction, "And whoever follow this rule, peace and mercy upon them."

Bibliographical Notes and Index

Bibliographical Notes

DESPITE the fact that my story of the Sisters of St. Joseph in Minnesota and North Dakota has been written for the pleasure of the general reader, I know that even the most casual reader at times wishes to verify the source of a printed statement. I have, therefore, adopted the expedient of assembling references and explanatory comments here according to chapter. By this means, I hope that the needs of scholars will be met, even though I have not listed a formal bibliography. Since the archives of the Sisters of St. Joseph of St. Paul at St. Joseph's Provincial House and at the College of St. Catherine are as yet unorganized and therefore somewhat inaccessible, I have also placed on file in the Manuscript Division of the Minnesota Historical Society and in the library of the St. Paul Seminary fully annotated lists of the newspaper references I have compiled in my research. While the largest bulk of material came from Minnesota newspapers, my long and tedious hours at a newspaper rack have done little more than scratch the virgin soil.

Every library in the Twin Cities has yielded a sizable amount of useful information which, while it adds to my surprise that the Sisters of St. Joseph have heretofore been so little known to the state's historians, also increases my apprehension that I have covered the ground inadequately.

The nebulous, unappraisable, but obviously most important source of my knowledge is the span of eight years — 1909 to 1917 — which I spent as a high school and college student in Derham Hall and the College of St. Catherine, and the period since September 1919 when I entered the novitiate. Of these experiences I am perhaps incapable of making exact citations, much less of telling others how I arrived at the conclusions herein set forth.

If my elaborations are too simple it is because I have tried to remember that the book is, after all, for the reader.

The archival collections most essential to my research were those of the Sisters of St. Joseph of St. Paul and St. Louis, the St. Paul Catholic Historical Society, the National Archives, the Baltimore Cathedral archives, the Richmond diocesan archives (microfilm copies of which are owned by Notre Dame and Catholic University), the Chicago Historical Society, the archives of Notre Dame University, the Library of the Catholic University of America, and especially the Manuscript Division and the Union Catalog of the Library of Congress.

CHAPTER I. THE SWELLING OF THE STREAM

The material on the vision is from J. W. Bond, *Minnesota and Its Resources* (Chicago, 1857), pages 243–51. The quotation on the means of grace is from the same volume, page 127.

There are no contemporary accounts written by the sisters for the early days either in St. Louis or in St. Paul. The accounts which have sometimes been cited as diaries are all, so far as I am aware, reminiscent narratives written long after the events. Mother St. John Fournier, writing in 1873, was the earliest recorder, but it was then twenty years since she had left St. Paul and it is quite possible her recollections might have been blurred by the fact that she was then the superior of the independent community of the Sisters of St. Joseph of Philadelphia.

One letter of Sister Francis Joseph Ivory, written October 29, 1894, is in the St. Paul archives of the Sisters of St. Joseph and a photostatic copy is in the Minnesota Historical Collections. The letter, eleven pages of handwriting, was written to Sister Ignatius Loyola Cox in response to a request for some notes on the early history of the sisters in St. Paul for Father Ambrose McNulty, who in turn was preparing a paper for the Minnesota Historical Society. Subsequently, upon the death of Father McNulty, Archbishop Ireland found the material among his papers and sent it to *Acta et Dicta* for publication, where it appeared in July 1914 (3(No. 2):253–89). This has been explained in my article in *Minnesota History*, 30:1–13 (March 1949), and, as I have noted there, I prefer to quote exactly from the sisters' reminiscent letters rather than to follow Sister Ignatius' prim style in reworking them to a more genteel text.

The motherhouse of the Sisters of St. Joseph of Lyons furnished me with a copy of Mother St. John Fournier's letter of 1873 describing the early American experiences. I have a photostatic copy of the same letter from the archives of the Sisters of St. Joseph of Philadelphia. The whole letter is printed in French and English as Appendix II (pages 326–57) in the recent work, edited by Sister Maria Kostka Logue, *Sisters of St. Joseph of Philadelphia* (Westminster, Maryland, 1950), with a somewhat tidier translation than mine.

Longer and more detailed letters from Sister Francis Joseph Ivory are preserved in the Carondelet archives of the St. Louis motherhouse. Sister Monica of St. Louis was preparing to write a book about the congregation in 1890 and for that purpose she corresponded with many of the older sisters. The book was never written, but the material was available to Sister Lucida Savage when she was writing her Catholic University doctoral dissertation from 1921 to 1923.

Three letters of Sister Francis Joseph are of special interest, dated August 12, 1890, September 10, 1890, and April 17, 1891. There are explainable inaccuracies in names in these letters and I have simply omitted the names of priests — such as Father Ffrench, with two f's — which occur in no other St. Paul record. In her letter of 1895 to Sister Ignatius, Sister Francis Joseph speaks of her shaking hands and fading eyes, which unquestionably influenced her style.

A curious and interesting item in the archives at Notre Dame University is a handwritten book containing all the parish records of Loretto in Father Demetrius Gallitzin's day. The volume was made by Father Ferdinand Kittell, successor of Gallitzin, and it is a duplicate of the one made for presentation to the Holy Father. There the record of Sister Francis Joseph's family may be read. It is of interest that a relative of Sister Francis Joseph is at present engaged on a genealogical history of the family.

The letter of Sister Ursula Murphy, dated January 28, 1895, is in the St. Paul archives and there are photostatic copies in the Minnesota Historical Society. The same location is true for all St. Paul historical letters.

The most competent brief account of the founding of the Sisters of St. Joseph at LePuy in 1650 and of the period of the

French Revolution is that to be found in the first chapter of *Sisters of St. Joseph of Philadelphia.* A fuller interpretation of the French background is provided by Sister Evangeline Thomas in *Footsteps on the Frontier: A History of the Sisters of St. Joseph, Concordia, Kansas* (Westminster, Maryland, 1948). Factually, the work of Sister Lucida Savage, *The Congregation of Saint Joseph of Carondelet* (St. Louis, 1923), is still quite reliable both for the French background and the American foundation. The most accessible general works of reference, such as *Religious Orders of Women in the United States* (Hammond, Indiana, 1930) and the *Catholic Encyclopedia* (1907–14), although they give fairly good sketches, have been superseded in many factual details by more recent research. The annual known as the *Catholic Directory* (with varying titles in the earlier years) from 1852 to 1950 yields increasingly accurate records of the growth of the Sisters of St. Joseph in the St. Paul province. The number of professed sisters and novices, the size, and the name of the superior of every institution is listed and some comparative figures are given.

No original study of the life of Mother St. John Fontbonne has yet been made by an American Sister of St. Joseph. *Simple et grande: Mère Saint-Jean Fontbonne* by Mère Stephanie of Lyons (Paris, 1929) has been translated and adapted by the Sisters of St. Joseph of Brentwood under the title *Mother St. John Fontbonne* (New York, 1936).

The correspondence between Bishop Loras and Bishop Provencher is amply quoted in the periodical *Les Cloches de Saint-Boniface,* 44:38–43 (February 1945), in an article entitled "Etablissement des Soeurs de Charité à la Rivière Rouge," by G. Dugas.

The same volume of *Les Cloches* carries a paper by Sister Mary Murphy, "Voyages des Soeurs Grises dans l'Ouest," in the April issue (pages 81–87) describing the trips the Grey Nuns made through Minnesota in 1846, 1850, 1853, 1855, and 1859. The same account in English is printed in *Papers Read before the Historical and Scientific Society of Manitoba, 1944–45* (Winnipeg, 1945) with the title "The Grey Nuns Travel West." An eight-thousand-word diary of the 1859 trip has been preserved.

Some inaccurate details are added to this story in a typed manuscript in the Minnesota Historical Society library, with the caption "The Little Grey Nuns." It gives a faulty report of the correspondence between Mark Fitzpatrick of St. Paul and the Grey Nunnery of Montreal upon the subject of the Grey Nuns' trips through St. Paul in 1838, 1844, 1845, and 1850. Mr. Fitzpatrick used the material in a series of articles in *Twin Town Topics,* vol. 1, no. 1 (June 6, 1935) and vol. 2, no. 12 (October 30, 1936).

I have relied upon the copies of the letters of Félicité de Duras, Comtesse de la Rochejacquelin, sent to me from the motherhouse in Lyons in 1949. None of the savory bits were edited out of these copies, which I assume to be the reason for my slight variations from the texts used in other books about the Sisters of St. Joseph. Among the documents copied for me in Lyons is one entitled "Notes envoyées de Lyon à la Sup. de Carondelet," dated November 4, 1890, giving recollections of the departure of the sisters for America in 1836 and of the life of the countess, who died in 1883.

The St. Paul Catholic Historical Society, whose collections are housed in the library of the St. Paul Seminary, owns the first drafts of many of the letters sent to the Paris and Lyons offices of the Society for the Propagation of the Faith and all the replies to Bishop Cretin and Bishop Grace. In addition, I have been able to use a large collection of carefully made French transcripts procured from the Library of Saint-Sulpice in Paris by the Most Reverend James L. Connolly in 1933–34. These will eventually be deposited in the Catholic Historical Collections, St. Paul Seminary.

The Minnesota Historical Society has a good showing in material of this kind including typed copies of the Detroit collection known as the Hickey Papers, rather faulty English translations of material relating to the Northwest in the offices of the Propagation of the Faith in France. There are term papers describing the St. Paul holdings in documents and letters. The society now has also a microfilm copy of my comparative calendar of Propagation of the Faith material available in Minnesota together with all the documents and letters I have referred to above and my typed copies of Minnesota material from the files of the Catholic Indian Bureau, Washington, made in 1934–35. There is also a fair collection of the *Annals,* some in French, some in English. The volumes of the Dublin edition containing letters of Bishop Loras and Bishop Cretin were procured by the Reverend E. D. Neill, when he was a consul in Dublin after the Civil War.

The Church Founders of the Northwest by the Reverend M. M. Hoffmann (Milwaukee, 1937) has been of considerable help to me for the biographies of Bishops Loras and Cretin. Sister Grace MacDonald has worked in many aspects of Minnesota history and she has been generous in giving me the benefit of her researches. In the National Archives I found several hundred pages of letters and documents relating to the Winnebago Indian schools in Minnesota and to the activities of various missionaries in the Northwest. All these I have had copied on microfilm. The Library of Congress copied from the *Catholic Directory* for 1850–86 (when the incomplete collection at the Minnesota Historical Society begins) the pages relating to the dioceses of St. Paul, Dubuque, Milwaukee, and St. Louis. These are in my possession on microfilm.

Bishop Cretin's diary is quoted in *Acta et Dicta,* 1(No. 1):39 (July 1907). Although this publication of the St. Paul Catholic Historical Society appeared irregularly and has not been published for a number of years, it would be difficult to name an aspect of diocesan history which has not had treatment in its pages.

The Minnesota Historical Society purchased for my use the film file of the *Boston Pilot* from 1838 to 1919.

New information about the life of Sister Appolonia, to whom the family name Meyer instead of Mirey has been attached in St. Paul records, is supplied in the Philadelphia history of Sister Maria Kostka Logue, pages 33–34, 42, 45, 50, 203.

I quote the Reverend E. D. Neill from the contemporary newspapers in the Minnesota Historical Society, checked against the handwritten manuscripts of his sermons and addresses in the same collections. The only discriminating biographical sketch is that by Dr. Solon J. Buck in the *Dictionary of American Biography.*

CHAPTER II. OF EVERY TRIBE AND TONGUE

Untangling the national and international complications involved in the Long Prairie mission has been a fascinating endeavor. The sisters were by no means the least interesting characters in the bizarre drama.

The *Irish Standard* for January 4, 1896, carried a history of Sinsinawa Mound and Father Mazzuchelli, who is described as a young gentleman of Milanese nobility, vested with full missionary apostolic powers from Rome.

Original lettera of Bishop Crotin, Father de Vivaldi, and Sister Cesarine are in the Catholic Historical Collections at the St. Paul Seminary. All the correspondence relating to Vivaldi's consular service in São Paulo I have obtained on microfilm from the National Archives. Census data from Wisconsin and Kansas have been supplied by the respective state historical societies as well as other biographical material concerning the activities of the former canon. The Salesian Fathers of Turin and Buenos Aires have searched their archives for his Patagonian period and they procured the volume written on his chaplaincy in Argentina by Cardinal Santiago Luis Copello in 1944.

Sister Grace MacDonald's studies are "Canon Vivaldi's Missionary Activities" in the *Iowa Catholic Historical Review*, April 1932, and "The Long Prairie Mission: A Letter of Canon Vivaldi" in *Acta et Dicta*, vol. 6, no. 1 (October 1933).

CHAPTER III. THEY THAT DWELL THEREIN

The extensive newspaper sources for this chapter are filed as indicated in the introduction to these notes. Monsignor Anatole Oster wrote his personal reminiscences of Bishop Cretin for *Acta et Dicta*, 1(No. 1):73–88 (July 1907).

The letter of Father Peyragrosse is quoted in full in French as Appendix III in *Sisters of St. Joseph of Philadelphia*. I hold a photostatic copy, dated July 13, 1853, and the translation in the text is mine. The same is true of the letters of Bishop Cretin to Mother St. John Fournier, which are quoted in part in the Philadelphia story.

A poor English translation of Father Fayolle's melancholy letter is among the transcripts of the Hickey Papers at the Minnesota Historical Society, Manuscript Division.

CHAPTER IV. THE GATE OF THE CORNER

The material in this chapter is derived from research in the life of Mother Seraphine Ireland over a period of twenty-five years. It developed from many interviews with Mother Seraphine and Sister Antonia and Sister Ste Hélène. I published one article in *Ariston* in November 1930, which was reprinted as a brochure in 1943. Another unpublished manuscript of mine is a fictionalized biography.

The baptismal records of the Ireland family were copied for me in 1934 and again on May 24, 1950, from the originals in the church in Kilkenny County, Ireland, at Burnchurch, Danesfort.

CHAPTER V. ONE IN FELLOWSHIP

The *Minneapolis Tribune* for April 23, 1950, carried a feature by Jay Edgerton on the hanging of Mrs. Bilanski, with quotations from the contemporary papers. Over the years this story has been used again and again by newspapermen. The Murray Papers at the Minnesota Historical Society, Manuscript Division, contain Mr. Murray's version. Mrs. Clara Hill Lindley quotes her mother's account of this affair in the book *Memories of James J. and Mary M. Hill*, which was published posthumously by her husband, E. C. Lindley (New York, 1948). The same volume is the one quoted throughout this book, although Mrs. Lindley published other memoirs of her parents.

CHAPTER VI. FRONTIERS BEYOND THE TOWN

The Sweetman Papers in the Manuscript Division of the Minnesota Historical Society contain information on John Sweetman's colony at Currie. These papers are classified as Irish-American Colonization Papers. The account of Mr. Sweetman's visit to Don Bosco in the interests of a foundation of Salesians in Currie is in Box 1.

In the same location is to be found the unpublished master's thesis of Howard E. Egan, "A History of Irish Immigration in Minnesota, 1865–1890," containing the quotation from Mother Seraphine on the colonies and the conversation of John Sweetman on Bishop Ireland.

Minnesota History, 9:331–46 (1928) contains an article on "The Sweetman Irish Colony" by Alice E. Smith. *Six Seasons on Our Prairies*, by the Reverend Thomas J. Jenkins (Louisville, Kentucky, 1884), describes the Catholic colonies, especially Avoca. The *Graceville Enterprise* for June 20, 1935, gives an account of the fiftieth anniversary of the founding of St. Mary's Academy. The history of the Kilkenny church appeared in the *Montgomery Messenger* for September 19, 1930. George Petersen wrote an excellent series of articles for the *Minneapolis Tribune* on the various colonies, October 27, November 3, November 6, 1942. Louis Larson's recollections of pioneering at Marshall are contained in *La Crosse County Historical Sketches, Series 6*. The histories of Lyon County by C. F. Case and Arthur P. Rose give descriptions of the colonies at Minneota and Ghent.

CHAPTER VII. BEHIND CONVENT WALLS

Sister Wilfrida's reminiscences are preserved in the archives of the motherhouse of the Sisters of St. Joseph, St. Louis. In 1921, when Sister Wilfrida was sixty-two, she wrote long, unstudied letters, which were never intended for publication, but merely to help Sister Lucida Savage of the St. Louis province in the preparation of the history of the Sisters of St. Joseph of Carondelet.

CHAPTER VIII. "THE CONSECRATED BLIZZARD OF THE NORTHWEST"

The literature on the career of Archbishop Ireland is extensive, but it is also elusive. Some excellent critical studies of certain aspects of the controversies with which the archbishop's name is always associated have been published during the past five years, although no full-length biography has yet appeared.

Of great value to any study of the period are the indexes to the *New York Tribune* (1875–1906) and the *New York Times* (1851–1905, with a break between 1857 and 1863). I own copies of these indexes on microfilm and fair files of the papers are available in Minnesota. I was able to complete my reading in the film files of the New York Public Library and the Library of Congress. There is a file of the *Chicago Tribune* at the Minnesota Historical Society library and the *Tribune* library in Chicago facilitated my search.

An index to the *Minneapolis Journal* (1899–1914) was made by W.P.A. workers in 1939. It is stored in the Minneapolis Public Library and my citations to the *Journal* follow that excellent guide, for every card of which I have made transcripts from the newspaper files. A similar guide to Chicago newspapers is stored in the Chicago Public Library, but it is less thoroughly done and for a less useful period. The whole file of the *Northwestern Chronicle* (1867–1903) is extremely valuable. It is available both in microfilm and in bound volumes. Until its removal to

Milwaukee in 1900, the *Northwestern Chronicle* was the official diocesan paper of St. Paul. The unofficial Catholic paper of Minneapolis, the *Irish Standard* (1886–1915), is most useful.

A collection known as the "Annals of Early Minnesota History," consisting of transcripts from Minnesota newspapers, which is stored in a basement at the Minnesota Historical Society, has two bulky folders on the Catholic church and numerous cross references. This W.P.A. project is incomplete and somewhat unreliable for coverage, but it is of immense value at least to the late 1870s. The folders on nationalities and the translations from Swedish language papers provide points of view which might not otherwise be obtained. The *North* and the *Loyal American,* anti-Catholic journals of Minneapolis, are interesting chiefly for their cartoons of Archbishop Ireland. Sister Callista Hynes, a Franciscan Sister of Rochester, Minnesota, used these papers and the *Irish Standard* in her master's dissertation on the American Protective Association in Minnesota, of which I have a microfilm copy.

In the Baltimore Cathedral archives there are five letters from Bishop Grace, three of them to Archbishop Martin Spalding and two to Cardinal Gibbons. Archbishop Ireland wrote sixty-six letters to Cardinal Gibbons, of which I have made typed copies. The Richmond diocesan archives for the period of Bishop Denis O'Connell's administration contain 154 items of Archbishop Ireland's correspondence, of which I have transcripts. They include letters to Monsignor O'Connell when he was rector of the American College in Rome and in the years following up to 1903 when he became rector at Catholic University; cables; and a few clippings written or inspired by Archbishop Ireland. The letters in the archives of Baltimore and Richmond have been quoted by a number of scholars, but we are perhaps still too close to the period of their writing to have all the necessary insight for their final interpretation. Materials in the possession of the archdiocese of St. Paul have not yet been released for the use of students.

The work of the Reverend Dr. Frederick J. Zwierlein, although curiously skewed, is the first bold exploration of sources and it is of tremendous value for everything except interpretation. His books are *The Life and Letters of Bishop McQuaid* in three volumes (Rochester, 1927) and *Letters of Archbishop Corrigan to Bishop McQuaid and Allied Documents* (Rochester, 1946). In the earlier work, Archbishop Ireland is fully, if adversely, treated in volume 2 by fourteen references and in volume 3 by a chapter of ninety-one pages and six other references. He is generously remembered in forty-five places in the later work. The valuable feature of Dr. Zwierlein's contribution is his exact citation and location of letters and documents and newspaper sources, especially from the archives of the archdiocese of New York and the diocese of Rochester.

The controversies listed are intertwined with each other and with other public and personal problems so that no definitive bibliography of each is possible.

SECRET SOCIETIES. Archbishop Ireland took the position that it was inexpedient to condemn any secret societies except the Masons. He believed that most of the organizations were harmless and not specifically anti-Catholic and that needless stirring up of rancor should be avoided. However, he thought that Catholics should be advised privately against membership. His letters to Cardinal Gibbons which specifically mention secret societies are listed by date and by their index number in the Baltimore Cathedral archives. The *Irish Standard,* March 7, 1896, quotes Archbishop Ireland's discussion of the meaning of the church discipline in the matter of secret societies.

SINGLE TAX. To Archbishop Ireland Henry George, the single tax, Dr. McGlynn, and their partisans were all part of a cause — keeping the working masses in the church. There is a note of weariness in his references to the George theories and the George propagandists which suggests that the economic aspects of the problem received scant attention from him. The most voluminous treatment of the problem by a Catholic is that of the Reverend F. J. Zwierlein in the third volume of his work on Bishop McQuaid, where the first eighty-three pages are given over to a chapter on "Dr. McGlynn." The presentation is biased and should be read against the more recent researches of the Reverend Henry J. Browne in *The Catholic Church and the Knights of Labor* (Washington, 1949). Two letters of Archbishop Ireland to Cardinal Gibbons mention Henry George.

THE KNIGHTS OF LABOR. Father Browne's dissertation is adequate citation. The *Irish Standard,* May 21, 1887, gives a detailed account of the previous Sunday's sermon at the Cathedral in which John Ireland made references to the temperance cause, the Knights of Labor, the Catholic University, and other matters which had occupied him while he was in Rome.

THE CATHOLIC UNIVERSITY. The series of volumes issued by the Catholic University Press on the history of the institution give ample treatment of Archbishop Ireland's part in the critical years. They are John Tracy Ellis, *The Formative Years of the Catholic University of America* (Washington, 1946), Patrick H. Ahern, *Catholic University of America, 1887–1896* (1949), Peter E. Hogan, S.S.J., *Catholic University of America, 1896–1903* (1949), Colman Barry, O.S.B., *The Catholic University of America, 1903–1909* (1950).

THE WORLD PARLIAMENT OF RELIGIONS. The Chicago Historical Society has a complete file of the various souvenir volumes issued in connection with the World's Columbian Exposition of 1893, including the speeches made at the religious meetings and the description of the exhibits in the Catholic educational display. The archives of the University of Notre Dame have an outstanding collection of manuscript material covering every aspect of Catholic participation in the exposition. There is also a frank discussion of attitude by Archbishop Ireland in numerous letters to Monsignor Denis O'Connell and to Cardinal Gibbons. The Minneapolis Public Library has a file of the rare *Revue des Deux Mondes*, which carried on the subsequent controversy over religious congresses.

THE APOSTOLIC DELEGATION. The press of the country, Catholic and secular, was vocal in its opposition to the appointment of an apostolic delegate to this country. Archbishop Ireland became a sort of protector to the first appointee, Archbishop Francisco Satolli, after the Columbian Exposition in 1893. Bishop John Vincent, father of Dr. George Vincent and founder of Chautauqua, wrote an insulting article in the May 1893 *Forum*, "The Pope in Washington," which was answered by Bishop Shanley at the North Dakota Chautauqua, Devils Lake, according to the *Northwestern Chronicle*, July 28, 1893.

CAHENSLYISM. The best critical work on the subject is that of John J. Meng in the *Catholic Historical Review*, January and October 1946. The Cahensly Memorial is extensively discussed in the *Northwestern Chronicle* for July 3, 1891. Foreignism is treated on July 17 and August 7, nationalism on June 5.

AMERICANISM. This controversy came to a head over the translation of the Paulist Father Walter Elliot's *Life of Father Hecker* into French. A misinterpretation of the French version was made by the Abbé Charles Maignen to convey the idea that doctrines of the church were being watered down to make them more palatable to Americans and more in accord with the American spirit of progress. Prompt denials that any such situation existed except among a few French rebels were made by all those involved in the accusations, but not before an encyclical condemning the errors had been issued; it was called *Testem Benevolentiae*.

The Reverend Thomas T. McAvoy is now in France making an extended study of Americanism. His articles on the subject are: "Americanism and Frontier Catholicism" in *Review of Politics*, 5:275–301 (July 1943), "Americanism, Fact and Fiction" in *Catholic Historical Review*, 31:133–53 (July 1945), and "'Americanism' Reviewed by Felix Klein" in *American Ecclesiastical Review*, 122:355–63 (May 1950). The last-named article is on volume 4 of the six-volume autobiography of the Abbé Felix Klein, a ninety-year-old priest who was in the thick of the Americanism controversy and who later twice visited St. Paul. John Ireland's letters indicate his attitude in the controversy.

THE FARIBAULT-STILLWATER PLAN. The full-length study of Daniel F. Reilly, O.P., *The School Controversy (1891–93)* (Washington, 1944), is said to have neglected the New York sources of the argument, but there is no such reticence in Dr. Zwierlein's *Letters of Archbishop Corrigan to Bishop McQuaid and Allied Documents*. Another useful study is the unpublished Notre Dame master's thesis of Brother Bonaventure Foley, C.S.C. (1944).

THE CARDINALATE. The struggle for a cardinal's hat for Archbishop Ireland has been treated in many books and articles. The older works are Maurice Francis Egan, *Ten Years near the German Frontier* and *Recollections of a Happy Life*; Maria Longworth Storer, *Roosevelt the Child* and *In Memoriam Bellamy Storer*; John Talbot Smith, "Archbishop John Ireland" in the *Dublin Review* for January 1921. John T. Farrell in three recent articles on the Spanish-American War period has made frequent allusions to the subject, but his conclusions concerning the character of Archbishop Ireland seem unwarranted to me after covering virtually the same primary sources and a great many more than he cites. His articles are to be found in the *Catholic Historical Review* for October 1947, March 1950, and April 1951.

Index